1961

PROFESSIONAL MANPOWER

AND

EDUCATION

IN

COMMUNIST CHINA

by

Leo A. Orleans
LIBRARY OF CONGRESS

NSF-61-3

Foreword

The development of Communist China as a potential major power is necessarily related to its scientific and technological capabilities. An assessment of these capabilities both for the present and future is dependent to a great extent on a study of its professional manpower resources and its educational system.

This National Science Foundation-sponsored study, prepared by Leo A. Orleans of the Library of Congress, examines the characteristics and training of Chinese professional manpower and their relationship to Communist China's technological development. The study represents more than 2 years of research and analysis applied to materials collected over a period of 4 years. It follows in the steps of a previously supported comparable study of Soviet professional manpower published in 1955 (now being revised).

It is hoped that this publication will not only increase our limited knowledge of this aspect of Communist China's development but will also encourage further study of this very important field.

ALAN T. WATERMAN,
Director, National Science Foundation.

Preface

Although the interest in professional manpower and education in Communist China has been constantly growing during the past decade, great gaps in knowledge continue to exist and the whole subject remains a relatively virgin area for research and analysis. The aims of the present study are to attempt to lay a foundation for the understanding of this Chinese riddle and, in so doing, to create, possibly, an interest and a reaction which would stimulate further study of these important and often controversial topics. Thus, this monograph does not contain "all the answers," but attempts to survey the available materials dealing with professional manpower and education in Communist China, analyze and summarize the most significant data and factors, and indicate the areas in which the greatest gaps in knowledge exist.

Anyone who has had experience working with Communist data or with Chinese data must appreciate the difficulties that beset the analyst when the most frustrating aspects of both are combined to become Communist Chinese statistics. It is not necessary to describe in detail the type of difficulties encountered in dealing with statistics of Communist China—most of them become apparent in the text. For almost every figure, there is a contradictory figure, often in the same source—a week, a month, or a year later—sometimes varying by as much as 100 percent. Sometimes this is due to changed concepts and the inability to pin down the inclusions and exclusions; at other times the difficulty is in the use and abuse of statistics; there are still other instances where there seems to be no adequate explanation. Sometimes a transition from one policy to another covers a period of several weeks and even months, so that contradictory statements may appear in concurrent issues of the same newspaper which at all times reflects Party views. Then there are the common phenomenon where independently reported components of a particular category never seem to add to a total reported in another source, percentual distributions that are reported for missing totals, and percentual growth that is given over an unknown base.

Despite these drawbacks, it must be admitted that educational statistics are usually more reliable, once the concepts are understood, than many other figures released by the Chinese Communists. Furthermore, it is a distinct impression that, excluding some obvious exceptions, these data are not withheld or perverted for the sole purpose of confusing the user. Rather, the major problem lies in the fact that, despite improvements in statistical techniques, tighter controls, and greater emphasis on reporting and recordkeeping, China remains a country in which statistics are grossly inadequate. The efforts of the state to improve quantitative data is hindered by China's size, by the magnitude of her population, and especially by the careless attitude toward statistics evident throughout most of her history.

Two more points pertaining to statistics: Although an effort was made always to utilize reported data when they were available, there are instances where the figures were presented, but alternate and seemingly more reasonable estimates were made. Also, although some of the figures were reported in the original source with great precision, they were rounded in the text because such precision does not seem to be appropriate to the general nature of Chinese statistics. If Communist sources cannot agree on the exact number of institutions of higher education in China, it would be ludicrous to present the number of students in these institutions to the nearest individual.

The reader may feel that the intensity of coverage of the various topics in this study is uneven. The feeling is justified. Usually this was dictated by the availability of data, as for example the more detailed treatment of the medical personnel as opposed to scientists and engineers. In other instances, it was a matter of selectivity necessitated by time limitations. For example, data available for a detailed analysis of the vacillations in Communist policies as they apply to education were not exploited fully, while an attempt was made to present a complete compilation of the statistics pertaining to education and professional manpower.

Because this study deals with current topics and statistics in a country that is in a state of constant flux, it was particularly difficult to draw a line and say that no matter what new data comes out tomorrow—no more changes! Such resolutions were broken several times, necessitating the reexamination and reinterpretation of sections or sentences because of major policy shifts or only short newspaper items. Whether fact or imagination, it appears that the flow of data increased considerably since the actual work was terminated. Because of this, there is always the danger that parts of the study may become obsolete before the printer's ink is dry.

The overwhelming mass of the source materials used was obtained from mainland newspapers, periodicals, and radio broadcasts. Most of them were used in translated form, as for example the translations supplied by the U.S. consulate general in Hong Kong (*Survey of China Mainland Press, Extracts From China Mainland Magazines,* and *Current Background*) and by the U.S. Joint Publications Research Service, Washington, D.C. Often it was thought necessary to go back to the original source to try and clarify a particular point; it was usually wasted effort. Because of the nature of most of the sources on which this study is based, a bibliography is not included and sources appear only in footnotes at the bottom of each page. Although a fairly large number of Russian sources were utilized, it is the conviction of the author that, for the most part, the Soviets—at least those outside their intelligence system—do not have data on China that are not obtainable in the United States. It is unusual to find facts and figures in Soviet books and journals that are not already available from Chinese sources, while critical analyses of any of the problems simply do not exist. Nevertheless, the many Russian books on China are important in that they conveniently integrate and summarize scattered data between two hard covers. On the other hand, the Chinese themselves do have illuminating and critical discussions in their own publications and they are quoted extensively in some of the chapters. While on the subject of quotations, it will become immediately apparent to the reader that many of these translations are rather awkward. Only minor changes were made in the often literal translations of the original texts, because by polishing them up, they lose some of the original flavor and color so often present in the "lingo" of the Chinese Communists. In lieu of a glossary of terms, an attempt was made to explain each word or expression, which has a special meaning in the present context, the first time it appears in the text.

Comparative data on China and the United States or China and the Soviet Union were kept to a minimum because it was felt that comparisons at this stage in China's development are meaningless and would have to be so qualified as to make them lose all significance. It means little to say that the United States is currently graduating 38,000 engineers, while Red China is graduating in the vicinity of 18,000 engineers annually, when the comparison may be between a graduate of the Massachusetts Institute of Technology and a graduate of a 3-year technical institute half of whose time has been spent in actual production work, not to mention political indoctrination and Communist-sponsored youth activities. Or perhaps, a comparison of the number of graduates of one of our agricultural colleges in the Middle West with one of the newly established "red and expert" universities in an interior village of China would be equally meaningless.

I would like to thank the National Science Foundation for the financial support which made this study possible, and numerous members of the staff of the Library of Congress who provided assistance during the preparation of the study. Specifically, at the National Science Foundation I wish to extend thanks to Mr. Thomas Mills, Program Director for the Scientific Manpower Program (Division of Scientific Personnel and Education), and Mr. Robert Cain, Project Director of Manpower Studies (Clearinghouse), for their decision to assign this project to my care. I wish to express special gratitude to Mr. Joseph P. Kozlowski of the Scientific Manpower Program, Foreign Manpower Studies, for his encouragement and help. I also wish to thank Mr. Alfred J. Holston, NSF Chief of Printing, for his expert processing of this study for publication. At the Library of Congress I would like to acknowledge the support of Dr. Roy P. Basler, Director of the Reference Department, and the assistance of members of his staff, in particular Miss Georgella Hefty, who handled many of the complex administrative and financial problems associated with the project.

The following individuals have kindly read and made valuable comments on the original manuscript: Mr. Michael K. Roof, of the Reference Department of the Library of Congress my good friend and severest critic; Dr. Edwin G. Beal, head of the Chinese Section at the Library of Congress; Dr. Theodore H. E. Chen, head of the Department of Asiatic Studies at the University of Southern California; Dr. Tek-cheung Chen; Dr. Alexander G. Park, Deputy Chief, Communism Analysis Division of the U.S. Information Agency; Dr. Paul K. T. Sih, Director of the Institute of Asian Studies at St. John's University; and Dr. Irene B. Taeuber, of the Office of Population Research at Princeton University.

Mr. Wang-chi, of the Library of Congress, supplied me with the list of institutions of the Academy of Sciences, appearing in appendix I. This list will appear as part of his projected publication entitled "Mainland China Organizations of Higher Learning in Science and Technology and Their Publications." Mr. David Johnson executed the fine cover.

I want to acknowledge with gratitude the "above and beyond" services of Mrs. Mary England, who provided editorial assistance in copy preparation for prepublication review and who indexed this monograph.

Finally, I would like to express sympathy to my wife, Dink, who has been both patient and understanding during my prolonged periods of seclusion.

Washington, D.C.   August 1960

L. A. ORLEANS

Contents

LIST OF TABLES

CHAPTER VI:

CHAPTER VII:

CHAPTER VIII:

CHAPTER I
Introduction and Highlights

China is undergoing perhaps the most drastic social, political, and economic changes that have been experienced by any country in modern history. Within a period of some 10 years this long-dormant giant has been transformed from a weak, divided, economically backward country, to a unified, regimented, and centrally controlled nation, which has not only, for a time, challenged the combined forces of the United Nations in Korea, but which has set as its immediate economic goal the overtaking of Great Britain in the output of many basic economic goods. China is a nation in a hurry, and the Communists are willing to pay any price necessary to accomplish their goals. Even the most cautious observers must admit that China's economic gains have been impressive, particularly when viewed, not against the often inapplicable standards of the West, but against the China of yesterday. To understand China's education, scientific, and manpower problems, it is helpful to have some notion of the general setting within which the internal changes are taking place.

Undoubtedly the primary factor responsible for China's progress is the establishment of effective controls reinforced by fear, which affords Communist leaders the means to exercise absolute determination over the nation's economy and the psychological and physical responses of its peoples. This control is pervasive and omnipotent. Everyone, from children in nursery schools to the aged in the so-called "happiness homes," feels the heavy hand of the state. In the rural communes, in the factories and mines, in the schools and research institutes, and even in their homes, people are under the authoritative guidance of well-dispersed Party members, militia, and the ubiquitous surveillance of block leaders, neighbors, and secret police. The individual must conform, must produce, and must accept the judgment of either the state or his immediate superiors. To maintain these controls, the Communists are careful to relax these restrictions when the potential reaction to a particular program may become too violent or when the results do not seem to follow the anticipated pattern. In practice, the Peking regime appears to have adapted Mao's military principle: "Enemy advances, we retreat; enemy halts, we harass; enemy tires, we attack; enemy retreats, we pursue." This has made it possible for China to abandon the ancient oriental fear

1

of "loss of face" and to experiment, reverse earlier directives, and contradict earlier policies without hesitation. For example, the push, the temporary retreat, and an intensified surge in creating urban communes; the frequent reversals in the policies toward intellectuals; the bland announcement in August 1959 that statisticians had been a "little overzealous" in reporting 1958 "leap forward" production figures; the vacillations with regard to birth control.

Under these circumstances, it is easy to assume that Communist China is one huge concentration camp and that were it not for this minute control of the individual's life, the people would revolt and the regime would collapse. This is a wishful conclusion for there are additional forces at work in China which give its leaders powerful alliances in their schemes. The most important of these is nationalism, and it is expressed in the pride and the hope of large segments of the Chinese population. No matter how heavy the burden on the individual, he cannot help seeing the changes around him and be proud that he has had some small role in creating them. There is also hope—not so much hope for himself, for that has long been dismissed by most of the people, but hope for his children and for his grandchildren. They are going to school and there is hope that they will be educated. There is hope that things must get better for they cannot get much worse, and it is the children who will benefit by these improvements: "Look at the Soviet Union," they say. There is hope for the country, for just think what can be accomplished in the next 20 years if the first 10 are representative; and once again the younger generation will reap the harvest. Realizing full well the extent to which nationalism, pride, and hope can be made to serve the objectives, the Communists play up these emotions loud, clear, and often, over radio, over the widespread public address systems, and in compulsory meetings.

But as is so often the case in Communist China, every assertion must be followed by the inevitable contradiction, for despite the strength of the regime, there are indications of both overt and covert opposition. There are scattered reports of localized revolts in many parts of China; there is, of course, the example of Tibet; there were the strong antiregime denunciations made during the short "thaw" in the spring of 1957 when the Chinese people had an opportunity to express their feelings. The atmosphere of tension exists at all levels of the society: Among the peasants, the national minorities, the intellectuals, and even in the military. Some of them are more serious than others, but at present none seem important enough to cause the Communists real concern. Some of these tensions are inherent in the daily life of any individual. They manifest themselves in an undertone of fears, anxieties, resistance to change, and in antigroup and antistate behavior. Such phenomena are, in fact, evident in democratic societies as well as totalitarian states, although many of them have been intensified under the conditions exist-

2

ing in Communist China. Other tensions, often in the nature of external challenges, seem to have been intentionally induced by the Communist leaders to accomplish certain specified internal goals: The regime's decision to accelerate collectivization in 1955 was accompanied by the "Liberate Taiwan" campaign and an upsurge in tensions on the mainland; to facilitate the transition to the commune system in 1958, the Communists initiated the Quemoy-Matsu issue; the germwarfare fabrications in early 1952 enabled the Communists to overcome a general apathy of the masses toward personal and environmental hygiene and launch a nationwide health campaign. These and other induced tensions provided the regime with the necessary excuse to coerce the population into higher productivity on the job, "voluntary" contributions of labor for numerous mass projects, and greater efforts in every prescribed activity.

Because of the shortage of trained specialists, one would normally assume that the regime would cater to those individuals who are capable of contributing more than anyone else toward making China a powerful force in world politics. This is not always the case. Almost all persons with a higher education fall in the category of intellectuals and are thereby suspect by definition. This, of course, has created a basic dilemma: The intellectuals are urgently needed but have never been completely trusted. Their skills are vital for the development of education and the economy; however, inquiring minds might question the universal validity of Marxism-Leninism and the infallibility of the Communist Party, as they most assuredly did during the "one hundred flower" period in 1957. In China the relationship between the Party and the professionals has been complicated by the background of the intellectual class. Ever since the basic reforms of the Chinese traditional educational system some 40 to 50 years prior to the Communist regime, education had been based upon Western models, while large numbers of outstanding scholars had studied abroad, particularly in the United States, where they had established academic and personal ties incompatible with Communist concepts. As a result of this dilemma, the state's attitude toward the intellectuals had vacillated from praise to scorn, from acceptance to open attack. At no time, however, did the Communists pretend to place any faith in the lasting or genuine political reliability of the intellectual.

The need to break down the spirit of the intellectuals became especially apparent after May of 1957, following the period of "blooming and contending." The wave of criticism toward the regime that swept the country during this one month was so severe that the Party was forced to an immediate about-face, initiating a prolonged rectification campaign and some of the most bitter attacks on China's intellectuals. They were subjected not only to concentrated dosages of political indoctrination and to humiliating public sessions of criticism and self-criticism but also to

3

ENROLLMENT FOR CHINA, UNITED STATES, AND SOVIET UNION,
1958–59

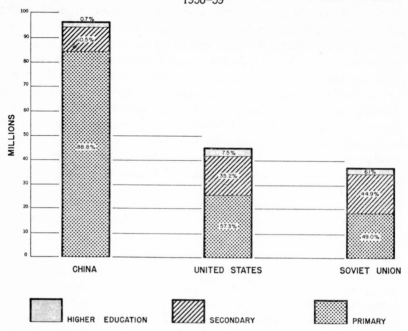

CHINA   UNITED STATES   SOVIET UNION

HIGHER EDUCATION   SECONDARY   PRIMARY

forced participation in physical labor—the final blow to the prestige of
any educated Chinese. Literally hundreds of newspaper accounts told
of students, of professors, and of members of the Academy of Sciences
going down to the communes in the "hsia-fang" movement for short or
long stretches of physical labor, thus "increasing the cultural level of the
peasants and at the same time learning to appreciate the value of working with one's hands."

These conditions could not have failed to produce a deterioration of
morale and performance among China's professionals; the politically
stultifying atmosphere has certainly affected the imagination and crea-
tiveness of individuals in the arts as well as the sciences. The criticisms
of the scientists against Party leadership, against organization of research,
and against working conditions in general have certainly been silenced.
It would seem, however, that given another opportunity to express their
views, the same complaints would once again be voiced.

It is in this atmosphere that the Communists have initiated their "leap
forward" in education, literacy, and science, and have succeeded, to
some extent, in raising the skills and the educational level of the population. It is because of the above factors that they have been able to
absorb about 100 million people into their regular school system and an
even larger number of people into various types of spare-time and on-the-
job training and literacy programs.

4

When the Communists took over the mainland in 1949, they inherited a country with an immense population of whom over 80 percent were illiterate, where education was a privilege, people with skills were few, technicians fewer, and higher personnel and scientists even more rare. The tasks of the new regime were well defined. They had to teach people to read and write; they had to expand the educational system to include as many children as possible in as short a time as possible; they had to supply the country with increasing numbers of semiskilled and skilled workers, with semiprofessional and professional personnel; they had to insure the present and future needs of the country with the skilled manpower needed to achieve their objectives.

In less than 10 years the Communist regime managed to increase the enrollment in primary schools by some 60 million and in institutes of higher education by some 500 percent. To do this the Communists have had to sacrifice quality—a problem of which they are well aware but consider inevitable at this time. The jump from illiteracy to a first rate educational system cannot be accomplished over a period of a few years; improvements will have to come gradually. The quality of education varies from year to year with shifts in policies and from one school to the next, but the general trend in quality seems to be in inverse proportion to quantity. As the numbers in schools increased, more and more shortcuts were taken. In an effort to achieve universal literacy, simplified characters were taught, and the standards for literacy were reduced. To expand primary and secondary education to include some 100 million children, the quality of instruction was sacrificed. To assure a continuing increase in the number of college graduates, requirements were reduced, and the student was assured success by a proper political attitude.

The "great leap forward" initiated in 1958 compromised education even further. Production became the key word, and everyone from the first grade to the college student had to contribute in some way toward production. While the regular students had less and less time to spend on their studies, more and more people were absorbed into the educational mill on a part-time basis. The so-called "red and expert universities" were also introduced in 1958 to instruct peasants and workers in advanced production techniques.

The above briefly describes the educational atmosphere in Communist China today. While stressing the need and importance of education, the regime minimizes the contributions of the educated. While the needs of the economy for technicians, engineers, and scientists are constantly proclaimed, the individual student finds the road to achievement filled with political, social, and economic obstacles. In effect the student is told: "Study, study, study, but remember that too much book learning is dangerous and a person with practical experience is more valuable than a scholar."

Although one would naturally assume that as a result of the proclaimed shortage of scientific and technical personnel and other intellectuals the Communists would try to cater to their needs and create the most favorable conditions for their work, this has not been the case. There has been a basic contradiction in the Party's relationship with the intellectuals, and despite the urgent need for them, the intellectuals have never been completely trusted.

Pressures to create intellectual conformity have been pervasive, and "ideological remoulding" has been forcefully applied. All intellectuals have been affected by these pressures, but those who received their training abroad or in foreign-sponsored schools have been given particular attention. Confessions and denunciations of the bourgeois West and of their own past histories were obtained from all the older intellectuals during the 1957 rectification campaign. The time-honored status of intellectuals, and despite the urgent need for them, the intellectuals have that to be "red" was of much higher value than merely to be "expert." An editorial directed at academicians stated that—

> . . . the ugly ideology of bourgeois intellectual individualism is seriously impeding the progress of our scientific, technological, cultural, and educational program. A leap forward in ideology is a prerequisite for a forward leap in science.

The result was a more complete subordination of all scientific research and of all the higher professionals to the Party.

These are the conditions under which the estimated 625,000 persons with higher degrees are expected to perform their duties and to lead the country into a new era. It must be noted, however, that although perhaps none of these individuals was able to live through this period completely unscarred, not all of them have been affected to the same degree by the rectification and by other policies directed against intellectuals. The most severe attacks have been directed against only one-fifth of this total number of professionals—those who received their education prior to 1950.

The distribution of these 625,000 individuals with degrees from institutions of higher education has been greatly affected by the emphasis placed on technological education. Whereas prior to 1950 engineers constituted approximately one-sixth of the population with higher degrees, they now constitute 171,700—more than a quarter of the total. The numbers who have been graduating in the fields of education and medicine have also shown sizable proportional increases, while the graduates in the sciences have increased in number but remained fairly constant in proportion to the total. Most of the emphasis on engineering, medicine, and education has been at the expense of such fields as law, social sciences, finance, and economics.

The general quality of the present college graduates in China is usually quite low. Those who received their training in the West prior to 1950 and the few thousand selected students who have been trained in the Soviet Union since then remain the core of the professional manpower.

Scientific research is conducted at the various institutes of the Academy of Sciences, at educational institutions, and at some of the industrial enterprises. However, there are two major limiting factors as to quality and quantity of the research performed. The number of highly qualified personnel capable of advanced scientific research is small, and the major emphasis in research is on its immediate application. From the practical point of view, it is more expedient at this stage of development for Chinese scientists to borrow existing knowledge from the more advanced nations and convert it to the special needs and the present level of Chinese technology. It is here that the Chinese scientist can make his greatest contribution.

There is an apparent shortage of technical personnel at both the professional and semiprofessional levels. Additional technicians could be put to good use and would make a considerable contribution to China's present economy and to its future rate of growth. However, they do not represent the solution to China's economic problems. Some form of balance must exist between the technical personnel and the overall level of a country's economic development. The growth in the numbers of engineers and technicians must go hand in hand with the gradual development of heavy industry, with greater yields from agriculture, with the production and importation of the necessary machinery and equipment, and with a faster rate of capital accumulation. To say that a shortage of technical and scientific personnel is a major factor in limiting the rate of China's development is to oversimplify the many problems that are facing her today.

What of the future of education, professional manpower, science, and technology in Communist China? Predictions and projections for China are extremely hazardous and vulnerable. Flimsy trends and indices are of little practical value in projecting either statistics or concepts even to a few years hence. What may seem to be a trend is often wiped out overnight by a new policy or by a different assessment of the statistics. Only broad general conjectures may be expected to weather the unpredictable nature of developments within Communist China.

At the primary level, universal education for the full 6 years is not likely to be attained in China in the foreseeable future; participation rate will probably continue to grow but at a much slower pace. Great emphasis will probably be placed on the vocational schools to fill out the needs for skilled manpower, and on the normal schools to increase the ranks of trained teachers. Because of increased enrollment in higher education during the past few years, the number of graduates will greatly increase despite the fact that enrollment will level off.

Raising the low standards of education will be extremely gradual. As the numbers at the various educational levels become stabilized, additional emphasis will be placed on quality; this will coincide with an increase in the number of more qualified teachers. At all levels, but especially in higher education, the quality of the graduate will be closely related to the degree of emphasis on labor and the time that students will be expected to contribute to production. The difference in standards and quality between urban and rural schools will persist.

The number of professionals with higher education is currently increasing at approximately 10 percent annually. This rate of increase may accelerate slightly during the coming years. The emphasis will continue to be on the technical and engineering personnel. The professional level of these individuals will in no sense be comparable to that of graduates of universities in the West. However, increasing numbers of select Chinese students will probably get advanced training in the Soviet Union and will achieve a fairly sophisticated level in their fields. For some time to come the emphasis will continue to be on the practical application of scientific knowledge to various types of production.

Finally, at the risk of being accused of being a neo-Malthusian, it is suggested that the extent of China's achievements, the fulfillment of her plans, the speed with which she will attain industrial and economic goals will, to a very large extent, depend on her ability to limit the excessive rate of growth of her population—one brief attempt at population control was abandoned as a national policy in 1958, presumably because of its failure. Despite the very impressive progress that Communist China has been able to achieve during the past 10 years, the burden of the fifteen or more million people added to her population every year may be too overwhelming for China to emerge as a modern industrial power.

CHAPTER II

Educational Policies and Problems

EDUCATION BEFORE 1950

Until the turn of the 20th century, education in China was centered on the teachings of Confucius, on classic literature, and on Chinese history. The emphasis was on the past and not on the present or the future. Education was available to a small minority of the population, primarily the children of officials and intellectuals. Except for a series of minor reforms beginning in 1901, the break with the past did not occur until 1905, when the age-old system of competitive civil examinations, with their stress on classical studies, was abolished. This first major departure from the classical tradition set the stage for the gradual introduction of such subjects as science, geography, and world history. Public education, which was completely new to Chinese culture, developed gradually, influenced by missionary schools and pedagogic practices from Japan, the United States, and Europe.

Due to the size of the population and inadequate financial support, the considerable progress in school reforms did not benefit the population at large; only a limited number of urban children felt the effect of the new policies.

After the revolution of 1911, the new Ministry of Education issued a statement which established as its main goals the enlargement of school facilities, especially for primary schools; increased emphasis on handicraft and trade schools; elimination of the ancient classics from the lower schools; and introduction of coeducation into primary schools. Between 1911 and 1928, primarily through the initiative of the National Educational Association, the school system in China underwent a number of reorganizations and reforms, but again little progress was made in extending education to the less-privileged segments of the population.

In 1928 the Kuomintang regime reiterated the emphasis on education proclaimed under the Chinese Republic. The initial statement of policy was followed by numerous directives changing and implementing the original decrees and allowing local variations. The new government increased teachers' salaries and generally improved their working conditions. In an attempt to find the ideal solution to the problems of education in China, schools were combined, divided, and reorganized. For example, at different times there were 4-year primary schools, 1- and

2-year primary schools, and 6-year primary schools—some divided into junior and senior levels and some not. Nevertheless, compulsory education was never achieved, and the best schools in every large town were the privately endowed institutions supported by individuals, guilds, missions, and other organizations. These are the schools from which a large proportion of the present professional and political leaders of China were graduated.

Two major obstacles to the introduction of universal education in China were closely related. One was simply the size of the total population; even a preliminary approach to the ideal of universal education would entail supplying teachers and other facilities for some 100 million children. The other was the lack of the necessary funds to establish such a system. Although financial support for all public schools was shared by the central, provincial, and county governments, there was never enough money even to maintain the schools already in existence, much less to expand the existing facilities. Also, the mass of the population was not psychologically ready for educational reform, especially when illiterate and impoverished parents were required to pay fees for the schooling of their children. Other obstacles, again related to general conditions within China, were the shortage of qualified teachers, inadequate transportation, and political and economic instability.

The development of higher education was also slow and sporadic. The first national university in China was created in 1898 as the Capital University, later called the Peking University. By 1912, the first year of the Republic, there were 4 universities and 111 independent colleges and specialized institutes in China, with a total enrollment of 40,114 students. Of the 108 institutions of higher learning in 1922, 50 were private, 31 provincial, and 27 national.[1]

As in the case of primary and secondary education, the Ministry of Education of the Nationalist Government, in attempting to establish a suitable system of higher education, proclaimed and amended numerous decrees and laws. The Ministry experimented with the length of training to be prescribed in universities, with types of higher educational establishments, and with the curriculums in the various faculties. In certain respects—and particularly in relation to the progress made at the lower educational levels—there was considerable advance in higher education during the Nationalist period. In the early 1940's there were 143 institutions of higher learning, subdivided as follows: 39 universities, 50 independent colleges, and 54 technical institutes.[2] The number of institutions continued to grow, and by 1947-48 there were 207 institutions of higher education with 155,036 students.[3]

[1] Chung Shih, *Higher Education in Communist China* (Hong Kong: 1953).

[2] *China Handbook, 1937–1944* (Chungking: Ministry of Information, 1944).

[3] *Chung-kuo Chiao-yu Nien-chien* [Chinese Educational Yearbook] (Shanghai: Ministry of Education, 1948).

General Nature of Reforms

China's constitution states that "citizens of the People's Republic of China have a right to education." In their attempt to make this right a reality, the Communists had to overcome most of the problems that had faced the previous regimes. The difficulties in attaining their goals are reflected in the often unsystematic and haphazard nature of the numerous educational reforms. Such success as they achieved was primarily the result of comprehensive centralized control over the population, the

STRUCTURE OF EDUCATIONAL SYSTEM (CIRCA 1960)

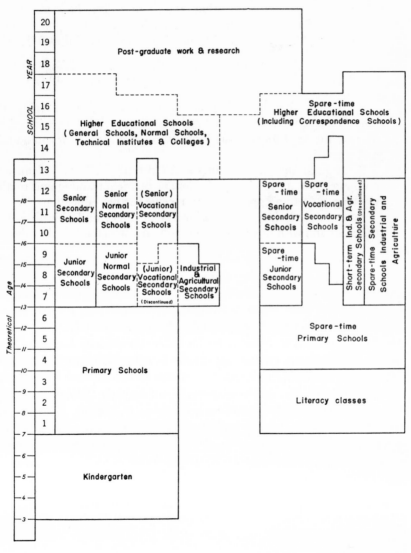

willingness to spend the necessary funds for the expansion of educational facilities and also the willingness to sacrifice quality in order to provide at least some education for the great masses of the population. Under the direction of the Ministry of Education and, of course, the indomitable leadership of the Communist Party, the educational system has undergone a number of major reorganizations and reorientations which have affected not only the administration and curriculums but the basic principles of education as well.

The basic educational reform of the new regime was adopted by the Administrative Council of the Chinese People's Republic on August 10, 1951. It provided for the types of schools, the length of the various courses, age limits, and requirements; however, for the most part, the system retained the structure that the Nationalists had given it. Most of the difference was in the approach and in the philosophy. Ch'ien Chun-jui, Vice Minister of Education, summarized it as follows:

1. It clearly and completely guarantees to all the people in the country, first of all the workers and peasants, an opportunity to receive education.

2. It establishes the appropriate position and system of technical schools, specialized schools and colleges, and special courses in order to meet the need for training large numbers of persons for national reconstruction.

3. It guarantees to all young and old-type intellectual elements an opportunity to receive revolutionary political training and to all working cadres an opportunity to receive further education.

4. It correctly integrates uniformity of policy and objectives on the one hand with flexibility of method and procedure on the other.[4]

The influence of the Soviet Union on the Chinese education system is undeniable. Although the attempt has been to learn from Soviet experience and try to adapt this experience to the peculiar conditions and needs of China, there have been numerous complaints of blind imitation of things Russian, although usually these criticisms have been quite specific and have not extended to the system as a whole. One of the more frequent expressions of resentment in connection with education refers to the wholesale translation of Soviet textbooks, many of which are obsolete, and many of whose methods and examples are quite foreign to the Chinese student. During the single year of 1953, 277 translations of Soviet textbooks were published for use in Chinese schools. The demand for Soviet technical and scientific literature has been even greater; between 1949 and 1955, about 2,000 titles were translated into Chinese.[5] The total number of Russian books translated into

---

[4] *Jen-min Chiao-yu* [People's Education], November 1951.

[5] Pin Min, *Istoriya Kitaysko-Sovetskoy Druzhby* [History of Sino-Soviet Friendship] (Moskva: 1959), p. 341.

Chinese is considerably larger: between 1950 and 1957, 190 million copies of 12,400 books were printed and distributed.[6]

The Party maintains rigid control not only over the educational system, as such, but over every school through Party representatives who have more authority than any of the professional educators. These representatives must approve the curriculum, all student activities, all promotions and graduations, appointment of teachers, and every other phase of school activity.

The political and practical education of youth is given an emphasis equal to that of the basic subject matter studied. Ideological indoctrination and orientation permeate every lesson. Time is set aside daily for group meetings and political discussions. In addition, there are usually weekly meetings for discussing such topics as "significant occurrences" that are of interest to the children, such as the celebration of the 40th anniversary of the Great October Revolution, International Women's Day, and Liberation Day.

To the Communists, education is far more than schooling. It is not distinguishable from indoctrination, propaganda, and agitation. Everything that produces an impact on the minds of men and brings about changes in behavior and thought must be considered a phase of education.[7]

Utilizing this concept of education, the Communists are able to report figures implying that perhaps a quarter of the population of China is attending some type of "educational" course. Although this total by no means implies that one-fourth of the Chinese people have experienced some type of formal education in the Western sense, the Communist Chinese have in fact made great progress in expanding the educational system of the country.

Two ministries under the State Council were established to take charge of education. The Ministry of Education was inaugurated in October 1949 and the Ministry of Higher Education was set up in November 1952. The latter was abolished in February 1958, leaving the Ministry of Education as the highest government authority for the control of all levels and types of education. The Ministry issues directives in respect to the administration and organization of schools, curriculums, textbooks, and methodology to education bureaus and educational and cultural offices in provinces, municipalities, and special districts. These bureaus and offices are nominally under the control of People's Committees at their corresponding levels, but actually they are under the leadership and close surveillance of individual members of the Communist Party.

---

[6] *Shih-chieh Chih-shih* [World Knowledge], No. 3, Feb. 5, 1958.

[7] Theodore Hsi-en Chen, "Education," *The New Leader*, May 4, 1959.

Although central direction and control persists, the recent trend has been more and more toward decentralization, giving local administrative organs and even individual schools (still under Party leadership) some authority in planning, organizing, financing, and maintaining the schools, depending upon local conditions and needs.

The Budget for Education

An editorial in a February 1958 issue of the *People's Daily*, speaking of educational requirements, stated that "the State is in no financial position at present to satisfy fully the needs of the people." [8] This statement could just as well have been made during any one of the preceding years for, although there has been a considerable increase in money allotted to education, funds have not kept pace with the growth of enrollment and the need for expansion of school facilities. Nevertheless, the importance attached to education may be seen from the fact that, despite this shortage, the state has managed to allocate an average of 7 percent of its growing national budget between 1951 and 1956 to education. In 1957 the figure increased to almost 10 percent, growing by some 40 percent over the preceding year while the total state budget decreased by about 4 percent.

As may be seen in table 1, over the years there have been, usually, only minor fluctuations in the proportion of the state budget going toward education. There have been, however, some sharp changes in the internal distribution of the educational budget among higher, secondary, and primary education. Because of the great demands and the shortage of funds, the Communists have often had to concentrate, from one year to the next, on one particular level of the educational system. In 1955 there was a decrease in the funds allocated for higher and secondary education and no increase in the funds for primary education. The year 1956 saw a radical drop in the money allotted for primary education and a proportional increase in the money for higher education and, especially, secondary education. Some of the shifts in emphasis have been internal and not visible from the overall figures. For example, during some years more money was spent to construct and expand vocational schools at the expense of normal schools and secondary general schools.

The slight drop in the educational budget in 1958 is the reflection of the newly initiated drives for "work and study" and "people's schools." One of the explicit reasons for these policies has been to reduce the budget for education and to make the people and the students themselves pay a larger share of the educational expenses. The following quotation points up the budgetary considerations involved in the more recent emphasis on spare-time education as exemplified in the agricultural schools:

[8] *Jen-min Jih-pao* [People's Daily], Feb. 10, 1958.

Money expended by the State to train a student in an ordinary junior middle school amounts to more than 180 yuan a year, whereas that needed for the education of an agricultural middle school student is less than 20 yuan. Similarly, the financial burden on the student's family is reduced from more than 100 yuan to some 30 yuan a year. To train the same number of students, an agricultural middle school requires fewer teachers than an ordinary junior middle school. Students of the agricultural middle schools, though not studying as many subjects, can more quickly apply what they learn to production because they work part time.[9]

Perhaps the most indicative measure of the stage of development and quality of education in Communist China is the amount spent annually per student at the various educational levels. From 1952 through 1955 only 12 yuan were spent annually per student in primary education. This already insignificant amount dropped to 8 yuan in 1956. Even so, these figures are exaggerations, for the educational budget includes both operating school expenses and costs of capital construction. The local budgets are not a factor here, for while schools at provincial or municipal levels are under the local budget and are administered by the corresponding administrative units, these budgets are included in the national total.

The annual expenditures per student in higher and secondary education are considerably greater but still extremely low. The average amount spent for a secondary-school student has been greater than that spent on a student in an institute or a university. The reason probably lies in the fact that the Communists took over relatively adequate facilities for higher education from the Nationalist Government but their expansion of secondary education—particularly secondary vocational education—has had to develop from a much more inadequate base. Thus, the capital expenditures for secondary education have been higher.

Between 1955 and 1956 the budget for science increased by over 500 percent, and by 1958 was approximately 1.2 percent of the state budget, or a fairly significant proportion of the total—considering the small number of scientists and the level of the economy. These funds are used to maintain the Academy of Sciences as well as to support research by the ministries, industries, and educational institutions.

In 1956 the budget of the Academy of Sciences was 66.7 million yuan [10] or 28.4 percent of the science funds, while in 1957 the total increased to 90 million yuan,[11] representing a slight drop to 27.5 percent of the science budget.

---

[9] *Peking Review,* No. 11, Mar. 15, 1960.
[10] *New China News Agency,* June 4, 1957.
[11] *Ibid.,* July 5, 1957.

TABLE 1.—*Communist China's Budget for Education and Science*

	1950	1951	1952	1953	1954	1955	1956	1957	1958
Total State budget (millions of yuan)	6,808	11,902	16,787	21,488	24,632	26,920	30,573	29,020	40,960
Budget for education:									
Millions of yuan	......	813	1,123	1,832	1,883	1,761	2,075	2,906	......
Percent of State budget	......	6.8	6.7	8.5	7.6	6.5	6.8	10.0	......
Higher education:[1]									
Millions of yuan	......	114	205	426	468	399	557	637	599
Percent of budget for education	......	14.0	18.3	23.3	24.9	22.7	26.8	22.3	......
Yuan per student	......	73	107	201	185	139	137	142	......
Secondary education:									
Millions of yuan	......	140	394	722	743	691	1,043	[5]2,269	[5]2,253
Percent of budget for education	......	17.2	35.1	39.4	39.4	39.2	50.3		
Yuan per student	......	71	125	201	175	177	201		
Primary education:[2]									
Millions of yuan	......	560	500	633	649	649	432		
Percent of budget for education	......	68.8	44.5	34.6	34.5	36.9	20.8		
Yuan per student	......	13	10	12	13	12	8		
Other:[3]									
Millions of yuan	......	......	24	51	23	22	42	......	......
Percent of budget for education	......	......	2.1	2.7	1.2	1.2	2.0	......	......
Budget for science:[4]									
Millions of yuan	......	8	11	32	34	38	235	327	384
Percent of State budget	[6]	[6]	[6]	[6]	[6]	[6]	.8	1.0	1.2

Blanks indicate figures are not available.

1 Also includes funds for sending students abroad and to operate the Academy for Minorities.

2 Also includes budgets for kindergartens and nurseries.

3 Funds for various spare-time schools, cultural studies, literacy classes, and other adult courses.

4 There are a number of other figures reported for several of the years. For example, the 1956 budget for science was reported to have increased by 253.7 percent over 1955 (*New China News Agency*, June 26, 1956), resulting in a 1955 figure of 93 million yuan. Similarly, the 1958 budget for science was reported to be 131.3 percent greater than in 1957 (*New China News Agency* Feb. 12, 1958), resulting in a 1957 budget of 293 million yuan.

5 Includes budget for both primary and secondary levels.

6 Infinitesimal.

NOTE.—The official exchange rate is 2.345 yuan to 1 American dollar. On the open market, however, the yuan usually "depreciates" by over 50 percent. This exchange rate is presented only as a rough guide. An uncritical conversion of yuan to dollars, or for that matter to any other currency, is quite meaningless and deceiving. Although there are many reasons for the unrealistic exchange, perhaps the most important are the tight Government controls over foreign trade, rationing of food and consumer goods and the isolation of mainland China from international price effects.

Sources: *T'ung-chi Kung-tso* [Statistical Work], No. 12, June 29, 1957; 2 reports by Li Hsien-nien, Minister of Finance, to the People's Congress (*New China News Agency*, June 29, 1957, and Feb. 12, 1958); *T'sai Cheng* [Finance], No. 8, Aug. 5, 1957.

The "Leap Forward" in Education

The year of the "great leap forward" throughout China was 1958. Not only did industrial and agricultural production take the "leap," but poets turned out more poems, athletes ran faster and jumped higher, and all the people of China took a "great leap forward" in Communist ideology. In the field of education, however, the "great leap forward" added to China's already severe problems. Education was extended to great numbers, but the emphasis on quantity led to a corresponding neglect of quality. When one considers that in 1958 alone, Chinese statistics report that the number of children in kindergartens increased from 1 million to 30 million, enrollment in primary schools from 64 million to 86 million, and enrollment in secondary schools from 7 million to 10 million, the effect on quality of the instruction offered can readily be inferred. In addition to the massive increase in the numbers of people being educated, the policy of simultaneous work and study and the introduction of "people's schools" and "red and expert universities" also contributed to the low quality of instruction.

The glorification of labor has been preached in the schools of China almost from the initial revision of the educational system under the Communists. From the middle 1950's the emphasis continued to increase, culminating in 1958 when the whole educational system was once again revised to incorporate production and physical labor as part of every student's curriculum.

The emphasis on combining education and labor is the result of three related policies and goals. The first is the continuing effort, intensified since the rectification campaign, to deemphasize the role and prestige of the intellectuals (see ch. VI):

> Because of the existence of the two separate classes of brain workers and brawn workers and the antagonisms between mental labor and physical labor [in the old society], the intellectual elements brought up in the old society generally cannot become laborers while laborers generally are not intellectual elements.[12]

Now, of course, since the ownership of the means of production has undergone Socialist transformation, "the gap between mental labor and physical labor is gradually narrowed down and will eventually disappear." One editorial pointed out that in the past some circles had overlooked the importance of labor training among elementary and secondary school students. These circles were said to have failed to understand the duties of Chinese elementary and secondary schools and the fact that most of the graduates of these schools would have to engage in labor while only a small portion would be able to pursue advanced studies.[13] Other editorials and articles criticized the attitude of many

---

[12] *Jen-min Chiao-yu* [People's Education], Apr. 1, 1958.

[13] *Jen-min Jih-pao* [People's Daily], Mar. 16, 1957.

students who considered it degrading to engage in farming and other types of manual labor. This was called an arrogant approach and a "feudalistic, aristocratic, and bourgeois view."

The second reason for the introduction of labor into all school curriculums is more utilitarian. In China everyone is a producer, and every pair of hands contributes to the economic race in order to decrease the time necessary for transforming China into an industrial nation. Particularly since the introduction of the communes, virtually every individual from 6 past 60 is required to contribute to the common goal.

The third reason is budgetary. During the early months of 1958, the emphasis on thriftiness was also given as a reason for the need for students to participate in labor. The Communists announced that the country could not afford to pay the way of ever-increasing numbers of youths through school. Thus, the stipends were lowered, and students in secondary general schools and in institutions of higher education were directed to work during their vacations and on their days off to help pay for the cost of their education:

> Since last year [1957], a number of students in China have performed various types of manual labor during vacation and extra-curricular hours and used the remuneration for their work to meet part or all of their tuition and living expenses. This combination of work and study is of momentous significance to bringing up students as socialistic and cultured laborers. . . . The State defrayed more than 300 million yuan in stipends for secondary school students alone during the period of the First Five-Year Plan.[14]

Like so many Communist policies, in which there is a gradual intensification and expansion of the original plans, this was just the beginning of the work-study system. The general emphasis on manual labor and production led first to the combination of production and education in secondary vocational schools, then to part-time and spare-time jobs for students, and finally, in 1958, to the "great leap forward" into an almost complete integration of education and production. Whereas in the past it was in most cases a decision of the individual student whether or not he took a job, on March 15, 1958, the Ministry of Education issued an official proclamation stating that the question as to whether a student should seek employment would be decided by the institution in which he was enrolled.[15] This proclamation stated that schools in the rural districts should sign contracts with farm cooperatives so that their students would have the opportunity of working on farms. These schools were also empowered to set up experimental farms of their own. In the urban areas, schools were to arrange for their students to work in factories or on construction sites or other such places under contracts signed with neighboring plants and enterprises. Schools were instructed to set up

---

[14] *New China News Agency,* Jan. 27, 1958.

[15] *Ibid.,* May 15, 1958.

experimental factories of their own, if possible; urban schools that lacked the necessary land were instructed to send their students to work in nearby farming cooperatives in the suburban districts.

By the summer of 1958 the policy was being implemented throughout the country:

> Factories and workshops have been set up by institutions of higher learning in various parts of China in accordance with the policy of combining education with labor. The factories and workshops have been set up in line with the specialized fields of the institutions in order to link teaching with scientific research and production. They are turning out a great variety of products including iron and steel, farm machinery, chemical fertilizers, paper, and such high grade products as precision machinery and electronic tubes. They are also designing and trial-producing machinery and equipment to contribute to the great leap forward in production.[16]

The same phenomenon was occurring in secondary schools and even in primary schools:

> Many primary schools have begun to attach themselves to factories, worksites, gardens, and other places of work to establish a permanent labor system. . . . The pupils also participate in domestic work and work beneficial to the public inside and outside their schools. Their work includes street sweeping, weeding of fields, and elimination of insect pests. At present, a primary school at Chunghua Road has teamed up with a chemical factory, a rope factory, a timber mill, and a flour factory. The pupils of the senior classes will take up timber carrying and ropemaking, while those of the intermediate classes will do lighter work such as rice grading and packing.[17]

In addition to setting up factories and workshops in educational institutions, there is even a more intense effort to get all types of enterprises and institutions to establish and operate schools:

> All factories, enterprises, scientific research organs, public offices, civic bodies, armed forces, people's communes, and cities and street organizations must operate schools. Facts demonstrate that they are capable not only of operating spare-time schools but also full-time and part-time schools; not only regular schools but also training classes; and not only specialized higher and medium-level schools but also the ordinary primary, middle, and normal schools.[18]

Although the big push to have enterprises, institutions and communities establish schools did not occur until the "leap forward," the initial steps in this direction were taken earlier in the form of *minpan* or people's

[16] *Ibid.*, July 24, 1958.
[17] *Chieh-fang Jih-pao* [Liberation Daily], Oct. 12, 1958.
[18] *Hung-ch'i* [Red Flag], No. 3, Feb. 1, 1960.

schools. Until 1956 only a fraction of 1 percent of the schools in China were not run by the state. Probably partly as a result of the growth in enrollment which occurred in 1956, the Communists decided that the state could not assume the full financial burden of expanding education and introduced a policy designed to induce schools to become self-supporting. The masses were directed to set up their own schools and to "promote education through industry and thrift"; if monasteries and ancestral temples were not available for school buildings, buildings should be erected with materials and labor donated by the masses; desks and chairs for use in the classrooms should be provided by the families of the students; since most of the students were participating in some form of production, their contributions would aid in the upkeep of the schools.

The following is a typical description of the activities in a rural people's secondary school:

> Students study half the day and do productive work the other half. On rainy days they have more time for study, but on fine days less time. Apart from their studies, they have to reclaim wasteland, till the land, look after the livestock. They have also built three classrooms and eight dormitories. Their study is quite exacting, as they have to go through basically the same courses as offered in an ordinary secondary school. . . . The day students go to school in the morning carrying with them sickles and baskets or receptacles for manure, so that when they go home after school every day they may cut grass or pick up manure on the way.[19]

The Communists have not been blind to the deficiencies of people's schools. For example, here is a statement made when there was still controversial discussion with regard to these schools:

> The private schools themselves have many unreasonable elements; the more obvious ones among them are: (1) High tuition affected the enthusiasm of laborers to send their sons and daughters to school; (2) the unreasonable wage system affected the development of unity and positiveness among the teachers, and bread capitalist and equalitarian thinking; (3) the loose system of control of personnel and finances caused unreasonable situations of more men than work and more work than men. These irrational elements directly affected the elevation of the quality of education and the manifestation of the potentialities of schools.[20]

Since to a large extent the establishment of these schools has been left up to the individual provinces and communities, their development has been erratic and scattered. Some provinces have encouraged this type of school while others have barely started. Although reports speak of people's schools "mushrooming everywhere," incomplete returns show

[19] *Jen-min Jih-pao* [People's Daily], Feb. 10, 1958.
[20] *Chieh-fang Jih-pao* [Liberation Daily], Jan. 25, 1956.

that only 25,600 primary schools with 1,610,000 pupils and 8,000 secondary schools with over 420,000 students were operating at the beginning of 1958.[21] The provinces in which private education has expanded most rapidly are Kweichow, Hopei, and Liaoning. In 1958, 30.5 percent of the total number of primary pupils were in private schools in Kweichow; in Hopei and Liaoning, more than 19 percent of the secondary school students were in schools set up by the people. Since 1958 the number of schools operated by the masses has rapidly increased, but most of them are of the spare-time variety, requiring little equipment and staffed by persons with minimal qualifications:

> Private schools may not have a high standard of quality, but the masses think they are better than no schools. Private schools should be set up and run according to the local conditions. They should be set up and run on a scale and maintained at a level permitted by these conditions, and no attempt should be made to make them uniform in quality. For uniformity can be achieved only at the expense of the quantity of schools, which means that there will be fewer opportunities for education for the masses.[22]

This is a most straightforward statement of the policy which emphasizes quantity over quality.

The "leap forward" in education did not stop at the primary or secondary level but extended to higher education. In 1958 people's universities also sprang up all over the countryside. The directive of the Central Committee of the Chinese Communist Party called for the proletarianization of higher education within 15 years, so that by that time all the young people and adults in the country who could meet the requirements and had the desire might acquire a higher education. The result has been the establishment of scores of so-called "red and expert universities." Both the organizers and the teachers in these "universities" are primarily individuals with the "proper political conciousness" rather than those with scholastic attainments. The fact that the level of these schools was brought down to the level of the masses was proclaimed as a step toward the raising of mass culture and not a lowering of educational standards. It is with great pride that reports proclaimed that at a particular "university" the "professor" was a model farmer who had not even completed primary school.

All "red and expert universities" are part-time schools. They are founded and supported by local authorities to serve production and are "closely connected with reality." The majority teach advanced agricultural methods, while political indoctrination is one of the basic ingredients of all the courses. There have been many reports on the numerical growth of such institutions. Only one example, however,

---

[21] *Jen-min Jih-pao* [People's Daily], Feb. 10, 1958.
[22] *Ibid.*

will suffice to illustrate the entire phenomenon. Between 1957 and 1958 the number of higher educational establishments increased from 227 to 1,065; in addition, "23,500 spare-time universities, and part-work part-study universities were established".[23] In this case, no distinction is made between regular higher educational institutions and "red and expert universities"—both are included. One county in Honan Province reported that during a period of 2 days, 44 "red and expert universities" were set up.[24]

Wyndham Newton, in the *Far Eastern Economic Review*, commented on the events transpiring in China in these terms:

> Proper University students and graduates, who have gone right through the normal avenues of promotion and education must resent almost as deeply as the faculties themselves the description of "university" as now applied to institutions established in a factory or directly related to work and study on the land—all the more so when quite uneducated persons who happen to be expert artisans or workers in some branch of technique like ant-killing become members of their faculties.[25]

In trying to build up the prestige of the new institutions the Communists inadvertently and indirectly indicated the level and quality of education in most regular universities:

> The Liming Machinery Works in Shenyang, for instance, has founded a work-while-you-study technological institute which is attended by workers and cadres with a middle school level. These students work 4 hours and study 6 hours a day. In 3 to 4 years they will be able to reach the academic standard of a college or university graduate.[26]

What is the net effect of the educational developments of the past few years? Undoubtedly the integration of production and education will contribute to the achievement of the goals of increasing production and lowering educational costs to the state. But what of the effects on the quality of education received by the youth of China? On September 19, 1958, the CCP Central Committee and State Council directed that "productive labor must be listed as a regular subject in the curriculums of all schools, and each student must participate in manual labor for a prescribed length of time." [27] Scattered sources refer to the "prescribed length of time" as being 4, 6, or 8 hours per week; however, this seems too little time to account for some of the "accomplishments" ascribed to

[23] *New China News Agency,* Sept. 1, 1958.

[24] *Jen-min Jih-pao* [People's Daily], Aug. 12, 1958.

[25] Wyndham Newton, "Chinese Universities To Become 'Proletarian'," *Far Eastern Economic Review,* Nov. 27, 1958.

[26] *College Students of New China* (Peking: 1958).

[27] *New China News Agency,* Sept. 19, 1958.

educational institutions. Many students must spend half their time, or even more, on actual production or in manual labor. For example:

> Young pioneers of Hsiao-feng Secondary School got busy throughout the night and in 3 days turned out 100 small carts. Decked out with small red flags, these carts, in neat rows, hauled over 4 million catties of manure to the farm cooperative.[28]

It would be safe to assume that this operation cut into the educational program of the students. Again:

> The integrated iron and steel works being set up by Northeast China Engineering College in Shenyang will turn out 10,000 tons of iron, 20,000 tons of steel, and 30,000 tons of rolled steel annually. Altogether, 100 factories and workshops have been set up by the more than 30 colleges and schools in Shenyang. The Shenyang Medical College is preparing to manufacture microscopes, medicinal preparations, and drugs and medical apparatus.[29]

And again: "In July and August this year [1958], Tsinghua University completed and planned 61 factories, shops, a designing company, and an engineering company."[30]

There are innumerable examples of the volume and scope of production undertaken within educational institutions and by students in factories and on the farms; usually, participation in these activities has been placed above educational goals and achievements.

There are a few indications that the enthusiasm for this policy may have carried its implementation too far. Some doubts have already been expressed: "Will this directive raise or lower the intellectual standard—that is, the quality of education and scientific research?"[31] Until now the answer has always been optimistic; after discussing the fantastic production accomplishments of some of the schools, the reports usually add, as they did in the case of Tsinghua University, that "teachers and students improved the teaching work and markedly improved the teaching quality." But the fact that the question was raised at all may be a sign of an eventual easing of the policy.

"Walking on Two Legs"

There is an important factor to be considered in the rather pessimistic picture of an educational system that in some respects seems to be moving backward. It is expressed by a currently popular slogan and places the preceding discussion into a frame of reference that gives some rationale to the educational policies of Communist China.

The slogan "walking on two legs" is an important practical rationalization of many of China's problems. Translated from Communist jib-

---

[28] *Kuang-ming Jih-pao* [Kuang-ming Daily], June 20, 1958.
[29] *New China News Agency,* Aug. 1, 1958.
[30] *Shih-shih Shou-ts'e* [Current Events], No. 20, Oct. 27, 1958.
[31] *New China News Agency,* July 11, 1958.

berish into its simplest form, it says, in effect, that in their present stage of development they are unable to use the best and most efficient methods of production, and are unable to give the people all they might want in terms of education, services, etc.; it is therefore necessary to strive to attain our goals by a variety of methods and through many diverse approaches.

To implement this principle, the Communists have unsuccessfully attempted to develop backyard furnaces at the same time that they were expanding modern steel plants; they are utilizing the experience of the traditional Chinese medical practitioners while continuing to present Western medical theories in many of the schools; they are using coolie labor to unload ships next to a dock with a modern crane; they are emphasizing science and so-called "scientific methods" among the peasants while they attempt to obtain true scientific achievements from a nuclear physicist in an institute of the Academy of Sciences.

Perhaps the most lucid example of "walking on two legs" is in the field of education. The Communist have stated the policy in this phraseology:

> We are guided by the principle of the coordination of uniformity and diversity, of popularization and acceleration of standard, and of overall planning by the central authorities and delegation of power to the localities. We have put into effect a program with equal emphasis on schools operated by the state and those operated by factories, mines, enterprises, governmental organs, civic bodies, armed forces, people's communes, cities, and street organizations; on full-time, part-time, and spare-time education; on popular education and vocational educational; on school education and self-education; and on tuition-free and tuition-paying education.[32]

This diversity in methods of education and types of schools reflects the official view that faces reality and indirectly admits that at present China is in no position to provide a first-class education to the scores of millions of children and youths of school age. At the same time it is acknowledged that even inferior education is better than none:

> The cultural revolution includes both the tasks of universalization and elevation. . . . Presently we are setting up, in great numbers, agricultural middle schools, and also elementary schools and spare-time middle and elementary schools administered by the people. The main purpose of these schools is universalization, and not too much is expected of these schools. . . . First we must energetically complete the universalization process, and immediately afterward, seek to consolidate and elevate.[33]

On this premise, millions of people are attending various types of schools on a part-time basis where they learn the rudiments of the three R's,

---

[32] *Hung-ch'i* [Red Flag], No. 3, Feb. 1, 1960.
[33] *Jen-min Chiao-yu* [People's Education], May 1, 1958.

obtain a certain political awareness, and perhaps go on to one of the "red and expert universities." This is one of the "legs." The other "leg" of the educational system continues to cater to the more promising urban student who will be expected to enter one of the better institutes or universities and who may go on to advanced studies at the Academy of Sciences. This practical approach to education has undeniable merits and seems to be well suited to the conditions within China. It is not the most efficient system; many qualified students do not have the opportunity to pursue their studies and are, in effect, wasted; but despite the limitations in the facilities, teaching personnel, funds, etc., it manages to provide a large number of people with an appreciation for education which will be passed on to the next generation, while giving a relatively small number of people the knowledge needed to be in the forefront of the drive toward industrialization and world status.

Prospects and Proposed Reforms

Over the past 10 years the most significant features of China's educational system have been: (1) Complete Party control over all aspects of education; (2) rapid expansion of the school facilities and even more rapid growth of enrollment; (3) the inferior quality of education received by the great majority of the students; (4) great emphasis on specialization, particularly at the middle and higher educational levels, which was intensified further with the integration of education with production; and (5) the willingness to use the trial-and-error method throughout the educational system.

What can be expected of the next 10 years? Certainly centralized Party control will not diminish. Enrollment will continue to grow, but at a much slower pace. The quality of mass education will not improve radically, and specialization will continue to be an important factor. At the same time, a greater number of promising students will be sent to the expanding facilities for quality training in the first-class, or so called "key," universities. There are already indications that new experiments are being conducted and that China's educational system may once again be ready for additional innovations.

Some indications of the possible future trends in this respect have been outlined in two speeches delivered by Vice Premier Lu Ting-yi (CCP Propaganda Department Head) and Minister of Education Yang Hsiu-feng, at the second session of the Second National People's Congress.[34]

The all-encompassing goals of the contemplated reforms are aimed at accelerating the learning process by reducing the years of study and at the same time raising the standards of education, controlling study hours, and increasing physical labor. The major points of the speedup

---

[34] *Peking Review,* May 10, 1960.

are: (1) For children to start school at 6 years of age instead of 7; (2) teaching of reading and arithmetic in the first grade; (3) introduction of algebra in the fifth grade; (4) transfer of mathematics, physics, and chemistry from the college level to the senior secondary schools; (5) transfer of the basic tools of scientific and technical study (such as analytical geometry, integral calculus, the theory of semiconductors, nuclear physics, and the study of rare elements and high molecular compounds) to the senior secondary level; (6) in general, reduction of the lecture hours and increase in homework. Their contentions were that these reforms would have important and beneficial results, but exactly how all the above subjects would fit into a 3-year senior secondary school was not discussed. The contemplated reforms would also reduce the existing 12-year system for elementary and secondary schools to 10 or even 9 years: This would "release" some 10 million senior secondary school students from 16 to 17 years of age for full-time production work; graduates who do not go on to full-time university work would continue their education on a spare-time basis.

Another suggestion was recently contained in the political journal *Red Flag:*

> At present, the full-time schools, still follow an old practice of starting the academic year in the fall. We believe this can be changed. The academic year, in fact, can begin both in the spring and fall, and matriculation can take place twice a year. This has to be done to meet the needs of children born in different months, and to make it possible for people of different background to enter school at any time they want.[35]

Because of the relatively informal and flexible structure of the educational system, this may not be as difficult to achieve in China as it would be elsewhere.

Both Lu Ting-yi and Yang Hsiu-feng, in the speeches referred to above, repeatedly urged caution and a practical sense in carrying out the new reforms. They recommended that preparatory experiments be made, that different conditions in different localities be taken into consideration, and that premature conclusions be avoided.[36]

The tentative schedule for these reforms is set at 10 to 20 years because the application of the "guiding ideology of Marx-Lenin-Mao to education cannot be solved all at once." On the basis of past experience, however, it may be predicted that if and when these policies are passed down to the local school administrations, there will be an acceleration

---

[35] *Hung-ch'i* [Red Flag], No. 3, Feb. 1, 1960.
[36] For a more detailed discussion of the proposed reforms, see Robert D. Barendsen, "Planned Reforms in the Primary and Secondary School Systems in Communist China," Information on Education Around the World Series, U.S. Office of Education, August 1960.

of the tempo of transforming schools to the new system. In an effort to please their superiors, local officials are notorious for pushing through policies and programs at a much more rapid pace than intended by the planners at the national level. Because of the speedup, performance records are set, but in most instances the end result is prolonged confusion and an actual delay in the implementation of the policy. There is no reason to believe that the activation of the present proposals will substantially produce more efficiency.

CHAPTER III

Primary and Secondary Education

PRESCHOOL FACILITIES

As is so often the case in present-day China, a conceptual change plays havoc with statistics. Data dealing with preschool facilities is a case in point; it must be split into two periods, pre- and post-1958.

Kindergartens and nurseries have never been widespread in China, and statistics on their development show that even as late as 1957, out of some 140 to 150 million children under 7 years of age, there were only about one and a half million in formal establishments of this nature. In general, the figures up to 1957 probbaly refer solely to urban child care facilities built and operated by factories, mines, business enterprises, government offices, and city-block cooperatives. Their main function was to permit the mother to work, so that while some of these facilities were located in residential neighborhoods, many were maintained on the premises of the particular institution where the mother worked.

Even during this period of relatively slow growth, there were not enough qualified personnel to staff preschool institutions, and most of the teachers were housewives or young girls who had undergone very short training courses. Nevertheless, in the more progressive kinder-gartens there was an attempt to include such training as physical educa-tion, language, knowledge of social and natural environment, art, music, and number study.

In 1958 the reported number of children enrolled in "kindergartens" increased almost thirtyfold over the preceding year, while the number in nurseries increased from half a million to over 47 million. Communist propaganda to the contrary, the figures for 1958 cannot be equated with those for 1957 and must be looked at independently. The growth coin-cided with the "leap forward," with the establishment of communes, and with the explicit policy of absorbing as many people as possible into the labor force. In the urban areas, more and more women entered plants and offices. In the rural areas, they were forced by the recruit-ment of millions of males into irrigation projects, roadbuilding and the like, to perform a much greater share of agricultural labor. Whereas in the past there had been some seasonal, informal accommodations to

TABLE 1.—*Development of kindergartens and nurseries, 1949–59*

Year	Kindergartens			Nurseries	
	Number	Enrollment	Instructors	Number	Participants
1949........				[1] 300	[1] 13,000
1950........					
1951........	[1] 1,800	[2] 140,325	[1] 2,000		
1952........	[1] 6,500	[3] 381,816	[1] 14,000	[1] 2,700	[1] 99,000
1953........		[3] 436,927			
1954........		[3] 424,965			
1955........		[3] 484,000			
1956........		[3] 562,000			
1957........	[1] 16,400	[1] 1,088,000	[1] 42,000	[1] 17,700	[1] 488,000
1958........	[1] 695,300	[1] 29,501,000	[1] 1,193,000	[1] 3,186,300	[1] 47,140,000
1959........	[4] 4,980,000	[4] 67,700,000			

Blanks indicate figures are not available.

[1] *Ten Great Years* (Peking: State Statistical Bureau, 1960).
[2] *New China News Agency*, Dec. 2, 1950.
[3] *Jen-min Shou-ts'e* [People's Handbook]. (Peking: 1957).
[4] *Shih-shih Shou-ts'e* [Current Events], No. 5, Mar. 6, 1959.

take care of children during the planting and harvesting seasons, the communes now provide year-round facilities for all children under school age.

The result is that the figures for 1958 and 1959 in no sense refer to what we would understand to be kindergartens. Although facilities for preschool child-care have expanded in the cities, the overwhelming increase has occurred in the countryside, where millions of children are watched over by illiterate or semiliterate old women or young girls while their mothers are working in the fields. They receive little, if any, instruction. Using averages, reported statistics indicate that there are about 45 children in each group, supervised by 2 adults.

The policy of instilling in all the love of labor is now introduced at the preschool level. In a newspaper discussion of kindergartens, one author felt it his duty to point out that "we should not regard children as laborers," but then proceeded to state that "play, schoolwork, and labor are three kinds of activity indispensable to the overall development of education in kindergarten." He pointed out that "some kindergartens took labor as their main activity and engaged the children in work to process goods for factories." This, he said, was wrong: Labor education should principally take the form of self-service—"wipe tables and chairs, arrange toys, irrigate plants, feed little animals, and the like." [1]

[1] *Shanghai Wen-hui Pao* [Shanghai Wen-hui Daily], June 20, 1959.

PRIMARY SCHOOLS

The development of primary schools in China has been rapid, particularly during the early years of the Communist regime. The highest growth occurred between 1950–51 and 1952–53, when the primary school enrollment increased by over 75 percent. On the other hand, during the next 4 years, enrollment increased by only 2 million. Between 1955–56 and 1956–57 there was a 10 million jump in the number of

PRIMARY SCHOOLS

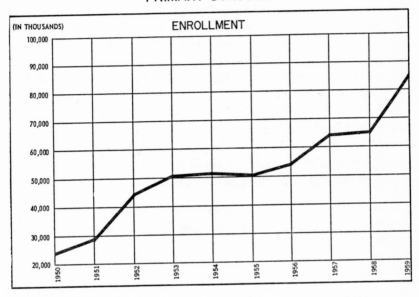

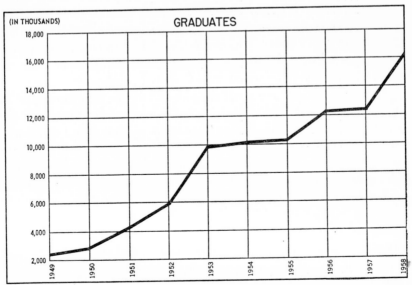

SOURCE: TABLE 2

children in school; there was a very slight increase in 1957–58; then there was the 22 million "leap forward" in 1958–59 enrollment (table 2).

Although there is usually variation in reported proportions of school-age children in school in any one year, the trend cannot be disputed, as evidenced by two sources: 50.7 percent in 1953, 61.3 percent in 1956, 85 percent in 1957 and 1958, and 87 percent in 1959 and 1960.[2] Although none of the reports is specific in what is meant by school-age children, they obviously refer to children of primary school age, or roughly between 7 and 12 years of age. The quoted percentages seem to be more or less consistent with estimated age distribution of China's population (ch. VIII, table 3); however, this consistency ignores one important fact: Because of the large number of overaged children attending primary schools, the actual number of pupils who are between 7 and 12 constitute a much smaller proportion of the total number of "school-age" children than reports would indicate. As the years go by, the increase in the participation rate will be much less rapid for two reasons: (1) There is a normal slowing up as the proportion in school approaches the school-age population, and (2) the increase in school attendance of children 7 through 12 will to some extent be counteracted by the decrease

TABLE 2.—*Primary schools, 1948–60*

[In thousands]

School year	Entrants	Enrollment	Graduates
1948–49			[1] 2,387
1949–50		[1] 24,391	[1] 2,829
1950–51		[1] 28,924	[1] 4,232
1951–52		[1] 43,154	[1] 5,942
1952–53		[1] 51,100	[1] 9,945
1953–54		[1] 51,664	[1] 10,136
1954–55		[1] 51,218	[1] 10,254
1955–56	[2] 17,500	[1] 53,126	[1] 12,287
1956–57		[1] 63,464	[1] 12,307
1957–58	[3] 16,169	[1] 64,279	[1] 16,225
1958–59	[4] 20,170	[1] 86,400	
1959–60		[5] 90,000	

Blanks indicate figures are not available.

[1] *Ten Great Years* (Peking: State Statistical Bureau, 1960).
[2] *New China News Agency*, Sept. 1, 1955.
[3] *New China News Agency*, July 1, 1957.
[4] *Ibid*, Feb. 13, 1958.
[5] *Ibid*, Jan. 22, 1960.

[2] *New China News Agency*, Sept. 19, 1959; *Hung-ch'i* [Red Flag], No. 3, Feb. 1, 1960.

in the number of overaged children.   In any case, it is unlikely that the announced target to achieve universal primary education by the mid-1960's will be attained.

A word of caution about the statistics on the number of graduates from primary schools, as presented in table 2: Both the magnitude of the figures and the discrepancy between them and other reports point to the probability that there is an element of double counting.   Since the majority of children, particularly in rural areas, have not been going beyond the lower primary school, they were counted as primary school graduates after completing 3 or 4 years of school.   Those who went on to senior primary school were counted again after completing the second 3 years of primary school.   This may be illustrated by comparing the enrollment with the graduates after subtracting the number of entrants for the current year.   Thus, by subtracting 17,500,000 entrants from the 53,126,000 enrolled in 1955–56, a figure of 35,626,000 is obtained, which represents an impossibly high 3:1 ratio between enrollment and graduates for a 6-year school.

Other figures in different sources reporting the number of primary school graduates seem more realistic and probably represent the actual number of graduates from the full 6-year elementary schools.   (From late 1951 to late 1953, primary schools consisted of only five grades.) For example, it was reported that during the period 1952–53 through 1955–56 there were 13,370,000 graduates [3] as opposed to a total of 42,622,000 derived from table 2.   Another report states that for the inclusive period 1949–50 through 1956–57,[4] there were 22 million primary school graduates, versus 67,932,000 in table 2.   In both instances there is a reasonably stable relationship between the two figures: 31.2 percent and 32.9 percent.   This relationship suggests that perhaps the differences have a basis and that the higher totals include anyone who had completed at least 3 years of primary school.

Prior to 1952 there was little standardization in the texts used in primary schools, and every province and many individual schools had their own books, depending on what was available.   Starting with 1952, there was an attempt to standardize textbooks, but in all probability there is still a considerable variety of books used in millions of primary classes throughout China.

Because of the special difficulties in learning the Chinese characters, the primary school curriculums assign half of the study time in grades 1 to 4 and one-third in grades 5 to 6 to the study of language (see appendix table B–1).   Ideally, during the 6 years in primary school the children should master 4,000 characters.   An hour a day is also devoted to arithmetic.   Both political training and practical extracurricular activities

---

[3] *New China News Agency,* Sept. 24, 1956.

[4] *Chiao-shih Pao* [Teachers' Biweekly], Oct. 1, 1957; translated by U.S. Joint Publications Research Service, in Rept. No. 753, Oct. 16, 1958: *Education in Communist China.*

also form an integral part of the curriculum. Particular emphasis on production was introduced in 1958 (see ch. II). It would seem reasonable to assume that because of the nature of agricultural work, the children in the rural areas are expected to contribute somewhat greater time to work than do their counterparts in the cities, whose usefulness in factories and other urban enterprises would be much more limited.

SECONDARY SCHOOLS

The secondary schools in China are divided into the general and the specialized secondary schools. The general (sometimes translated as "ordinary") secondary schools are essentially academic in character and consist of 3-year junior and 3-year senior schools, or a total of 6 years. The specialized secondary schools are subdivided into two types: The normal or teachers' schools and the vocational schools. Theoretically, both are divided into the lower and higher levels of 3 years each. Actually, the structure is not that precise: Depending on the particular course and scool, the term of study may fluctuate anywhere from 2 to 6 years.

The simple diagram below may be useful in following the unfortunately (but inevitably) involved discussion of the secondary schools:

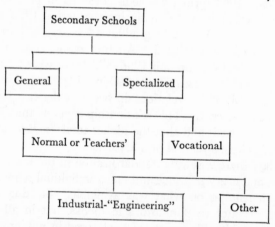

The prescribed ages for most of the secondary schools are 13 through 18 years, although once again there are many overaged children in the schools. In the movement from primary to junior secondary schools and from the first level to the second level of the secondary schools, students are required to take examinations to determine their eligibility. Since the number of vacancies in the various levels are limited, many children are eliminated, and only the most promising students are advanced. Here, too, there are exceptions: It was decided that children of workers and peasants whose grades were equal to those of others should have preference in enrolling in secondary schools. "In some localities a plan was adopted whereby select elementary students were sent to secondary schools without entrance examinations in proportion to the parents who were proletarian or poor hired peasants" [5]—a devious way of making it possible to assure the proper political background in the relatively small proportion of students who move up the educational ladder.

Secondary General Schools

The secondary general schools supply the overwhelming majority of students who go on into higher education. Table 3 presents the enrollment of both levels of general schools and the annual number of graduates. The development of these schools has been more rapid than that of the specialized secondary schools—either the normal (or teachers'

TABLE 3.—*Secondary general schools, 1949–60*

[In thousands]

School year	Enrollment			Reported total enrollment [1]	Graduates [1]
	Junior	Senior	Total		
1948–49......	....	....	....	....	280.0
1949–50......	[2] 831.8	[2] 207.2	1,039.0	1,039.0	296.0
1950–51......	[2] 1,067.0	[2] 238.0	1,305.0	1,305.0	284.0
1951–52......	[2] 1,383.7	[2] 184.4	1,568.1	1,568.0	221.0
1952–53......	[2] 2,230.5	[2] 260.4	2,490.9	2,490.0	454.0
1953–54......	[2] 2,571.6	[2] 359.5	2,931.1	2,933.0	644.0
1954–55......	[3] 3,109.0	[3] 478.0	3,587.0	3,587.0	969.0
1955–56......	[4] 3,320.0	[5] 582.0	3,902.0	3,900.0	939.0
1956–57......	[6] (3,830.0)	[7] 366.1	4,196.1	5,165.0	1,299.0
1957–58......	[8] 4,340.0	[8] 780.0	5,120.0	6,281.0	1,313.0
1958–59......	[9] 7,340.0	[10] (1,180.0)	....	8,520.0	....

Blanks indicate figures are not available.

[1] *Ten Great Years* (Peking: State Statistical Bureau, 1960).

[2] *New China News Agency*, Dec. 2, 1950.

[3] *Current Background*, Nov. 26, 1956 (Hong Kong: U.S. consulate general).

[4] *T'ung-chi Kung-tso T'ung-hsin* [Statistical Work Bulletin], No. 20, Oct. 29, 1956.

[5] *New China News Agency*, Aug. 31, 1955.

[6] Average between 1955–56 and 1957–58 enrollment in junior secondary schools.

[7] *New China News Agency*, June 20, 1956. This figure appears to be out of line with the other reported data.

[8] *Chiao-shih Pao* [Teacher's Biweekly], Jan. 1, 1957, as quoted in U.S. Joint Publications Research Service, *Nontechnical Education in Communist China*, Rept. No. 198, Jan. 24, 1958.

[9] *New China News Agency*, Sept. 18, 1959.

[10] Difference between total and junior enrollment in secondary schools. Undoubtedly an exaggerated residual.

[5] *Fu-tao-yuan* [Instructor], No. 10, Oct. 12, 1959; translated by U.S. Joint Publications Research Service, in Rept. No. 1165–D, Feb. 12, 1960.

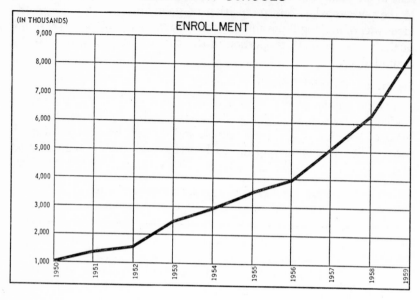

ENROLLMENT

(IN THOUSANDS)

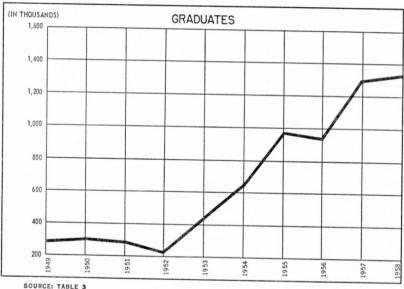

GRADUATES

(IN THOUSANDS)

SOURCE: TABLE 3

schools) or the vocational schools. The sharp increase in the enrollment between 1957 and 1958 may be attributed to the creation of
the so-called agricultural middle schools "and other industrial schools"
(falling within the secondary general-school category) on the communes. Although this type of school would more appropriately fall
under the vocational heading, enrollment statistics suggest that in most
instances they are included in the secondary general schools. In 1958

these schools had 2 million students,[6] comprising 70 percent of the total increase over the previous year. No further breakdown of this figure is available; however, the increase has been especially apparent at the junior secondary level, where in a single year the number of students increased by 3 million. Undoubtedly the "middle schools" in the communes are limited to the first three grades and the overwhelming majority of the senior secondary general schools are still located in the urban areas.

Although the secondary general schools now number 20,000,[7] those on the communes are in no way comparable to those in the cities. The rural schools "closely combine theory and practice" and "carry out extensive research on their own farms." A sample investigation of secondary agricultural schools in Kiangsu Province in 1959 showed that they were "inadequate and inferior in their material equipment and teaching staffs as compared to the secondary general full-time schools." [8] Of course the article then goes on to state that "under the leadership of the Party, with the support of the masses and the strenuous efforts of the teachers and students," the schools are constantly improving. The same article mentions one interesting reaction to agricultural schools: "What is the use for farmers to study farming?" The obvious answer, according to the Communist, is increased production and the fact that the students learn more than just farming. For example, one secondary agricultural school has opened six special courses: ". . . agricultural techniques, tool manufacturing, animal husbandry, veterinary medicine, civil engineering, gardening, and silkworm raising." [9] It would appear safe to assume that a completed primary education is not necessarily a prerequisite for these schools. It is even safer to assert that these schools confuse the educational statistics even further.

The reported number of graduates from secondary schools clearly refer to both the junior and senior levels, for in every year the number exceeds the total enrollment of the senior schools alone. In other words, the graduates of the 6-year secondary course are counted twice: Once after the junior level and once more after they complete the senior level. There are several figures, however, that report the two levels separately and make it possible to isolate the graduates from senior secondary schools from the total number of graduates. One source reported that in the period 1949–50 through 1956–57, the graduates from junior secondary schools numbered 4.4 million, while those from senior secondary schools numbered 720,000.[10] The sum of these 2 figures is almost identical to the total for these years shown in table 3: 5,120,000 versus 5,106,000. Thus, the higher level graduates constituted 14.1

[6] *Ten Great Years* (Peking: State Statistical Bureau, 1960).

[7] *New China News Agency,* Feb. 11, 1960.

[8] *Hung-ch'i* [Red Flag], No. 9, May 1, 1959.

[9] *Ibid.*

[10] *Nash Drug Kitay* [Our Friend China] (Moskva: 1959), p. 527.

percent of the total secondary graduates. Senior secondary graduates for the 4 reported years 1952–53 through 1955–56 constituted 13.1 percent of the total graduates (table 4). Similarly, the reported 216,000 senior graduates for 1950–51 through 1953–54 constituted 13.5 percent of the 1,603,000 secondary graduates for the same years.[11] This relative stability lends some credence to the year-by-year estimates of graduates from senior secondary schools presented in table 4.

Students in secondary general schools have been spending approximately 30 hours per week in classwork (see appendix table B–2). Since 1958 an increasing amount of their time has been spent in production; however, it is difficult to determine precisely to what extent these extra-curricular activities have limited classwork. It seems probable that much of the productive work expected of students in the cities is contributed outside of the school hours, except as it may relate to specific courses. Because of the nature of agriculture, the contribution of the students in rural schools is probably more seasonal and more intensive than in the

TABLE 4.—*Graduates from senior secondary schools, 1950–59*

Year	Graduates	Year	Graduates
1949–50..............	[1] (46, 200)	1954–55..............	[2] 106, 000
1950–51..............	[1] (44, 300)	1955–56..............	[3] 156, 000
1951–52..............	[1] (34, 500)	1956–57..............	[1] (202, 600)
1952–53..............	[2] 58, 400	1957–58..............	[4] (221, 700)
1953–54..............	[2] 72, 100	1958–59..............	[5] (242, 000)

[1] For the years in which a breakdown is available, there is a fairly close correlation between senior secondary graduates and the total number of reported secondary graduates: 1952–53, 12.9 percent; 1953–54, 11.2 percent; 1954–55, 10.9 percent; and 1955–56, 16.6 percent. It was then possible to utilize this relationship to estimate some of the missing years. It is reported that for the period 1949–50 through 1956–57, there were 720,000 graduates from senior secondary schools (*Nash Drug Kitay* [Our Friend China], Moskva: 1959, p. 527). By subtracting the reported graduates 1952–53 through 1955–56, a residual of 327,500 is obtained, to be distributed between 1949–50, 1950–51, 1951–52, and 1956–57. It was distributed in proportion to the total number of graduates in the appropriate years.

[2] *T'ung-chi Kung-tso T'ung-hsin* [Statistical Work Bulletin], No. 20, Oct. 29, 1956.

[3] *New China News Agency*, Apr. 4, 1956. This figure of 156,000, by the way, fits in rather uniquely with data from 2 other sources. In the same year there were 787,000 graduates from junior secondary schools (*New China News Agency*, June 20, 1956). The sum of these 2 figures (943,000) corresponds almost exactly with the 939,000 graduates reported in *Ten Great Years* (Peking: State Statistical Bureau, 1960).

[4] Assumes the same rate of increase among senior secondary graduates as reported for total secondary graduates.

[5] Assumes an identical rate of increase between 1957–58 and 1958–59 as between 1956–57 and 1957–58.

[11] *New China News Agency*, June 12, 1954.

urban areas. In October 1958 students from over 20,000 secondary schools were asserted to be running "170,000 small factories, producing over 4,000 simple machines and 1,700,000 tons of organic and chemical fertilizer. They have more than 16,000 experimental farms and are getting good harvests." [12] This is very impressive until one stops to consider that the figures imply that every school has an average of over eight "small factories"; that each school built an average of one-fifth of a "simple machine," which need not be anything more than an agricultural implement; and that probably all of the fertilizer was organic and not chemical.

As for the regular curriculum in secondary general schools, about 40 percent of the total class time is devoted to Chinese language and literature, history, and political education. About 26 percent of the time is allotted to mathematics and physics, and 17 percent to geography, biology, and chemistry. The remaining hours are devoted to physical education, music, and art. One obvious gap in many of the schools is the absence of training in foreign languages. Until recently, students went to special language schools, and only a limited number of secondary schools provided language courses in the regular curriculum. In 1959, however, Yang Hsiu-feng, Minister of Education, quoted Chou En-lai as stating that "foreign language courses should be required throughout high school." [13] Undoubtedly the number of city schools offering language courses will increase in the future.

Secondary Specialized Schools

Secondary specialized schools are divided into normal (or teachers') schools and vocational schools (which embrace industrial courses often translated as "engineering" and also courses in public health, finance and economics, agriculture, and forestry).

Normal (or Teachers') Schools

Like the secondary general schools, normal schools are theoretically divided into 3-year junior and 3-year senior schools. Actually, the length of the courses does not seem to be that precise—some courses may run anywhere from 2 to 4 years at each level. Entrants to the junior level must have completed the 6-year primary school, while entrants to the senior normal schools must have graduated from either the general or the normal junior secondary school. Theoretically, graduates from both levels of the normal school are required to serve in primary schools for a specified number of years, after which time the graduates of senior normal schools may then be promoted to teach in the junior level of the

---

[12] *Fu-tao-yuan* [Instructor], No. 10, Oct. 12, 1959; translated by U.S. Joint Publications Research Service, in Rept. No. 1165–D, Feb. 12, 1960.

[13] *Hsin-hua Pan-yueh-k'an* [New China Semimonthly Journal], No. 11, June 10, 1959.

SECONDARY SPECIALIZED SCHOOLS

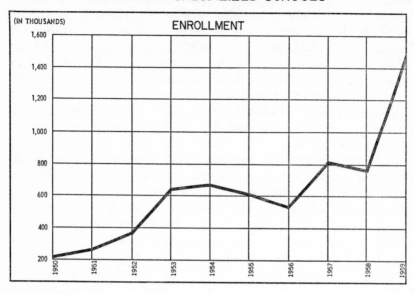

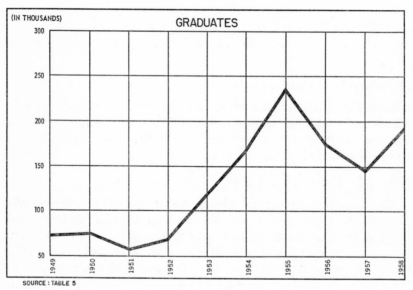

SOURCE : TABLE 5

secondary general schools.   Actually, because of the shortage of teachers, many go on to teach in the secondary general school system, upon graduation, without the primary school experience.   Presumably to avoid the possibility of teenagers' teaching students who are virtually the same age, the Ministry of Education decreed in 1955 that candidates for normal schools must be at least 15 years old and not more than 30.[14]   A

---

[14] *Jen-min Jih-pao* [People's Daily], June 17, 1955.

further comment on the quality of normal-school students (future teachers), is the fact that the most promising students are channeled into the secondary general schools. Thus, the normal schools find themselves with average and below-average students as well as with reputations as second-rate schools; this, in turn, prompts fresh graduates from primary schools to seek admittance to the schools with the greater prestige—the general schools.

The curriculums in normal schools are very similar to the ones in secondary general schools (see appendix table B–3), except that there are courses in educational techniques and time is allotted for practice teaching. To some extent the curriculums vary with the type of normal school. In 1954, for example, the following distribution of some 369,000 students and 791 schools was reported: 357 senior normal schools training teachers for junior secondary and junior normal schools, with 111,291 students; 7 schools training kindergarten teachers, with 6,755 students; 427 junior normal schools for future primary school teachers, with 251,132 students.[15] The same source stated that among these students there were 95,266 women, or only 25.8 percent of the enrollment in secondary normal schools.

Despite the acute need for more and more teachers, normal-school education has been developing at a relatively slow pace (table 5). It was not until 1958–59 that enrollment in these schools doubled. Although data are reported on the total number of graduates from specialized schools, it is not broken down between secondary normal and secondary vocational schools. An estimate of the distribution of graduates between the two types of schools is presented in table 6. It indicates that over a 10-year period only approximately 740,000 graduated from secondary normal schools. When this figure is compared with the report that the number of teachers at all school levels increased from 930,000 in 1949 to 2,500,000 in 1958,[16] it becomes apparent how many persons become teachers without attaining a secondary education.

It is anticipated that the shortage of qualified teachers will persist for at least a decade in the cities and even longer in the countryside; therefore enrollment in secondary normal schools may be expected to increase for some time to come. Despite the need and the increase in absolute numbers, the proportion of normal-school students to the total number in specialized schools has been declining steadily from 66 percent in 1949–50 to 41 percent in 1955–56. It is estimated that in 1958–59 this decline was arrested and that enrollment in normal schools was 42 percent of the total specialized-school enrollment (table 5). On the other hand, there seems to be no shortage in teachers for spare-time

---

[15] *Jen-min Chiao-yu* [People's Education], October 1954.
[16] *Jen-min Jih-pao* [People's Daily], Oct. 8, 1959.

TABLE 5.—*Secondary specialized schools, 1948–59*

[In thousands]

School year	Enrollment			Reported total enrollment	Graduates
	Normal	Vocational	Total		
1948–49......	....	....	....	....	[1] 72. 0
1949–50......	[2] 151. 7	[2] 77. 1	228. 8	[1] 229. 0	[1] 75. 0
1950–51......	[3] 159. 4	[3] 97. 8	257. 2	[1] 257. 0	[1] 57. 0
1951–52......	[3] 219. 8	[3] 162. 9	382. 0	[1] 383. 0	[1] 68. 0
1952–53......	[2] 345. 2	[2] 290. 4	635. 6	[1] 636. 0	[1] 118. 0
1953–54......	[2] 369. 0	[2] 299. 4	668. 4	[1] 668. 0	[1] 169. 0
1954–55......	[2] 308. 0	[2] 300. 0	608. 0	[1] 608. 0	[1] 235. 0
1955–56......	[2] 219. 0	[2] 318. 1	537. 1	[1] 537. 0	[1] 174. 0
1956–57......	[4] 273. 4	[5] 337. 0	610. 4	[1] 812. 0	[1] 146. 0
1957–58......	[6] 320. 0	[7](458. 0)	....	[1] 778. 0	[1] 191. 0
1958–59......	[8](620. 0)	[8](850. 0)	....	[1] 1, 470. 0	[9](213. 0)

Blanks indicate figures are not available.

[1] *Ten Great Years* (Peking: State Statistical Bureau, 1960).

[2] *Jen-min Shou-ts'e* [People Handbook] (Peking: 1957), p. 584.

[3] *New China News Agency*, Dec. 2, 1954.

[4] *Jen-min Chiao-yu* [People's Education], Aug. 1957.

[5] *New China News Agency*, June 20, 1955.

[6] *Kuang-ming Jih-pao* [Kuang-ming Daily], Jan. 1, 1957.

[7] Subtracting enrollment in normal schools from the total in specialized schools.

[8] The reported enrollment in specialized schools (1,470,000) was split between normal and vocational schools in proportion to the average distribution between the 2 types of schools over the preceding 3 years.

[9] The relationship between enrollment and graduates in any given year varies from 17.8 percent (1951–52) to 38.7 percent (1954–55) and is therefore deemed unuseable for estimating graduates from enrollment. However, there is a much closer correlation between enrollment of one year and the graduates of the following year. Excluding the 2 extremes, this proportion varies from 24.9 percent (1950–51 graduates as percent of 1949–50 enrollment) to 30.8 percent (1952–53 graduates as percent of 1951–52 enrollment). The average of 27.4 percent for the 8 years in which the necessary figures were reported was then applied to enrollment in 1957–58 to estimate graduates for 1958–59.

schools, where qualifications for teaching have been reduced to correspond to the available supply. For example, "Wuhan city has adopted various methods to train new teachers for the growing needs in workers' spare-time educational work. The Wuhan Teachers Institute, the Wuhan Teachers College, and the short-term teachers-training classes operated by some of the city's factories and enterprises began classes recently. The schools expect to train more than 1,000 teachers for spare-time senior and junior middle schools within a period of 2 or 3 to 6 months" [17]—another example of "walking on both legs."

[17] *New China News Agency*, Mar. 23, 1960.

[In thousands]

Year	Total graduates [1]	Normal [2]	Vocational [2]
1949–50	75	50	25
1950–51	57	36	21
1951–52	68	39	29
1952–53	118	64	54
1953–54	169	93	76
1954–55	235	119	116
1955–56	174	71	103
1956–57	146	65	81
1957–58	191	79	112
1958–59	(213)	90	123

[1] *Ten Great Years* (Peking: State Statistical Bureau, 1960).

[2] For want of a more precise method, the reported graduates from specialized schools were split between normal and vocational schools in proportion to the enrollment in the 2 types of schools. The reported number of graduates from vocational courses are reported for several years but are not used because they do not fit other related data. In some instances it may be a question of inclusions; in others, it may be a planned figure but not reported as such. For example, it was reported that in 1956–57 there were 137,000 graduates from secondary vocational schools (*New China News Agency*, June 26, 1957). This is impossible because the total number of graduates from both vocational and normal schools was reported at 146,000. Similarly, in 1957–58, 158,000 secondary vocational students were expected to graduate (*New China News Agency*, July 1, 1957), while the reported number of specialized graduates was 191,000 or only 30,000 larger. It is therefore presumed that the above method gives a more realistic picture over a period of years. However, the figures should not be considered definitive for any specific year.

Vocational Schools

There is perhaps more confusion in the data dealing with secondary vocational education than with any other type of training. There is a strong impression that this confusion is not limited to persons outside China—that the Chinese themselves are bogged down in the fluid and ambiguous system that was set up and frequently revised for the training of middle-level technical specialists.

The often vague terminology and imprecise categories make it necessary to depend on a close familiarity with quantitative data to seek the proper interpretation of the material. For example, the Chinese term "chuan-yeh" is used to signify both types of specialized schools (normal and vocational) and vocational schools as such. This confusion is magnified in translation. The broad category of specialized schools, the vocational schools, and the industrial (or engineering) courses of vocational schools are interchangeably translated as "vocational," "technical," "trade," or "specialized" schools.

Originally, the vocational schools were set up in two 3-year levels, like the other secondary schools. This does not seem to be the case at present, and the earlier distinction between lower and higher vocational schools has been abandoned. Even when the distinction was apparently in effect, separate data on enrollment in the two levels was rare, while at present it seems to be nonexistent. One source did give such a break-down for 1954,[18] showing the following enrollment for junior and senior vocational schools respectively: 1950–51, 22,651 and 75,172; 1951–52, 38,912 and 124,028; 1952–53, 77,109 and 213,337; 1953–54, 56,282 and 243,712. The initial reaction is that the figures were inadvertently reversed, since the enrollment in the senior classes is from three to four times greater than in the junior classes. The text, however, suggests that these figures are presented correctly for in 1953, in the process of reorganizing secondary vocational schools, a policy was adopted of "grad-ual retrenchment and cessation of student recruitment for the junior vocational schools." The numbers in the junior level did in fact decrease, but this did not affect the enrollment at the senior level, which kept increasing. The most direct evidence of the abandonment of the two-level system is in the reports of the established length of study for the various specialties in vocational schools:

> The secondary vocational schools, which train technicians of intermediate grade in more than 200 professions, will enroll grad-uates of junior secondary schools. Schooling period for courses of industry is 3 to 4 years; for courses of agriculture, forestry, public health, and other professions, 3 years; and for courses of accounting and economic planning, 2½ years.[19]

In other words, entrants must have already completed 3 years of the secondary school before starting on a 2½- to 4-year course in a voca-tional school. Even this does not seem to be universal, however, for in some instances primary graduates may go into "certain" vocational courses.

Another difficulty is in the fact that there is a considerable amount of overlapping between on-the-job training, spare-time education, and cer-tain vocational schools. This is especially true of industrial and technical training which during the past few years has become so closely inte-grated with industrial enterprises. To a lesser extent, this condition exists in all other types of vocational schools.

At present most of the vocational schools are of three types. The first is established directly by one or more industrial enterprises and is supposed to improve the cultural-technical level of the workers in the given enterprises. The second type is attached to a particular plant or enterprise—that is, an existing school is given to a particular enterprise, which administers it, facilitating the organization and training of workers

---

[18] *Jen-min Chiao-yu* [People's Education], October 1954.
[19] *New China News Agency,* June 15, 1956.

and employees for its specific requirements. The third type of vocational school is still more or less independent but maintains a semiformal relationship with one or more enterprises because of the requirement for all students to participate in production. The makeup of the student body is to some extent revealed in the following announcement:

> In order to fulfill the student-enrollment quota in the secondary vocational schools this year, the Ministry of Higher Education appealed to all places to strive to augment the sources of students and to mobilize junior secondary school graduates from the past few years to submit their applications. It also appealed to all factories, mining enterprises, government organs and people's organizations to encourage their young workers having a cultural level equivalent to junior secondary school to enter secondary vocational schools.[20]

The confusion has been intensified by the fact that most of the workers attend some type of school, while all the students participate in some form of productive activity in the enterprise associated with or running the school. It is therefore difficult to compare the enrollment in spare-time vocational training with data given for vocational schools. Table 7 presents the distribution of vocational school students by field of specialization prior to the 1958 integration of education with production.

The extent to which the State depends on vocational schools versus on-the-job training may be gleaned from the fact that during the 3 years 1954–56, the enterprises under the Ministry of Textile Industry trained 37,656 persons on the production line and 8,250 workers in vocational schools.[21] Although this example may not be typical, it is nevertheless indicative of the emphasis.

Despite this confusion of concepts and numbers, it is clear that, realizing the shortage of intermediate technical personnel, the Communists have tried to emphasize secondary vocational education. The reported enrollment in these schools has grown from 77,100 in 1949–50 to 337,000 in 1956–57 and at present is probably approaching 1 million (table 5). Nevertheless, considering the need, the progress has not been impressive: Over a 10-year period the secondary vocational schools had graduated only an estimated 740,000 (table 6). During this 10-year period there was a major shift in emphasis in the field of training in vocational schools: In 1949–50, only 27.8 percent of the students were taking training in technical and industrial courses; in 1955–56 the percentage had reached 55.8; and in 1957–58 it increased to 58.9 (table 5). It is estimated that by 1957–58, roughly 300,000 graduated from technical and industrial courses of secondary vocational schools, or about half of the total number of graduates from vocational schools (table 8).

---

[20] *Ibid.*, June 17, 1957.

[21] *Wo-kuo Kang-t'ieh, Tien-li, Mei-t'an, Chi-hsieh, Fang-chih, Tsao-chih Kung-yeh Ti Chin Hsi* [Past and Present of China's Iron and Steel, Electric-Power, Coal, Machine-Building, Textile, and Paper Industries] (Peiping: July 1958).

TABLE 7.—*Vocational schools: enrollment by field, 1949–56*

[Numbers in thousands]

Field	1949–50		1952–53		1953–54		1954–55		1955–56	
	Number	Percent	Number	Percent	Number	Percent	Number	Percent	Number	Percent
Engineering..........	21.4	27.8	111.4	38.4	129.7	43.3	151.7	50.6	177.6	55.8
Agriculture and forestry............	21.7	28.1	66.6	22.9	68.7	23.0	58.7	19.6	53.3	16.8
Public health.........	15.4	20.0	59.4	20.5	57.7	19.3	58.6	19.5	57.3	18.0
Finance and economics............	14.8	19.2	52.3	18.0	42.3	14.1	28.8	9.6	26.0	8.2
Fine arts and others...	3.8	4.9	.7	.2	1.0	.3	2.2	.7	3.9	1.2
Total............	77.1	100.0	290.4	100.0	299.4	100.0	300.0	100.0	318.1	100.0

Source: *Jen-min Shou-ts'e* [People's Handbook] (Peking: 1957), p. 584.

TABLE 8.—*Estimated number of graduates from technical and industrial courses of secondary vocational schools, 1950–58*

[Numbers in thousands]

Year	Vocational schools		Technical and industrial courses		
			Enrollment		Graduates [3]
	Enrollment [1]	Graduates [2]	Number	Percent of total	
1949–50......	77. 1	25. 0	[4] 21. 4	27. 8	7. 0
1950–51......	97. 8	21. 0	[5] 29. 0	29. 7	6. 2
1951–52......	162. 9	29. 0	[6] (55. 5)	34. 1	9. 9
1952–53......	290. 4	54. 0	[4] 111. 4	38. 4	20. 7
1953–54......	299. 4	76. 0	[4] 129. 7	41. 9	31. 8
1954–55......	300. 0	116. 0	[4] 151. 7	50. 6	58. 7
1955–56......	318. 1	103. 0	[4] 177. 6	55. 8	57. 5
1956–57......	337. 0	81. 0	[7] (207. 8)	61. 7	50. 0
1957–58......	458. 0	112. 0	[8] (282. 6)	61. 7	69. 1

[1] See table 5.

[2] See table 6.

[3] The assumption is made that the graduates of industrial courses will constitute the same proportion of the total graduates in vocational schools as their enrollment constitutes of the total enrollment. For example, in 1954–55 students in industrial and technical courses constituted 50.6 percent of the total enrollment in vocational schools; therefore this percentage is applied to the total number of graduates in the same year (116,000), obtaining the total of 58,700 graduates from industrial and technical courses.

It was reported that from 1949–50 through 1955–56, 177,000 persons graduated from "engineering" courses of vocational schools (*Jen-min Jih-pao* [People's Daily], Mar. 18, 1957), compared with the 191,800 obtained by the above method. A figure of 300,000 seems to be acceptable as an indication of the order of magnitude of the total number of graduates from technical and industrial courses of secondary vocational schools between 1949–50 and 1957–58.

[4] *Jen-min Shou-ts'e* [People's Handbook] (Peking: 1957.).

[5] *Kuang-ming Jih-pao* [Kuang-ming Daily], Oct. 5, 1955.

[6] Interpolating the percentage of total enrollment between 29.7 percent and 38.4 percent.

[7] For 3 years between 1952–53 and 1955–56 the reported enrollment in technical and industrial courses of secondary vocational schools grew by 16.4 percent, 17.0 percent and 17.1 percent. It is assumed that between 1955–56 and 1956–57 it grew at 17 percent.

[8] The percentage of total enrollment in industrial courses in 1957–58 is assumed to be identical with 1956–57 (61.7 percent).

As mentioned earlier, more and more of these schools are established and operated by individual plants of industrial ministries. As early as 1955 the Ministry of Heavy Industry was operating some 30 vocational schools with about 40,000 graduates.[22] The curriculums in these schools include courses in petroleum drilling, transportation, internal combus-

---

[22] Kuang-ming Jih-pao [Kuang-ming Daily], Aug. 6, 1955.

tion engines, processing and grading of coal, manufacture of agricultural machinery, operating and repairing lathes, mechanized loading and unloading equipment, heating equipment, etc. Graduates of secondary vocational schools were required "not only to have a basic knowledge of Marxism-Leninism and a general education but also to master certain specialized technical knowledge," and "not only to understand theories but also to carry out actual operations." [23]

There have been criticisms specifically directed at this type of school. One editorial stated that, as a result of excessively rapid development, many such schools are very poorly equipped and that the quality of the graduates is "generally too low to meet the requirements of the ministries concerned." This criticism leveled at vocational schools in 1956 could undoubtedly be reinforced today, after the "leap forward." The nature and level of these new schools may well be imagined from the following quotation:

> In 7-days' time, beginning March 18, 1958, without using a penny from the state funds, Nanking Municipality set up 263 vocational middle schools, enrolling a total of 17,000 students. Thus was accomplished in a few days what otherwise might take 5 to 10 years. . . . Of the 263 schools, 117 were set up within the city area to train personnel for work in machine, motors, and chemical industries, as well as for the production of food, woodwork, needlework, printing, and hygiene.[24]

Despite this spurt in the creation of so-called vocational schools, which has been duplicated throughout the country, it would seem that the authorities are placing more reliance on spare-time education for the workers and on-the-job training as opposed to vocational schools. After the initial increase in vocational-school enrollment during the early 1950's, there was relative stability for a number of years. The enrollment again went up only when vocational education became integrated with production. Although the creation of scores of schools over a short period of time may continue to show increases in enrollment, the emphasis will be on raising the educational level of persons already in the labor force.

ADULT EDUCATION

Under the general heading of "spare-time and part-time education" the Chinese Communists lump virtually all the educational activities outside the regular school system. The statistics on the number of persons attending the different types of adult-education classes have been of the most casual variety, often varying by more than 100 percent. It is therefore surprising that in 1959 the Chinese were able to publish a summary statistical table on enrollment in spare-time and anti-illiteracy classes. These integrated data are presented in table 9 despite the existence of contradictory figures.

---

[23] Chi-hua Ching-chi [Planned Economy], Sept. 23, 1956.

[24] *Jen-min Chiao-yu* [People's Education], May 1, 1958.

TABLE 9.—*Spare-time and illiteracy students, 1949–58*

[In thousands]

Year	In spare-time higher schools	In spare-time second-ary vocation-al schools	In spare-time second-ary schools	In spare-time primary schools	In anti-illit-eracy classes
1949........	0. 1	0. 1	....	....	657. 0
1950........	. 4	. 1	....	....	1, 372. 0
1951........	1. 6	. 3	....	....	1, 375. 0
1952........	4. 1	. 7	249. 0	1, 375. 0	656. 0
1953........	9. 7	1. 1	404. 0	1, 523. 0	2, 954. 0
1954........	13. 2	186. 0	760. 0	2, 088. 0	2, 637. 0
1955........	15. 9	195. 0	1, 167. 0	4, 538. 0	3, 678. 0
1956........	63. 8	563. 0	2, 236. 0	5, 195. 0	7, 434. 0
1957........	75. 9	588. 0	2, 714. 0	6, 267. 0	7, 208. 0
1958........	150. 0	....	5, 000. 0	26, 000. 0	40, 000. 0

Blanks indicate figures are not available.

Source: *Ten Great Years* (Peking: State Statistical Bureau, 1960).

The Literacy Drive

By far the largest proportion of adults attending classes are learning to read and write.   Illiteracy among the Chinese population has been and still is one of the important stumbling blocks to Communist plans for industrializing the nation.   In a speech at the 20th meeting of the 3d session of the 1st National People's Congress, Minister of Education Chang Hsi-jo reported that "at present the country's illiterates still account for 78 percent of the total population." [25]   In 1956 it was reported that nearly 50 percent of the employees in the plants and mines and 60 to 70 percent of the employees in the coal mines and in construction fields were illiterate.   The problem facing the Chinese was summarized in one article which stated that among the youth in the rural areas, about 70 percent were illiterate or semiliterate, while the Ministry of Education planned on wiping out illiteracy among only 3,080,000 persons during 1955: "At this rate of progress, it will take nearly 60 years to wipe out illiteracy completely among the 180 million youth in the country.   That is to say, even in the generation of our grandsons there will still be illiterates." [26]   However, either the pace was accelerated or the standards were lowered, because by 1959 the percentage of illiterates and semiliterates among the youth had reportedly been lowered to 30 to 40 percent.[27]

The word "youth" is used advisedly by the Communists.   Although there is no way of knowing specifically the age limits set for this group,

[25] *New China News Agency,* June 20, 1956.

[26] *Chung-kuo Ch'ing-nien* [China Youth], No. 21, Nov. 1, 1955.

[27] *Chung-kuo Ch'ing-nien Pao* [China Youth Daily], Sept. 25, 1959.

the major emphasis in the elimination of illiteracy is on the young people. The 180 million referred to above, for example, approximates the number of persons between 15 and 29 years of age (approximate ages of the Chinese Youth League). At this stage of the literacy drive, older people, particularly in the rural areas, are not deemed sufficiently important or adaptable to warrant the expenditure of time and money on their education.

Despite the difficulties, the Communists are making every effort to send as many young people as possible to school to learn to read and write. Exactly how much progress they are making is difficult to say, since the data are contradictory and muddled. Typical of the nature of the data are figures reported for 1958. On February 27, 1958, the New China News Agency announced that 28.4 million peasants were attending literacy classes. Three months later, on May 20, 1958, the same agency reported 61 million studying in spare-time literacy classes. Table 9 shows 40 million people in such courses. Another report stated that 200 million illiterates are to become literate within 7 years.[28] In line with the overall goal, the Committee for the Elimination of Illiteracy of the State Council announced in a March 1956 resolution that the target for eliminating illiteracy among cadres in Government organs was 2 to 3 years; for eliminating 95 percent of the illiteracy among workers in factories, mines, and enterprises, 3 to 5 years; and for eliminating most of the illiteracy among rural and urban inhabitants, 5 to 7 years.[29]

The regime is hoping for a cumulative effect in its literacy campaign. Everyone who has learned to read and write is urged to pass on this knowledge to someone else. In some localities even the primary-school children are expected to teach their elders what they learn in class.

Some adverse effects of the campaign are described in the following quotation from a speech by Minister of Education Chang Hsi-jo at the 20th meeting of the National People's Congress:

> Since the central authorities established 5 to 7 years as the time limit for the basic eradication of illiteracy, many provinces and municipalities have reduced the limit to 4 to 5 years. Many an industrial agency stipulated that the eradication of illiteracy among the workers be accomplished within 2 to 2½ years. Certain lower level units even went beyond these demands. Consequently, certain cadres responsible for illiteracy eradication in the mines and plants, in their attempt to fulfill their plans, resorted to coercion and harsh orders. For example, in certain areas, it was the adopted practice to impose fines or punishment upon those who failed to attend classes. In other areas, "literacy stations" and "literacy roadblocks" were established to coerce the masses into studying. All these erroneous methods are harmful to production, to the

---

[28] *Ta-kung Pao* [Ta-kung Daily], Dec. 7, 1955.
[29] *Chinese Home Service* (News Agency), Mar. 9, 1957.

health of the masses, and to the development of the task of eradicating illiteracy.[30]

An additional problem for the literacy drive, particularly in the rural areas, is that of retention. If an individual does in fact learn the number of characters required for him to be considered literate, he is not likely to retain this knowledge unless he puts it to use. Under present conditions, the Chinese peasant has little, if any, opportunity or inclination to practice his newly acquired knowledge.

One important question to be answered in connection with the literacy drive is: At exactly what point does a person become literate? For example: What is the qualitative significance of the claim that between 1949 and 1957, 22 million illiterates have learned to read and write? [31] Although criteria are seldom expressed, one report stated that the standard for minimal adult literacy is 1,500 characters for peasants and 2,000 characters for workers,[32] or less than half the number expected of primary-school graduates. With knowledge of so few characters, it is possible to read only the most simple types of texts. But to have raised 22 million illiterates even to this minimum standard of literacy through spare-time study must be considered a major accomplishment.

China is now in the process of implementing two important linguistic reforms, both of which are designed to simplify the written form of the language and thus to facilitate its study. Both have been the subject of heated discussion for many years. The first is the introduction of simplified versions of Chinese characters. Although several hundred characters have already been revised and are used in new texts, they do not eliminate the hardship completely. The second reform involves the introduction of a romanized alphabet. The greatest obstacle to the use of the more or less phonetic roman script is the fact that China has so many dialects, and the introduction of this script must be accompanied by the difficult task of teaching the Peking dialect throughout the country. The purpose of this linguistic reform is often misunderstood since "it is never intended to replace the Chinese characters with the phonetic alphabet," but only to speed up the learning process. "Fifteen to twenty hours is allowed for learning the whole alphabet, and then 100 hours for learning 1,500 Chinese characters. After this, by the set standard, one has ceased to be illiterate. . . . Thus, the fruits of anti-illiteracy work will be secured, and people will cease to be illiterate permanently and without any possibility of becoming illiterate again later on." [33]

In summary, it may be stated that the effort to eliminate illiteracy has affected a large part of the population and that progress has been made.

---

[30] *New China News Agency,* June 20, 1956.
[31] *Ibid.,* Sept. 21, 1957.
[32] *Ibid.,* Dec. 8, 1959.
[33] *Jen-min Jih-pao* [People's Daily], Feb. 12, 1960.

However, the reports that scores of millions of adults in China have become literate during the past 9 or 10 years are undoubtedly either exaggerations or the result of such minimal requirements that virtually anyone who has attended literacy classes is now termed "literate." The area where the effort to reduce illiteracy has met with undoubted success is in the expansion of elementary education. With some 90 million children attending primary schools, it would seem safe to assume that the next generation will have a considerably higher proportion of literates.

Other Facilities for Adult Education

In addition to attending literacy courses, peasants and, especially, workers in cities are attending classes either to obtain the equivalent of a primary or secondary education or to improve their productive capabilities. Some are even attending so-called "spare-time higher educational institutions," which are probably not comparable to the regular colleges and universities. Classes for on-the-job and spare-time training are generally sponsored and operated by the industrial plants, mines, and other enterprises and institutions, and have undergone several reorganizations since 1950.

The recent emphasis given this type of training is reflected in the creation of a Spare-Time Education Commission, an organ of the State Council, responsible for directing this form of education throughout the country. The notice proclaiming the establishment of this commission stated that—

> . . . in order to successfully carry out spare-time education work of such an enormous scale throughout the country, it is necessary for educational departments, cultural departments, industrial and communications departments, agricultural departments, finance and trade departments, scientific research department, planning departments, military affairs departments, trade unions, young Communist leagues, and women's associations to exert persistent and indefatigable efforts in a mutually coordinated and cooperative manner in making overall arrangements under the unified leadership of the Party committees at all levels.[34]

Workers' and peasants' schools, to a large extent, parallel the general primary and secondary schools, following a similar curriculum but with greater emphasis on political education and on the study of current events. Table 9 presents an integrated series on enrollment in the various types of spare-time courses. These data contradict most of the previous figures that from time to time have been reported in the press. In part, this confusion may be the result of the many reorganizations in the adult-education system and in the very loose and arbitrary utilization of the terms. Also, because most of these schools are run by individual enterprises and institutions, it is very possible that complete

---

[34] *New China News Agency,* Feb. 22, 1960.

statistics on this form of education have never been available and table 9 presents estimates made especially for the publication which reports them.

As an example of the confusion, it was reported in 1955 that 51,000 workers and peasants were attending the country's 87 short-term secondary schools.[35] Table 9 reports 1,167,000 students in spare-time secondary schools for the same year. Although the difference may be in the use of "short-term" [su-ch'eng] versus "spare-time" [yeh-yü], indications are that both terms are often used interchangeably, despite the fact that "short-term" schools have been almost completely replaced by "spare-time" schools.

Similarly, a teachers' newspaper reported 543,000 persons in 1957 in junior and senior secondary classes for adults—508,000 and 35,000, respectively.[36] The figure presented in table 9, presumably for the same group, is 2,714,000. There are many other examples of this nature. The suspicion is that there has been little integration of the data dealing with adult education. Industrial ministries may have reported enrollment in factory-run schools under the category "spare-time education"; schools run by the Ministry of Education may have reported enrollment in its own schools under the category "adult education" or "accelerated courses." In any event, the figures in table 9 seem to be fairly reasonable approximations of the general magnitude of the adult-education program. It must be stressed that these figures are generally not included in the enrollment reported for the regular schools. This exclusion may be illustrated by considering the reported figures for secondary schools. If spare-time students in the numbers reported above were to be included in the total enrollment, they would constitute close to 60 percent of the total enrollment in 1958–59 (5 million out of 8.52 million). Also, the increase in enrollment in spare-time secondary schools between 1954 and 1955 was greater than the total enrollment increase in the secondary general schools.

Probably typical of the spare-time secondary schools for peasants are those in Kiangsu Province. Here, the peasants study 3 hours during the slack farming season in winter and early spring. Secretaries of Party committees attached to the communes are responsible for the political course. Technical personnel of commune agrotechnical stations are responsible for the courses in agricultural knowledge and techniques. Specially assigned personnel selected from the masses are responsible for the cultural courses.[37]

The quality of courses for adults is on a very low level:

> Spare-time education for employees is not sufficiently systematized and is not on a regular basis. It lacks an adequate teaching

[35] Ibid., Mar. 5, 1955.
[36] Chiao-shih Pao [Teachers' Biweekly], Feb. 8, 1957.
[37] New China News Agency, Mar. 16, 1960.

system and curriculum, and the quality of teaching is poor. Employees are not guaranteed a regular fixed time for study. There is a shortage of secondary school and university teachers; they in turn are not given regular and adequate guidance. Leadership in spare-time education by government educational departments has been generally weak. . . . Owing to deficiencies in long-term planning and management, employee spare-time education has become routine and static.[38]

To improve this situation, the Ministry of Education issued a notice in 1957 urging all schools and organizations concerned to reorganize, consolidate, and elevate the standard in spare-time education.[39] Despite this proclamation, spare-time schools are still below the educational standards existing in the regular schools. Even in Shanghai, where conditions should be better than in other parts of the country, a recent investigation disclosed that only 22 percent of the 35,761 persons giving spare-time classes were professional teachers.[40]

There are also many workers who attend technical schools and courses which are operated by the enterprises and, also, many more who manage to improve their technical skills through on-the-job experience. One of the difficulties encountered in a more rapid development of on-the-job training was discussed in a newspaper editorial. It stated that some of the leading personnel of industrial departments in China are of the opinion that because of the heavy production schedules of factories and mines, it is "impossible to start the training of technical specialists early." Moreover, it continued, the "erroneous attitude of relying on Soviet experts" still remained in a number of factories and mines. The editorial then emphasized the need immediately to start training technicians at their place of work and to establish an independent industrial system "with the unselfish assistance from Soviet experts."[41]

It would seem reasonable to assume that the largest proportion of people who manage to improve their technical skills do so through on-the-job experience rather than in schools. It is, of course, impossible to estimate either the number of such people or the extent of their progress.

One serious problem in connection with education for workers is seldom mentioned in the Chinese press. Although, for the most part, adults attend classes only after a full day's work, many enterprises have set up schedules whereby a worker has to work for 6 hours and go to school for 2 hours. Sometimes this ratio may be 3:3, while in other instances a person may have an opportunity to work 10 hours but cannot

---

[38] *Jen-min Jih-pao* [People's Daily], Dec. 3, 1955.
[39] *Chinese Home Service* (News Agency), Feb. 21, 1957.
[40] *China Reconstructs*, Oct. 1959
[41] *New China News Agency*, Mar. 24, 1957.

do so because he is enrolled in a school.   A strong deterrent to spare-time education must be the fact that the worker gets paid only for the hours on the job—if he spends 2 hours of an 8-hour day in class, he loses one-quarter of his paycheck.

CHAPTER IV
Higher Education

General Nature of the System and the Problems

In May 1950 the first conference dealing with problems of higher education was called, and the basic program for the reorganization of the existing system was discussed and outlined.   Because of the shortage of technicians and specialists, one of the first reforms undertaken by the new regime was to convert gradually from a general system of university education to specialized institutes and to reduce the curriculums from 4–5 years to 3–4 years.   In 1955, however, a decree again changed the length of study in many fields to 5 years, although some special institutes continued to have 2-year, 3-year, or 4-year curriculums.   In the field of medicine the change to 5 years was introduced in 1954.

When the Communists took over control of the Chinese mainland, the country had slightly over 200 institutions of higher learning.   In 1957–58 there were approximately 236 universities and institutes of higher education.   The figure is approximate because the Communists themselves are undecided as to the exact number, different sources listing figures that vary from 5 to 10 or more schools.   This is also true of the more detailed breakdown of such institutions.   One representative distribution lists them as follows: 17 general universities, 10 polytechnical universities, 40 engineering institutes, 31 agricultural and forestry institutes, 37 medical colleges, 5 institutes of finance and economics, 5 institutes of law and political science, 8 language institutes, 57 teachers' (normal) colleges, 17 institutes of fine arts, 6 physical-training institutes, and 3 others.[1]   Although many of the new universities and institutes have been established in the interior provinces of China, they still predominate in the large cities of the coastal provinces.   Peking is undoubtedly the educational center of the country, with 50 institutions of higher education enrolling 121,000 students.[2]

The "leap forward" in higher education resulted in the usual distortion and confusion of statistics, and the latest reports inform us that the "number of universities and colleges trebled during 1958 and 1959, the

---

[1] *Student's Directory of Higher Education* (Peking: Ministry of Higher Education, 1958).

[2] *New China News Agency,* Oct. 29, 1959.

2 successive years of the big leap forward, bringing the total up to 840." [3] It is clear that the latter figure includes not only the bona fide institutions of higher education but also some of the more advanced "red and expert universities" and spare-time universities in industrial enterprises that have been set up as part of the peasant- and worker-education program. (See ch. II for a description of "red and expert universities.") The care that must be exercised in utilizing these statistics is apparent from the following quotation which illustrates an instance in which "red and expert universities" were obviously included:

> Here we will cite the example of Kaifeng, Honan Province. Between July 1 and 14 [1958], 162 agricultural cooperatives in 22 townships [hsien] founded 256 colleges and 695 research institutes with 3,266 departments attended by 201,700 students. [4]

Despite the loose definition of higher institutions, the data on enrollment and on the number of entrants and graduates usually excludes the "red and expert universities" but does include the spare-time students. Unless specifically stated to the contrary, everything that follows on higher education excludes the "red and expert universities."

Only the universities provide the student with a general education somewhat comparable to that attained by a student in the West, and even there the tendency is toward overspecialization. The institutes, for the most part, turn out narrow specialists whose courses outside their particular field seldom include more than those required to make them "red" as well as "expert" in one particular specialty (see ch. V). This is also true of normal colleges, which are supposed to train teachers for secondary schools. The so-called "multiplicity of courses" has been eliminated; probably partly due to this reduction of requirements, the number of 2-year normal colleges has been greatly expanded. In these pseudoinstitutions of higher education, many of the courses were combined, as for example biology and chemistry, and history and political science. In 1954 more than 75 percent of the normal-college graduates were the product of the 2-year system. [5]

It is interesting to note a few of the problems dealing with the system of integration of work and study as it pertains specifically to higher education. There it met considerably more opposition than at any other level. (The general aspects of the work-study policy are discussed in ch. II.) This opposition is not surprising because, according to the Communists, the majority of students in higher education during the earlier period of the regime had been brought up in "bourgeois and petty bourgeois families and their bourgeois viewpoint" had not been "completely transformed." These "rightists" students and teachers con-

---

[3] *Ibid.*, Jan. 27, 1960.

[4] *College Students of New China* (Peking: 1958).

[5] *Jen-min Chiao-yu* [People's Education], Oct. 1954.

tinue to maintain that "it is better to read more books than to participate in labor" and that they "could not learn anything from the peasants."

Although student objection to productive labor was quite widespread, the integration of study and work was carried out more smoothly in the fields where there was some natural relationship between theory and practical training and where students could be assigned work which had either direct or at least marginal relationship with their studies—such fields as engineering, agriculture, and medicine. The transition was more difficult among students in such fields as arts, history, and philosophy:

> Some students in the department of history say: "The hoe will not unearth the emperor Ch'in Shih Huang." Students in departments of foreign languages say: "The Latin alphabet has no connection with productive labor." And so on. In a word, it is claimed that there are exceptions to the need for the thorough implementation of the principle of combining education with productive labor.[6]

The answer to this is given in typical Communist jargon: "If we hold as correct the dialectical materialist theory of the universality of contradiction, we cannot but accept the fact that this theory of 'exceptions' is erroneous." Furthermore, a hoe can, in fact, "within a definite scope enrich the historical knowledge of the students." In what sense the scope is enriched is not discussed.

It is also clear that productive labor which is the result of brain and not brawn may not be substituted in the work-study program: Only physical labor, which throws students in direct contact with the masses, is considered beneficial in creating the new well-rounded Chinese intellectual. Of course, special efforts that do not require physical labor are also expected from the students, as illustrated by the following passage:

> The students of the Chinese Language Department of Peking University took collective action to write a new history of Chinese literature during the great leap forward last year. . . . A new edition of the *History of Chinese Literature* containing 1,200,000 words compared with the former edition of 700,000 words had been published about the time of the National Day this year. This deed is a vivid illustration of the marked success the masses can achieve in scientific research work. It also shows how utterly unrealistic is the view that "the scientific research campaign is much ado about nothing" and that "scientific research carried out by the masses has only quantity but no quality."[7]

Actually, quality is usually incidental in these mass literary projects, and the emphasis is placed on the fact that the new volume has almost twice as many words in it.

---

[6] Lun-t'an [Forum], No. 2, April 1959; translated by U.S. Joint Publications Research Service in Rept. No. 2060–N, Dec. 7, 1959: *Selected Political and Sociological Translations on Communist China.*

[7] *Kuang-ming Jih-pao* [Kuang-ming Daily], Oct. 26, 1959.

The national policy of "walking on two legs" also has a special meaning for higher education. Although quality education cannot be provided for all, there are certain key institutions that attempt to give exceptionally qualified students the best education available in China. One such institution is the University of Science and Technology, which was established in 1958 in the western suburbs of Peking. It is reported that this new type of university differs from most of the existing polytechnical institutions in that its chief purpose is to train research workers in the most advanced branches of science. The Chinese Academy of Sciences and the Ministry of Education assume joint responsibility in guiding its work, and Kuo Mo-jo, who heads the Academy, is its president.

The new university has 13 departments: Nuclear physics and nuclear engineering, technical physics, applied geophysics, chemical physics, radio electronics, radioactive and radiative chemistry, thermal dynamic engineering, high polymer chemistry and physics, applied mathematics and computing technique, dynamics, geochemistry and rare elements, biophysics and automation. The teaching staff comes mainly from top-level research workers of the Academy of Sciences. Enrollment during the 1958–59 school year was 1,600.[8]

However, the principle of combining work with study holds for this university as well. The professors and students of the university set up "five factories, an electronic computer plant, an electronics instrument plant, etc.—even before the academic year began." [9]

There are few detailed discussions of the curriculums in institutions of higher education. Furthermore, there have been several radical reorganizations of approaches and methods of instruction and also little uniformity between various institutions. The brief description below (based on the Northeastern Polytechnical Institute of Shenyang) seems to be more or less typical of the current setup in higher technical institutions.[10] The curriculum consists of four component parts, inseparable from each other: Political and ideological training of the students; technical (special) studies; productive work; and military training and physical education.

The curriculum for political and ideological training includes such subjects as the course and policy of the Party, the history of the Chinese revolution, the history of the international Communist movement, and political economy and philosophy. During a period of nine semesters, 560 to 600 hours are set aside for these subjects. Compulsory attendance at political lectures and participation in discussion groups is not included in this time.

---

[8] *Peking Review,* Sept. 30, 1958.

[9] *Ibid.*

[10] *Izvestiya Vysshikh Uchebnykh Zavedeniy, Tsvetnaya Metallurgiya* [Bulletin of the Higher Educational Institutions, Nonferrous Metallurgy], No. 5 (Moskva: 1959).

The study of technical and scientific subjects is closely coordinated with productive work. For example, physics is no longer taught as a distinct and integrated subject. Instead, a student majoring in electrical engineering will study electricity; one majoring in mechanical engineering will study only those aspects of physics which are directly pertinent to his field, etc. Similarly, analytical chemistry is combined with technical analysis, and physical chemistry with electrochemistry. New theoretical courses have been devised for each specialty. Also, that part of the material which can be assimilated by the student during the course of his productive work is not included in the lectures. During a 12-hour workday, the student spends 4 hours in production at adjoining plants, 4 hours in independent work (discussions of lectures, homework, etc.), and 4 hours in academic studies. An average of 1 hour per day is set aside for physical education and military training.

A significant change has also been made in conducting examinations. The evaluation of a student's knowledge in a given discipline is determined on the basis of the opinions of the party organization, instructors, and students, taking into account the ability of the student to solve specific production problems, the level of his theoretical knowledge, and the political consciousness of the student. Following a written examination, the students form themselves into groups to discuss the answers of

TABLE 1.—*Higher education, 1948–60: Entrants, enrollment, and graduates*

School year	Entrants	Enrollment	Graduates
1948–49			[1] 21,000
1949–50		[1] 117,000	[1] 18,000
1950–51	[2] 35,000	[1] 137,000	[1] 19,000
1951–52	[2] 35,000	[1] 153,000	[1] 32,000
1952–53	[2] 65,900	[1] 191,000	[1] 48,000
1953–54	[2] 71,400	[1] 212,000	[1] 47,000
1954–55	[2] 94,000	[1] 253,000	[1] 55,000
1955–56	[3] 96,200	[1] 288,000	[1] 63,000
1956–57	[4] 165,600	[1] 403,000	[1] 56,000
1957–58	[5] 107,000	[1] 441,000	[1] 72,000
1958–59	[6] 152,000	[1] 660,000	[7] 62,200
1959–60	[8] 270,000	[8] 810,000	

Blanks indicate figures are not available.

[1] *Ten Great Years* (Peking: State Statistical Bureau, 1960).
[2] *Survey of China Mainland Press*, July 8, 1955 (Hong Kong: U.S. consulate general).
[3] *New China News Agency*, Sept. 9, 1955.
[4] *Jen-min Jih-pao* [People's Daily], Mar. 17, 1956.
[5] *Chinese Home Service*, Mar. 16, 1957.
[6] *Chung-kuo Ch'ing-nien* [China Youth], No. 13, July 1, 1958.
[7] *Jen-min Jih-pao* [People's Daily], July 16, 1959.
[8] *New China News Agency*, Jan. 22, 1960.

their fellow students and to make evaluations. Then an evaluation is made by the instructor.

Entrants

The annual quotas for enrollment in the institutions of higher learning are set by the state. All such institutions must participate in the plan of "unified enrollment" and are not allowed to enroll students on their own:

> The unified enrollment for institutes of higher learning is handled by the national, regional, provincial, and municipal enrollment committees and offices for the examination areas set up by the departments of education, public health, and personnel; and the institutes of higher learning under the leadership of the Party committees and governments.[11]

New entrants are assigned to fields of study according to a detailed plan provided by the Ministry of Education. For example, for the 1954–55 school year, 37.42 percent of the entrants were to go into engineering, 6.34 percent into science, and 2.17 percent into finance and economics.[12]

Every province and municipality has an enrollment-work committee which is composed of the presidents of all institutes of higher learning in the area and which is subordinate to the regional department of education. This committee is responsible for administering entrance examinations and for registration, selection, and placement of the successful candidates. There are 77 cities in China which hold college entrance examinations (7 in the north, 10 in the northeast, 18 in the east, 26 in the central-south, 10 in the southwest, 4 in the northwest, and 2 in Inner Mongolia).

Presumably to strengthen and unify leadership in the college enrollment work throughout the nation, the National Committee of College Enrollment was inaugurated in Peking on March 19, 1956. The committee consists of 30 members who are the responsible persons of the relevant departments of the Central Government and some higher institutes of Peking.[13] (See appendix F for text of regulations governing enrollment.)

All the young people who want to sit for entrance examinations for the institutions of higher education must first pass a physical examination at the medical center in their locality or neighboring locality. They may then register at nearby designated places for entrance examinations to qualify for admission to institutes of higher learning. Although candidates theoretically have a choice of schools and specializations, they must "indicate their desire to subordinate themselves to planned distribution."

---

[11] *Cheng-ming* [Contend], No. 2, Feb. 10, 1958.
[12] *New China News Agency,* May 20, 1954.
[13] *Ibid.,* March 19, 1956.

Planned distribution was said to have been abolished in 1957 and selection by students to have been established entirely on a voluntary basis.[14] By 1958 it was reported that students did have a choice of schools and specializations and that planned distribution had accounted for only 17 percent of the total enrollment back in 1955 and only 6.3 percent in 1956. Other statements make the above report seem most unlikely. The explanation may lie in the phrase "planned distribution on a voluntary basis"; probably all students or prospective students "volunteer" to permit the state to decide their fate.

On July 2, 1957, "political quality"—to be measured primarily in terms of "knowledge of and performance during the rectification and antirightist campaigns"—formally became the primary consideration in the selection of candidates for higher education. The new regulation of the Ministry of Education also authorized exemptions from matriculation examinations and "priority considerations" for applicants of worker or peasant origin who demonstrated their political and labor capabilities and could satisfy certain minimal academic requirements. Defending the new system, the Party newspaper stated editorially that although such applicants might be inferior in "book knowledge," their greater experience in class struggle and production work would actually raise the standard of new students.[15]

In case several candidates have similar qualifications and grades on the entrance examinations, first consideration is given to workers, peasants, and current-year graduates from secondary schools. Next in order of priority are demobilized servicemen, employees who have participated in revolutionary work for 3 years, and then children of martyrs and national minority students, together with overseas Chinese and students from Hong Kong and Macao.

A continuing problem with regard to recruitment for higher education is the shortage of qualified applicants as a result of the inadequate number of graduates from senior secondary schools. The following excerpt well states the problem:

> In order to supply all kinds of higher construction personnel needed by the state, higher institutions have been greatly extended since the liberation. But the sources of students are extremely wanting. Apart from mobilizing senior secondary school students to apply for admission into higher institutions every year, we had on many occasions to mobilize and send people holding working posts to sit for the matriculation examinations and to expand sources of students in other ways. This year, in view of the demand of the situation of the nationwide leap forward, higher institutions have to enroll a greater number of students. Because the sources of students are still lacking, it is required that all those senior secondary school students due for graduation this year [1958] who are

---

[14] *Cheng-ming* [Contend], No. 2, Feb. 10, 1958.

[15] *Jen-min Jih-pao* [People's Daily], July 3, 1957.

able to study further, actively apply for admission into higher institutions.[16]

In the summer of 1956, 41 percent of 351,000 applicants were that year's secondary school graduates; 22 percent were workers in government departments, factories and mines, and other enterprises. The residual is unspecified. Also, 65,800 primary-school teachers were to take part in entrance examinations for teachers' colleges.[17] The last statement is of dubious validity, since the great majority of primary-school teachers do not have a completed secondary education. Although teaching experience may possibly be substituted for formal education, special courses would still have to be set up to suit the average level of achievement attained by these primary-school teachers.

Lengthy discussions have taken place to resolve many of the problems involved in recruiting college students. In the process of increasing the number of entrants, not enough care has been taken to insure the quality:

> The very fact that there were large numbers of students leaving their schools in the middle of their courses of studies has proved that accepting unqualified students by force of circumstances could only lead to the incurrence of heavy wastage in manpower and material to the country and cause the students to suffer.[18]

Another point under discussion is the large number of persons failing the entrance examinations, particularly among candidates already on the job who had left school several years earlier and wish to return to school. For example, in 1955, "three quarters of the cadres on active duty failed in their examinations." [19]

Although the number of entrants into the institutions of higher education has increased from 35,000 in 1950 to a planned 270,000 in 1959 (see table 1), the trend has not been consistently upward. The greatest drop occurred between 1956 and 1957, when the number of entrants into universities and institutes decreased from 165,000 to 107,000. This drop was explained or accounted for by the statement that the plan for admitting new students followed the development of production and the country's needs: Sometimes more students were needed and sometimes fewer. Also, it was during this period that much of the discussion occurred about the quality of students in higher education. Accepting the smaller number of entrants was perhaps designed to improve the quality of these students. Despite this drop, the number of entrants into higher institutions still exceeded the number of graduates from the higher secondary schools (general, normal, and vocational) in the spring of the same year.

---

[16] *New China News Agency,* Apr. 7, 1958.

[17] *Ibid.,* July 13, 1956.

[18] *Kuang-ming Jih-pao* [Kuang-ming Daily], Aug. 16, 1955.

[19] *Jen-min Jih-pao* [People's Daily], Mar. 17, 1956.

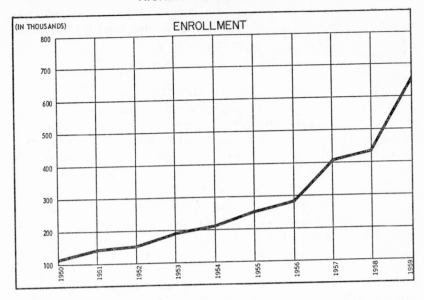

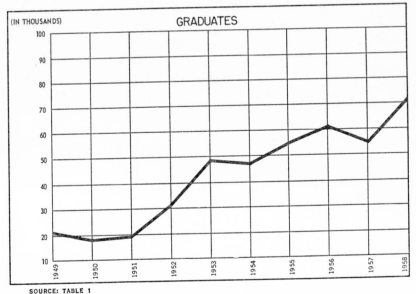

SOURCE: TABLE 1

One curious fact about the social background of the college students: Whereas peasants and workers constitute the overwhelming proportion of the total population of China, it is proclaimed with pride that the proportion of students of worker and peasant origin in higher education had increased from 20.46 percent in 1952–53 to 29.20 percent in 1955–56, and to 36.42 percent in 1957–58.[20] This means that despite the

[20] *Peking Review,* May 20, 1958.

pressures on the intellectual, the capitalist businessman, and the like, the sons and daughters of these "reactionaries" still constitute the great majority of the students in higher education after some 8 years of the Communist regime.

Enrollment

There has been a steady growth of enrollment in universities and colleges in China since 1949 despite some sizable fluctuations from year to year in the number of entrants. This growth has been a continuation of the expansion of higher education actually started by the Nationalist government in the middle 1940's. Although not typical for that early period, the growth in enrollment between 1945–46 and 1946–47 was greater in percentage than between any other 2 consecutive school years since then. As was the case at all other educational levels, the greatest increase since 1950 occurred between the school years 1957–58 and 1958–59—the year of the "forward leap"—when enrollment increased by 50 percent. A 22-percent leap was registered between 1958–59 and 1959–60, from 660,000 to 810,000 (see table 1). If the trend continues, enrollment in higher educational institutions should reach about 1 million persons by the 1960–61 school year.

TABLE 2.—*Comparison of enrollment on spare-time basis with full-time basis in institutions of higher education, 1950–59*

Year	Enrollment		Spare time as percent of total
	Total [1]	Spare time [2]	
1950–51...............................	137, 000	400	0. 3
1951–52...............................	153, 000	1, 600	1. 0
1952–53...............................	191, 000	4, 100	2. 1
1953–54...............................	212, 000	9, 700	4. 6
1954–55...............................	253, 000	13, 200	5. 2
1955–56...............................	288, 000	15, 900	5. 5
1956–57...............................	403, 000	63, 800	15. 8
1957–58...............................	441, 000	75, 900	17. 2
1958–59...............................	660, 000	150, 000	22. 7

[1] See table 1.
[2] See table 9, ch. III.

Enrollment in higher level spare-time courses has been showing continuous growth, roughly following the trend established by the enrollment of full-time students. Admittedly, the level of training in spare-time classes is lower than it is in the regular full-time classes, and probably fewer students complete higher education on the spare-time basis than on the full-time basis. This may to some extent explain the relatively wide discrepancy between the number enrolled and the number graduating from institutions for higher education (see table 1). With the "leap forward" in production there is a greater tendency to enter the labor force and continue further education on a part-time basis, and the exclusion of spare-time students from statistics on higher education would seem to run contrary to the intent of China's propaganda policies.

Table 3 presents the distribution of the enrollment in higher education in numbers, by fields, for both the pre- and post-Communist periods; table 4 makes a conversion to percentages of those figures by 5-year periods (see also chart on p. 70). The greatest increase has been in the enrollment of students in engineering: By 1957–58 they constituted over 40 percent of the total enrollment. Most of this increase was at the expense of law, the political and social sciences, economics, and the arts, each of which showed either a decrease or a relative stability in numbers at the same time that total college enrollment soared. Although the number of students studying physical sciences almost tripled between 1952–53 and 1957–58 (from 9,600 to 27,100), their proportion to the total enrollment remained virtually the same.

Considerable growth also occurred in the normal or teachers' colleges, whose enrollments comprise almost one quarter of the total for higher education. The emphasis has been on the independent normal college, and many such colleges that existed as parts of universities have gradually become independent.

Simultaneously with the increase in the enrollment in institutions of higher education, there was an increase in the number of faculty members. It is reported that at the end of 1957 there were 68,000 faculty members, of whom 45,000 were added during the First Five-Year Plan.[21] This is an impressive growth in numbers—but a growth at the expense of competency, inasmuch as the majority of the teaching personnel rank as assistants or lower.

Graduates

The institutions of higher education in China have graduated nearly half a million persons in all fields of specialization since 1949, or an average of about 45,000 persons per year. A detailed breakdown of the graduates and their major fields is presented in table 5.

The common interrelationships between entrants, enrollment, and graduates are more tenuous in China than elsewhere. This condition is only partially due to the inadequacy of the data; a more important reason is probably the degree of fluctuations in the prescribed number of years required to complete the studies in different fields of specialization. It may take as few as 2 years to complete a normal college, while specific curriculums in the field of engineering or medicine may take as long as 5 or 6 years. Table 6 (p. 76) juxtaposes the reported and the implied

---

[21] *Jen-min Chiao-yu* [People's Education], Oct. 1957.

TABLE 3.—*Higher education: enrollment by field, 1928–58* [1]

School year	Engineering	Science	Agriculture and forestry	Health	Political science and law	Education	Finance and economics	Literature and arts	Total
1928–29	2,777	1,910	1,035	977	9,466	1,661	1,695	5,464	24,985
1929–30	3,144	2,191	1,294	1,138	11,431	2,082	1,667	6,171	29,118
1930–31	3,734	2,872	1,419	1,350	15,899	2,561	2,025	7,706	37,566
1931–32	4,084	3,530	1,413	1,800	16,487	4,231	2,156	10,066	43,767
1932–33	4,439	4,159	1,557	1,852	14,523	3,368	2,867	9,372	42,137
1933–34	5,263	4,722	1,690	2,458	12,913	4,004	3,167	8,703	42,920
1934–35	5,910	5,324	1,831	263	11,029	4,059	3,033	7,921	39,370
1935–36	5,514	6,272	2,163	3,041	8,794	2,741	2,951	9,596	41,072
1936–37	6,989	5,485	2,590	3,395	8,253	3,292	3,143	8,364	41,511
1937–38	5,768	4,458	1,802	12,386	7,125	2,451	1,846	4,140	39,976
1938–39	7,321	4,802	2,257	3,623	7,024	3,027	2,809	4,852	35,715
1939–40	9,501	5,828	2,994	4,322	8,777	3,796	3,690	5,137	44,045
1940–41	11,226	6,090	3,675	4,271	11,172	4,823	5,199	5,920	52,376
1941–42	12,584	6,202	4,673	4,607	12,085	5,919	7,231	6,156	59,457
1942–43	13,129	5,852	5,038	5,108	12,598	7,626	7,691	7,055	64,097
1943–44	14,582	6,099	5,599	5,714	15,377	8,804	9,039	8,455	73,669
1944–45	15,047	6,177	6,042	6,343	15,990	10,466	9,742	9,102	78,909
1945–46	15,200	6,480	6,380	6,291	17,774	11,709	9,697	9,967	83,498
1946–47	24,389	9,091	9,364	11,452	28,276	18,389	13,851	14,524	129,336
1947–48	27,579	10,060	10,179	11,855	37,780	21,439	17,698	18,446	155,036
1949–50	30,300	7,000	10,400	15,200	7,300	12,300	19,400	14,600	116,500
1950–51	38,500	....	....	17,400	....	13,300	....	....	138,700
1951–52	48,500	....	....	21,400	....	18,200	....	....	155,600

1952–53	66,600	9,600	15,500	24,700	3,800	31,800	22,000	17,100	191,100
1953–54	80,000	12,400	15,400	29,000	3,900	41,100	13,500	16,900	212,200
1954–55	95,000	17,100	15,900	33,900	4,000	55,000	11,200	20,900	253,000
1955–56	109,600	20,000	21,600	36,500	4,800	63,000	11,400	21,100	288,000
1956–57	150,000	25,000	.....	.....	.....	99,000	.....	.....	408,000
1957–58	177,600	27,100	37,200	54,800	9,300	92,600	12,700	23,300	434,600

Notes and sources

Blanks indicate figures are not available.

1 The pre- and post-Communist categories are not absolutely comparable and there may be instances in which minor variations in inclusion occur. For the most part, however, the comparisons are valid. For the years 1928 through 1939 the category "others" was reported by the Ministry of Education. The total in this category for the 31 years consisted of 2,261 individuals and was omitted from the table.

1928–48: Chung-kuo Chiao-yu Nien-chien [China Educational Yearbook] (Shanghai: Ministry of Education, 1948).

1949–50 and 1952–56: Jen-min Shou-ts'e [People's Handbook] (Peking: 1957).

1950–52: New China News Agency, Dec. 2, 1954.

1956–57: Jen-min Jih-pao [People's Daily], Mar. 18, 1957.

1957–58: Jen-min Chiao-yu [People's Education], Oct. 9, 1957.

Forestry and agriculture: Communist figures for "forestry" and "agriculture" were combined to correspond with the pre-Communist category "agriculture."

Health: Includes doctors, dentists, pharmacists and other medical personnel with some level of higher education.

Political science and law: Prior to 1950 the category "law" also included political science and all the social sciences.

Education: From 1938 to 1948 this category was split into "education" and "teacher training"; these figures have been combined in the table.

Finance and economics: Equated with the pre-Communist category "commerce."

Literature and arts: Includes liberal arts and fine arts.

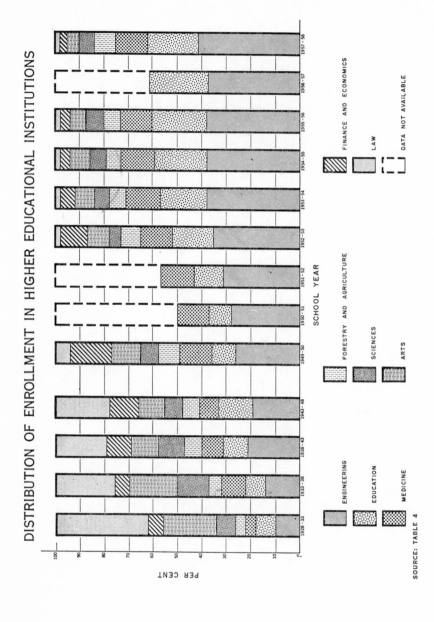

DISTRIBUTION OF ENROLLMENT IN HIGHER EDUCATIONAL INSTITUTIONS

PER CENT

SCHOOL YEAR

FINANCE AND ECONOMICS

LAW

DATA NOT AVAILABLE

FORESTRY AND AGRICULTURE

SCIENCES

ARTS

ENGINEERING

EDUCATION

MEDICINE

SOURCE: TABLE 4

70

TABLE 4.—*Higher education: enrollment by field as percent of total, 1928–58* [1]

School year	Engineering	Science	Agriculture and forestry	Health	Political science and law	Education	Finance and economics	Literature and arts	Total
1928–32	10.2	8.3	3.8	4.0	38.2	7.8	5.9	21.8	100.0
1933–37	14.4	12.8	4.9	10.5	23.5	8.1	6.9	18.9	100.0
1938–42	21.0	11.3	7.3	8.6	20.2	9.8	10.4	11.4	100.0
1943–47	18.6	7.3	7.2	8.0	22.1	13.6	11.6	11.6	100.0
1949–50	26.0	6.0	8.9	13.0	6.3	10.6	16.7	12.5	100.0
1950–51	27.8	......	......	12.5	......	9.6	......	......	100.0
1951–52	31.2	......	......	13.8	......	11.7	......	......	100.0
1952–53	34.8	5.0	8.1	12.9	2.0	16.7	11.5	9.0	100.0
1953–54	37.7	5.8	7.2	13.7	1.8	19.4	6.4	8.0	100.0
1954–55	37.5	6.8	6.3	13.4	1.6	21.8	4.4	8.2	100.0
1955–56	38.1	6.9	7.5	12.7	1.7	21.9	3.9	7.3	100.0
1956–57	36.8	6.3	......	......	......	24.3	......	......	100.0
1957–58	40.9	6.2	8.6	12.6	2.1	21.3	2.9	5.4	100.0

Blanks indicate figures are not available.

[1] Calculated from table 3. For 1928 through 1947, data were combined into 5-year periods.

GRADUATES FROM HIGHER EDUCATIONAL INSTITUTIONS

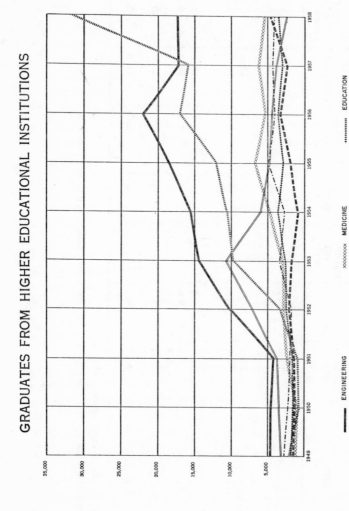

ENGINEERING   MEDICINE   EDUCATION

AGRICULTURAL   SCIENCE   LITERATURE & ARTS

FINANCE & ECONOMICS

SOURCE: TABLE 5

figures for the number of graduates. The relationship is far from perfect, but there is a degree of plausibility for most of the years, which lends credibility to the data compiled from a number of sources. Because withdrawals, failures, etc. are not excluded from the implied number of graduates, these figures should theoretically be larger than the reported number of graduates. This is the case for all but 3 years. The explanation for the gross irregularity in 1957–58 is probably in the questionable validity of the number of entrants in 1958–59, for while enrollment was increasing by 219,000, only 152,000 new students were reportedly admitted. Working from enrollment and graduates to the entrants, their number in 1958–59 should be 291,000, or 139,000 more than reported.

There are several observations to be made with regard to the distribution of the graduates. Perhaps the most important point is that the proportion of graduates in engineering has been consistently lower than their proportion in the student body and that this gap seems to have been widening during the past years. For example, in 1957–58 engineering students constituted 41 percent of the enrollment while during the same year engineering graduates constituted only 24 percent of the total. The fact that graduates are a reflection of earlier enrollments does not explain the above difference, because for the 6 years prior to 1957–58 the proportion of engineering students never dropped below 30 percent. Perhaps the explanation lies in the higher rate of dropouts among engineering majors and longer course of study.

A reverse relationship exists between graduates and enrollment among education majors. For the past 6 years, the proportion graduating has been considerably higher than the proportion enrolled in this major. The main reason here is that most of the courses in normal colleges last only 2 to 3 years.

Another striking factor associated with the distribution of graduates from institutions of higher education is the radical fluctuation that is often apparent between 2 consecutive years (see table 5). Some of these fluctuations seem plausible, while in other instances a reasonable explanation is difficult to reach. In the latter category is the jump in the proportion of graduates in the field of education from 28.5 percent in 1956–57 to 43.9 percent in 1957–58. This increase in graduates in 1 year is suspicious and does not reflect a similar increase in enrollment during the preceding several years. It may be the result of a change in definition; for instance, all persons regardless of major who are assigned to teaching are enumerated as majors in education. There are other examples of fluctuations which are not as radical and which probably reflect changes in policy, in duration of courses, vascillating requirements, and perhaps other more obscure factors.

The graduates have little, if any, voice in what they will do and where they will go upon graduation. The disposition of the graduates is determined by the State Economic Commission and approved by the State

TABLE 5.—*Graduates of institutions of higher education: number and percent, by field of specialization, 1949–58*

Year	Engineering		Science		Agriculture and forestry		Health	
	Number	Percent	Number	Percent	Number	Percent	Number	Percent
1948–49..............	4,752	22.6	1,584	7.5	1,718	8.2	1,314	6.3
1949–50..............	4,711	26.2	1,468	8.1	1,477	8.2	1,391	7.7
1950–51..............	4,416	23.2	1,488	7.8	1,538	8.1	2,366	12.5
1951–52..............	10,213	31.9	2,215	6.9	2,361	7.4	2,636	8.3
1952–53..............	14,565	30.3	1,753	3.7	2,633	5.5	2,948	6.1
1953–54..............	15,596	33.2	802	1.7	3,532	7.5	4,527	9.6
1954–55..............	18,614	33.8	2,015	3.7	2,614	4.8	6,840	12.4
1955–56..............	22,047	35.0	3,978	6.3	3,541	5.6	5,403	8.6
1956–57..............	17,162	30.6	3,524	6.3	3,104	5.5	6,200	11.1
1957–58..............	17,499	24.3	4,645	6.4	3,513	4.9	5,393	7.5
Total..............	129,575	30.1	23,472	5.4	26,031	6.0	39,018	9.1

Year	Education		Finance and economics		Literature and arts		Others		Total	
	Number	Percent	Number	Percent	Number	Percent	Number	Percent	Number	Percent
1948–49	1,890	9.0	3,137	14.9	2,521	12.0	4,084	19.5	21,000	100.0
1949–50	624	3.5	3,305	18.4	2,306	12.8	2,718	15.1	18,000	100.0
1950–51	1,206	6.4	3,638	19.1	2,169	11.4	2,179	11.5	19,000	100.0
1951–52	3,077	9.6	7,263	22.7	1,676	5.2	2,559	8.0	32,000	100.0
1952–53	9,650	20.1	10,530	21.9	3,306	6.9	2,625	5.5	48,000	100.0
1953–54	10,551	22.5	6,033	12.8	2,683	5.7	3,276	7.0	47,000	100.0
1954–55	12,133	22.1	4,699	8.5	4,679	8.5	3,406	6.2	55,000	100.0
1955–56	17,243	27.4	4,460	7.1	4,025	6.4	2,303	3.6	63,000	100.0
1956–57	15,948	28.5	3,651	6.5	4,294	7.7	2,117	3.8	56,000	100.0
1957–58	31,595	43.9	2,349	3.3	4,131	5.7	2,875	4.0	72,000	100.0
Total	103,917	24.1	49,065	11.4	31,790	7.4	28,132	6.5	431,000	100.0

Source: *Ten Great Years* (Peking: State Statistical Bureau, 1960).

TABLE 6.—*Comparison of reported and implied number of graduates from institutions of higher education, 1950–59*

Year	Directly reported [1]	Indirectly implied [2]	Year	Directly reported [1]	Indirectly implied [2]
1949–50....	21,000	15,000	1954–55....	47,000	61,200
1950–51....	18,000	19,000	1955–56....	55,000	50,600
1951–52....	19,000	27,900	1956–57....	63,000	69,000
1952–53....	32,000	50,400	1957–58....	56,000	−71,000
1953–54....	48,000	53,000	1958–59....	62,200	100,000

[1] *Ten Great Years* (Peking: State Statistical Bureau, 1960).

[2] Derived from data in table 1. The method used may best be illustrated by following a step in the calculation. To the enrollment in 1952–53 (191,000) are added the entrants for 1953–54 (71,400). Had no one graduated, this is the number of persons who would be enrolled. By subtracting the 1953–54 enrollment (212,000) from this sum (262,400), the implied number of graduates, withdrawals, and dropouts for 1952–53 is obtained (50,400).

Council. The detail in which this plan is worked out may be seen from the following plan for the assignment of the 1956 graduates:

1. 15,163 or 24.31 percent of the total number of graduates are to be sent abroad, or to the Academy of Sciences, to the Third Bureau of the Ministry of Geology, or to the Bureau of Technology, or are to work as research students and instructors in institutions of higher education. Of these, 4,932 are graduates of engineering courses, which is 22.78 percent of the total number of engineering graduates.

2. 15,438 or 24.74 percent of the total number of graduates are to be assigned to departments and agencies of the Ministry of Heavy Industry. Of these, 11,412 are graduates of engineering courses, which is 52.71 percent of the engineering graduates.

3. 8,706 or 13.96 percent of the total number of graduates are to be assigned to light industry, communications and transportation, agriculture, forestry, water conservancy, finance and economics, and education and culture.

4. 1,651 or 2.65 percent of the total are to be assigned to the Chinese People's Liberation Army.

5. 21,425 or 34.34 percent of the total are to be assigned to the various provinces, autonomous regions, and municipalities under national administration.[22]

The directive of the State Council that announced the above plan also warned the various ministries that work assignments for higher school students should be given only after their graduation. It seems that in the past certain ministries and departments violated this rule and assigned many students to work prior to their graduation and without

[22] *Jen-min Shou-ts'e* [People's Handbook] (Peking: 1957).

first obtaining permission from the Central Government. The Council also complained that in 1955 the distribution plan had not been followed properly and that an adverse effect on production had resulted; henceforth, it ordered, there must be strict adherence to the plan.

Advanced Studies

It is virtually impossible to estimate the number of persons holding advanced degrees in China today. The reason for this becomes apparent from the following discussion of the problems involved.

Advanced degrees were not awarded in the universities of pre-Communist China. Students seeking advanced degrees went abroad, primarily to Japan, the United States, or Europe. Although some data are available on the number of persons who have studied abroad (see table 7), the distribution between graduate and undergraduate students was not given. Another difficulty is that these data do not give the number completing their studies but report only the number of students who studied abroad in a specific year; therefore an individual who spent 2 or 3 years abroad would be double or triple counted. Finally, not all these students were awarded degrees. It is also suspected that the figures in table 7 are not complete. Japanese data, for example, on the number of Chinese students who studied in Japan suggest some major omissions in the Chinese sources, which may be the result of political considerations. One source gave the following as the number of Chinese (including persons from Manchukuo) studying in Japan: 1,421 in June 1932; 1,357 in May 1933; 2,168 in June 1934; 3,527 in June 1935; 5,652 in June 1936; and 5,934 in June 1937.[23] Although some of these individuals may not have been attending institutions of higher education, probably the majority were.

Because of the nature of the data, because of mortality, because many educated individuals managed to leave before the Communists sealed off the country, the number of persons with advanced degrees in China at the time that the new regime was established can only be surmised. If a guess is appropriate, it would seem that in 1950 there were about two or three thousand persons in China with advanced degrees obtained abroad.

The present situation with regard to advanced degrees in China is somewhat vague. Although the plan to award advanced degrees in Chinese universities was announced in 1956, it is believed that this plan was never put into effect and that no higher academic degrees have been awarded. There appears to have been no mention of graduate students since 1957. There are students who complete a 4- or 5-year university curriculum and remain to do additional research and often act as instructors. In all probability they are the same individuals who are referred to as graduate students (see table 8).

---

[23] *Chugokujin Nihon Ryugaku Shi Ko* [History of Chinese Students Studying in Japan] (Tokyo: 1939).

TABLE 7.—*Chinese students attending universities abroad, 1931–47*

School year	Number	School year	Number
1931–32................	450	1939–40................	65
1932–33................	576	1940–41................	86
1933–34................	621	1941–42................	57
1934–35................	859	1942–43................	228
1935–36................	1,083	1943–44................	359
1936–37................	1,002	1944–45................	305
1937–38................	366	1945–46................	8
1938–39................	92	1946–47................	730

Notes and sources

1931–36: *Statistical Abstract of the Republic of China* (Nanking: Directorate General of Budgets, Accounts and Statistics, Executive Yuan, 1940).

1936–42: *Kao-teng Chiao-yu Chi-k'an* [Higher Education Quarterly], vol. III, No. 4, Dec. 31, 1943.

1942–47: *Chung-kuo Chiao-yu Nien-chien* [China Educational Yearbook] (Shanghai: Ministry of Education, 1948).

Data are available that contradict these figures. For example, a survey conducted by the National Tsing Hua University Research Fellowship Fund and the China Institute in America (*A Survey of Chinese Students in American Universities and Colleges in the Past One Hundred Years*, New York: 1954) reports almost consistently higher totals for the United States than the figures in this table report for students in all countries. The same source states that, between 1925 and 1953, 9,617 Chinese students received degrees from American universities.

TABLE 8.—*Graduate students, 1950–56*

School year	Number	School year	Number
1949–50................	[1] 629	1953–54................	[1] 4,249
1950–51................	[1] 1,261	1954–55................	[2] 4,800
1951–52................	[1] 2,168	1955–56................	[2] 4,800
1952–53................	[1] 3,520		

[1] *New China News Agency*, Dec. 2, 1954.
[2] *Current Background*, Nov. 26, 1956 (Hong Kong: U.S. consulate general).

Perhaps the most competent graduate study-research program was instituted by the Academy of Sciences in 1955 (see section on the Academy in ch. VI). Upon completion of the 4-year graduate program either at the Academy or at a university, the student earned the title of "fu-po-shih" [associate doctor]. According to regulations issued by the Ministry of Higher Education, candidates for the title of associate doctor must be under the age of 40, graduates of polytechnical colleges or universities, with 2 years of experience in scientific or technical work. Exceptions may be made under the last two requirements for exceptionally qualified candidates, but all applicants must pass the entrance examination.[24]

The Communists also continued the previous practice of sending students abroad for study, the difference being that since 1950 the overwhelming majority of the students have gone to the Soviet Union for their training. A special examination is held by the Ministry of Higher Education to insure the quality of students going abroad. A sample of the reports dealing with their number reveals the difficulty in making a reasonable estimate for this group. It was reported that between 1949–50 and 1954–55, 5,000 students were sent out of the country for study.[25] Another report states that from 1953–54 through 1956–57, 7,099 persons went abroad to study, while 801 returned.[26] Four months later one Chinese journal stated that "between 1950 and 1957 the Soviet Union gave us great help in connection with higher education and trained over 7,000 teachers and over 6,000 students and postgraduates." [27] Still later, the Communists reported that between 1950 and 1959 the mainland regime sent 14,000 students to the Soviet Union and that 8,500 of that number had returned to China.[28] While presenting these seemingly contradictory figures, a few points of possible agreement must be mentioned. The 5,000 sent between 1949–50 and 1954–55 and the 7,000 sent between 1953–54 and 1956–57 seem fairly compatible with the 14,000 sent abroad between 1950 and 1959; the 6,000 trained students (obviously returned) between 1950 and 1957, and the 8,500 returned students between 1950 and 1959 are also in fair agreement.

Another difficulty arises in trying to determine what proportion of the students sent abroad were undergraduates and what proportion were sent abroad only after graduating from a higher institution. Referring to 1955, an announcement stated that 80 percent of the students returning from abroad were postgraduates and 20 percent were undergraduates.[29] This does not seem to be a representative distribution, especially since it includes only returning students, and refers to persons who left China in 1951 or 1952 and probably completed their undergraduate work prior to 1949. It would be surprising if graduate students constituted more than a third of the total number of students who went abroad to study during the past 10 years. This same report gives the following distribution of the students returning from the Soviet Union in 1955: "Thirty of these students took up the study of engineering, while the others took up specialized courses on communications and transportation, architecture, medicine, finance, and economics. . . . In addition

[24] *An-shan Jih-pao* [An-shan Daily], July 20, 1956.

[25] *New China News Agency,* July 8, 1955.

[26] *Jen-min Chiao-yu* [People's Education], Oct. 9, 1957.

[27] *Shih-chieh Chih-shih* [World Knowledge], No. 3, Feb. 5, 1958.

[28] *Jen-min Jih-pao* [People's Daily], Oct. 4, 1959.

[29] *New China News Agency,* Aug. 4, 1955.

to taking up the study of foreign languages, they usually took up courses lasting from 3 to 4 years." It must be noted here that one of the major obstacles to successful study in the Soviet Union is, of course, the language barrier.

In view of the foggy data and the vague concepts, it is difficult to determine precisely the level of educational attainment of persons that are reported to have earned postgraduate degrees. Most probably anyone who remained at the university for an additional period of time to participate in further study or research is included. Undoubtedly, anyone who had done any postgraduate work abroad, or possibly simply studied abroad, is considered to have earned a higher degree. In any case, Communist China has managed to produce only a few really highly qualified scholars, and the postgraduate studies can in no way be equated with advanced study engaged in by students in the West.

Probably the advanced-degree level of competence is now being achieved by a limited number of persons working at the various institutes of the Academy of Sciences and at some of the better universities with more advanced personnel and facilities. The University of Science and Technology, opened in Peking in 1958, may be one such institution. Most of the students in the field of science and engineering probably attain competence through work and research in the laboratories, industrial plants and other establishments and not as a result of a formal system of education that awards higher degrees.

CHAPTER V
Quality of Education

General Conditions

The rapid growth of enrollment in the schools, the increased number of graduates, and the larger budgets for education describe only one side of the story of educational development in Communist China. One must also examine the quality of present-day education in China, an aspect freely discussed by the Communists but often neglected by Western observers who concentrate on the impressive numbers and indexes. And yet it is here—in the quality of instruction and the adequacy of the educational plants such as buildings, laboratories, books, and other equipment—that the outstanding weaknesses of the educational system are revealed.

The Communists have been prone to criticize their own system, and in this chapter the qualitative aspect of present-day Chinese education is presented largely through citations of the official press, necessitating only minimal judgment on the part of the author. The overall conditions may be seen from the following excerpt from an educational journal:

> Guided by the "rather more than less" and "no need to fear disequilibrium" ideas, the target of enrollment was increased at each level. On this account the development of educational work was not in keeping with the basic conditions for developing and insuring the development of this work—teachers, school premises, equipment, and regular expenses. As the enrollment was raised at each level, the problem became ever more serious. To fulfill the State target of secondary school enrollment, for instance, the Kiangsu provincial government was already taxed to the limit of its teachers and material and financial means, yet the target was raised further by nearly 5,000 students at the administrative district and hsien [county] levels. Also, whereas the Ministry of Education formulated a preliminary scheme for popularizing compulsory education in 7 to 12 years, some hsien tried to beat the target date and attempted to popularize compulsory education in 2 years or even in several months. The result was that new chaotic conditions were developed because teachers and funds were not available, adding many difficulties to the future plans.[1]

The already "chaotic" conditions described above worsened still further with the "leap forward" in 1958. It was also during this year

---

[1] *Jen-min Chiao-yu* [People's Education], Jan. 9, 1957.

that the already-mentioned slogan "walk on two legs," initially introduced in the economic field, was effectively utilized to rationalize the detrimental effects of the rocketing enrollment and the work-and-study program (see ch. II).

Determined to raise the overall educational level of the population but realizing the magnitude of the problem, the Communists decided to compromise by attempting to give the largest portion of the population some semblance of an education (requiring minimum expenditure of capital and time away from production) and at the same time to give more adequate training to a smaller group and a thorough education to a select handful of politically and scholastically qualified individuals. This is referred to as "walking on two legs," although "on many legs" would be more precise because it also means that some schools will be run by the government while others will be run by plants, offices, and communes; general and vocational education will be equally emphasized; there will be simultaneous development of child and adult education; there will be equal emphasis on schooling and home study, on free and nonfree education. This, it is maintained, is the only way to achieve greater, faster, better and more economical results ("much, quick, good, cheap") in education during this "cultural revolution."

In view of this presumably acceptable justification of the deficiencies in the educational system, there has been much less criticism of it since 1958. This, of course, does not mean that the conditions have actually improved and, as a matter of fact, in many instances they grew worse. The quotations in this chapter are not necessarily in chronological order, but are chosen to illustrate a point and are usually representative of the whole period.

Teaching Personnel

The very rapid growth of enrollment at all levels of education has had several inevitable results. Most acute has been the severe shortage of teachers, which has resulted in a lowering of the necessary qualifications for teaching personnel and a consequent deterioration in the quality of instruction. In 1956, 39 percent of the primary-school teachers did not even have a completed junior secondary education—or, in other words, they had less than 9 years of schooling.[2]

Typical of the problem is this description of the situation in Kiangsu Province—a province which should be more capable of dealing with the problem than most:

> The shortage and inferior quality of teachers at all school levels is especially serious in the secondary schools. Due to the very small number of higher normal-school graduates, the provinces and municipalities must supply most of the teachers required by the secondary schools. For example, Kiangsu, which in compari-

---

[2] *T'ung-chi Kung-tso T'ung-hsun* [Statistical Work Bulletin], No. 20, Oct. 29, 1956.

son with the country as a whole had relatively good sources for obtaining teachers, has had to supply more than 90 percent of the secondary school teachers in 1956. Through employing graduates of 1-year training classes who had been primary school teachers with the equivalent of a senior secondary school education, 36.8 percent of the deficit was made up. By accepting 119 intellectuals, 3.6 percent was supplied. This still left more than half of the necessary teachers to be supplied by special districts [ch'u] municipalities [shih], and counties [hsien]. After they recruited the remaining small number of intellectuals, their only other resource was to promote primary school teachers with the equivalent of senior secondary school education to secondary school teachers and relatively good junior secondary school teachers to senior secondary school teachers. This lowered the quality of teaching.

The primary schools suffered the most from this procedure. In Kiangsu Province, more than 2,000 graduated from normal schools in 1956. Since most of these entered higher schools or the short-term training classes to prepare for secondary school teaching, only 300, or 3 percent of the number required, were assigned to the primary schools. In 1956, 1,110 or 50 percent of the primary school teachers in Soochow Special District with the equivalent of senior secondary school education were promoted to junior secondary teachers. . . . In the primary schools, some teachers were not much older than the students, and their teaching and ability to maintain discipline were poor. . . . Many teachers in junior secondary and senior secondary schools are primary school teachers and normal-school graduates, and their education does not meet teaching requirements.[3]

The national picture was at least as bad:

The quality of the present teacher is poor. Junior secondary school graduates have a low level of knowledge in culture and science. The scientific knowledge of the secondary technical school teachers has to be improved as well as their teaching methods.[4]

Still another source reported the serious situation:

With the development of general education, the shortage of secondary and primary school teachers has become more and more serious. It has now become a major problem in the educational development during the years of 1956 and 1957. It is estimated that the shortage of secondary school teachers will amount to about 90,000 persons, and of primary school teachers, to about 200,000. Obviously this is a very serious problem.[5]

The conditions are made even worse by the shortage and incompetence of administrative personnel: "School expansion has been so rapid

---

[3] *Jen-min Chiao-yu* [People's Education], Jan. 9, 1957.

[4] *Jen-min Jih-pao* [People's Daily], Mar. 13, 1957.

[5] *New China News Agency,* June 20, 1956.

that leadership has not kept abreast of requirements, and some schools do not have principals or directors to guide the teachers." [6]

What are the prospects for the future? Is this a temporary phenomenon or will these conditions continue for some time? The Communists provide this answer:

> According to a preliminary estimate, by 1962 we must enroll approximately 100 million children of school age and about 10 million overage children who have never attended school. By then, the number of primary school teachers and staff members should reach 2,820,000, or 1,170,000 more than the present number. * * * However, our normal schools can only graduate a little more than 700,000 teachers in the next 7 years. Since this is not enough, the way to solve the problem is to establish short-course normal classes and short-course normal schools to enroll senior and junior secondary school graduates and to assign them teaching posts after a 1-year period of training.[7]

If this 1956 proposal was adopted, it has prevented half a million badly needed graduates of senior and junior secondary schools from entering the labor force in other fields of economic endeavor.

There are reports that many of the primary and secondary school teachers are attending classes to improve their qualifications. However, Vice Chancellor Chien Wei-chang, of Tsinghua University, stated that—

> At present, a large number of teachers are engaged in study courses, but how much they have learned is still a questionable matter. Furthermore, the departments concerned have never conducted any inspection of their progress. . . . If there is no guarantee that we can acquire enough teachers, then it is impossible to conduct the schoolwork properly.[8]

The absorption of additional millions of students into the elastic educational system in 1958 and 1959 has created an intensification of the problem. The suggested solution has been to encourage people to teach concurrently with other jobs. The principle is: Whoever is capable should act as a teacher. Although this resulted in a certain easing of the shortage, it did draw into the educational system, and particularly into spare-time courses, individuals who have little to pass on to their students.

Physical Facilities

The situation is no better with regard to school buildings, equipment, and other paraphernalia necessary for the efficient operation of schools. Chang Hsi-jo, Minister of Education, stated in 1957:

> From the viewpoint of an increase in the number of school buildings, the floorspace doubled that of the preliberation period, but

---

[6] *Ibid.*

[7] *Shih-shih Shou-ts'e* [Current Events Handbook], No. 4, Feb. 25, 1956.

[8] *Chinese Home Service* (News Agency), May 21, 1957.

from the standpoint of the needs of the people, it is still inadequate. This is entirely correct, because the state's finances and material are limited so that excessive expenditures for education are impossible. This will exist for many years. This contradiction can only be gradually solved following development of the national economy. . . . It is not a question of whether more schools should be built but of whether it is possible or impossible.[9]

As a result of the shortage of school buildings, classes are being held in all types of makeshift accommodations—even out of doors when no other space is available. For example:

> Kiangsi Province has enrolled 31,000 secondary school students and solved the problem of school premises for only 12,000. Some schools in Kiu-kiang municipality have to give lessons on the drill grounds. The office rooms and students' dormitories of Yen-tse-chi junior secondary school in Nanking are large thatched sheds which leak and are flooded with water when it rains. There are no dining rooms, and taking meals in corridors and classrooms is quite a common thing.[10]

The space problem is vividly illustrated by statistics on school-building construction shown in table 1. Over a period of 9 years, the Communists built over 33.5 million square meters of floorspace for all types of schools; however, the main emphasis has been on schools for higher education. Whereas during the 9-year period 1950–58, secondary school enrollment increased 8.4 million (see ch. III), there were only 17.7 million square meters of school premises built—only 2.1 square meters per additional student; in premises for higher education, new

TABLE 1.—*New school building construction, 1950–58*

[In square meters]

Year	Higher	Secondary	Primary	Total
1950...................	190, 000	240, 000	110, 000	540, 000
1951...................	520, 000	630, 000	130, 000	1, 280, 000
1952...................	1, 020, 000	1, 570, 000	230, 000	2, 820, 000
1953...................	1, 510, 000	2, 490, 000	220, 000	4, 220, 000
1954...................	1, 530, 000	2, 510, 000	460, 000	4, 500, 000
1955...................	1, 330, 000	1, 610, 000	770, 000	3, 710, 000
1956...................	2, 050, 000	2, 500, 000	490, 000	5, 040, 000
1957...................	1, 920, 000	2, 810, 000	700, 000	5, 430, 000
1958...................	1, 650, 000	3, 360, 000	1, 040, 000	6, 050, 000
	11, 720, 000	17, 720, 000	4, 150, 000	33, 590, 000

Source: *Ten Great Years* (Peking: State Statistical Bureau, 1960).

[9] *Ibid.,* Mar. 16, 1957.
[10] *Jen-min Chiao-yu* [People's Education], Jan. 9, 1957.

85

floorspace amounted to 22.4 square meters per additional student during this period. One reason for this high figure is that in addition to laboratories, gymnasiums, etc., the total probably includes a larger proportion of dormitories for students in higher educational institutions.

Table 2 presents the annual increase in the number of students at the secondary and higher levels and compares this increase with the square meters of school premises constructed during that year.

The most critical situation exists in primary schools, where school construction has lagged far behind increased enrollment: For every additional square meter of school premises built during this period for this level, enrollment increased by almost 14 students. There are several explanations for this phenomenon. In the first place, the figures in table 1 refer only to state-constructed schools, while many primary schools were built with local funds. In the second place, as the above quotations indicate, many classes are held outdoors, in abandoned monasteries, and in other makeshift quarters. Nevertheless, these factors cannot make up for the existing lack of school buildings. A

TABLE 2.—*Comparison of enrollment and school construction: secondary and higher education levels, 1950–58*

Year	Secondary education			Higher education		
	Annual increase in students	Square meters of floorspace built	Square meters per student	Annual increase in students	Square meters of floorspace built	Square meters per student
	(In thousands)	(In thousands)		(In thousands)	(In thousands)	
1950........	296	240	0. 8	20	190	9. 5
1951........	389	630	1. 6	16	520	32. 5
1952........	1, 175	1, 570	1. 3	38	1, 020	26. 8
1953........	475	2, 490	5. 2	21	1, 510	71. 9
1954........	594	2, 510	4. 2	41	1, 530	37. 3
1955........	242	1, 610	6. 7	35	1, 330	38. 0
1956........	1, 540	2, 500	1. 6	115	2, 050	17. 8
1957........	1, 082	2, 810	2. 6	38	1, 920	50. 5
1958........	2, 931	3, 360	1. 1	219	1, 650	7. 5

Source: *Ten Great Years* (Peking: State Statistical Bureau, 1960).

comparison of school construction and enrollment in primary schools produces ridiculous results. For example, between 1950–51 and 1951–52, the number of children in primary schools increased by over 14 million (see ch. III, table 2), while during 1951 (not identical period, but both covering a year) the state constructed only 130,000 square meters of school buildings for such students—approximately 1 square meter of floorspace for every 108 students!

Essential equipment for teaching is also lacking. This is especially true in secondary industrial, agricultural, and public health schools which require laboratories and shop-type facilities:

> Some schools have no laboratory instruments and students cannot carry on experiments. They have no instruments. In some schools there are not enough books to go around. Lack of desks, clocks, athletic and teaching equipment is even more widespread.[11]

There is also a shortage of living accommodations for teachers and school administrators: "The shortage of living quarters for teachers and staff persons has affected their work and health. One assistant principal of Nanking lives with seven others (three persons per room), while another lives with nine others." [12]

These conditions have natural consequences in the quality of teaching and in the quality of response from the students. Even in the city of Peking, where one would expect conditions to be better than in most other areas, students were doing poorly in 1954:

> There still exists at present many serious shortcomings and problems in our secondary and primary school education in Peking, mainly that the quality of education and the record of students in many schools are very poor. In 1953, 70 percent of the city's senior secondary school graduates failed to pass the entrance examinations to institutions of higher learning.[13]

And in the lower schools:

> Last year [1953], 51 percent of the senior primary school graduates failed in their entrance examinations to junior secondary schools in Peking. . . . Apart from this there are still a number of students who hold the erroneous viewpoint of despising physical labor and the laboring people, and others who do not observe school discipline. Causes for this are many, but the main factor is that the educational department has not, in the past, adopted truly effective measures to raise the quality of education simultaneously as it strove to expand enrollment.[14]

Many of the primary and secondary schools have adopted the two-shift system, and some even a three-shift system. In some classes, the number of students increased to 60 or even 75. Some of the side effects of the overcrowded schools are also creating difficulties:

> Owing to a shortage of school buildings, a great number of secondary and primary schools will adopt the two-session system under which two classes will use the same classrooms, and some schools will allow three classes to use two classrooms in rotation.

---

[11] *Ibid.*

[12] *Ibid.*

[13] *Jen-min Jih-pao* [People's Daily], June 28, 1954.

[14] *New China News Agency,* June 29, 1954.

In other words, secondary and primary school students will spend one-third or one-half of their time outside school. How to educate these students when they are outside school is now a new problem. . . . Take Shanghai—already there are reports in the press that some youths and children wander about the streets, engage in fights, commit thefts, and run away from their homes; this has unfavorably affected their character and health.[15]

Withdrawals

Another serious problem facing the Communists is that many students withdraw from school before their studies are completed. There are several reasons for this, the most important of which is economic. Prior to the introduction of the communes, the greatest proportion of withdrawals was reported in the rural areas, where an extra worker meant more work points for the family and therefore a greater income from the now-defunct agricultural producers' cooperatives. The *Wen-hui Daily* commented on this situation:

> In the past year the withdrawals of secondary and primary school students from schools has been extremely serious. According to incomplete statistics compiled up to November of last year [1955], the number of secondary school students withdrawing or taking leave from schools during the school term of 1954–55 throughout the entire country reached some 144,000, representing 3.9 percent of the total number of secondary school students; and the number of primary school students withdrawing or taking leave from schools was 2.9 million, representing 8.9 percent of the total primary students. . . .
>
> Since winter of last year [1955], the trend of withdrawals from secondary schools and primary schools in the various places not only has not abated but has even increased. According to the most recent information supplied by seven provinces, from the beginning of the school term this spring to the end of February [1956], some 9,000 students had withdrawn or taken leave from 189 secondary schools, representing an average of 10 percent more students withdrawn from school in rural areas than in urban, more in higher classes in primary school than in lower, more in the first and second years of junior secondary than in the third or graduating years.[16]

In a speech before the National People's Congress in 1956, the Minister of Education reported 140,000 withdrawals from junior secondary schools but a much higher figure of 5.1 million from primary schools.[17] He went on to say:

> At present, in the secondary and primary schools in general, more than 10 percent of their students have withdrawn from schools or

[15] *Jen-min Jih-pao* [People's Daily], Oct. 4, 1954.

[16] *Wen-hui Pao* [Wen-hui Daily], Mar. 28, 1956, quoted by Union Research Service, vol. 3, No. 11, 1956.

[17] *New China News Agency,* June 20, 1956.

suspended their studies. In certain areas the number of these students amounts to more than 50 percent. This is a very serious situation. There are many reasons for this. A major reason is that following the creation of agricultural cooperatives, the farmers developed their production and requested the young students to return to productive labor in the villages. Also, certain people may have been temporarily unable to solve the problem of school expenses.[18]

Although the last sentence in the Minister's speech, referring to the economic factor, is made to appear as an afterthought, actually the financial responsibilities associated with school attendance are very important in the high withdrawal rate:

One student in school requires a minimum of 60 yuan for tuition, board, instruments, and miscellaneous expenses per semester, or 120 yuan a year. Generally the maximum wage per workday is 1 yuan. Based on 200 workdays per year, the income will be 200–300 yuan per year. If a family has few working members, it is difficult to pay 120 yuan. Because most secondary schools are in rural areas, this situation should be taken into account.[19]

One reason why 1956 was a particularly bad year for withdrawals was that student subsidies were decreased as a first step toward converting from subsidies to scholarships. The junior secondary school subsidy was reduced by 18 percent in 1955, and the sum granted in 1955 was scheduled for reduction by 14 percent in 1956 and by 10 percent in 1957. The senior secondary school subsidy was reduced by 28 percent in 1955, and the sum granted in 1955 was scheduled for reduction by 24 percent in 1956 and by 20 percent in 1957.[20]

Problems of Vocational Schools

Both the press and the various enterprises which hire vocational school graduates have complained about the inadequacies of these schools. One of the major complaints is that in the process of setting up technical schools, the imitation of the Soviet "technicum" (secondary technical school) has been too mechanical, without regard to China's economic, agricultural, and industrial conditions. Although most of the secondary vocational schools are supposed to educate at a level comparable to that of the senior general secondary schools, 56 percent of the instructors have not graduated from an institution above the level of the senior secondary schools, and virtually all are lacking in practical production experience. There are no textbooks for more than two-thirds of the curriculums.[21] Here, as in other schools, there is a shortage of instructors, but in the case of vocational schools there is a particular

---

[18] *Ibid.*

[19] *Chung-kuo Ch'ing-nien Pao* [China Youth Daily], July 13, 1956.

[20] *Ibid.*

[21] *Jen-min Jih-pao* [People's Daily], Mar. 10, 1957.

and additional reason for this shortage: It seems that most college graduates consider it degrading to teach in secondary technical schools and would prefer either to do research in higher institutions or to go into industry.

Under these circumstances it is not surprising to find the following criticism in the *People's Daily*:

> Although in the last 2 to 3 years, the quality of the graduates has improved, many industrial enterprises still report that the middle-class technical cadres are not able to satisfy the requirements of the production work because the graduates have a very narrow knowledge of industry and management and are unable to do independent work. The reasons are: The study load of students is very heavy, the relations between school and production are not good (practical training requirements are not satisfactorily filled), and the leadership of the school cadres and the work in political thought are also poor.[22]

A unique problem of secondary vocational schools is that controls are constantly changing and management is especially poor. Perhaps an extreme but not atypical example is that of the Tientsin Industrial School, a large secondary vocational school constructed in 1949. Inefficiency and changes of dual control have affected the school unfavorably. Originally it was under the control of the Tientsin Municipal Local Industry Bureau and the Local Industry Control Bureau of the North China Administrative Committee. Later, it was transferred to the Tientsin Municipal Heavy Industry Bureau and the Third Ministry of Machine Building. At present it is under the direction of the Tientsin Municipal Machine and Electric Equipment Industry Bureau and the Ministry of Electrical Equipment Industry. The former does not have a single full-time cadre to manage teaching and administration of the school, while the latter does not control the school directly and ignores it. As may be expected, the result is a policy so indefinite and fluctuating that the types of specialization and skills to be taught at the school are not firmly established. For example, during the last semester of 1955, the school received a directive that the specialization in industrial power installation should be changed to a specialization in generators. In 1956, after all the necessary changes in teaching staff, equipment, and the like had been made, the school was told to revert to the original specialization. This vacillation occurred more than once.

> The leadership organs simply want students. They are not concerned with the quality of students or with the type of training. There is a shortage of teachers in the school. The qualifications of the teachers are not high; probably half of them are secondary technical graduates. . . . The students need production practice, but a suitable plant cannot be located. . . . The school principal

---

[22] *Ibid.*

is too busy conducting meetings, does not direct teaching, and the school standards are low. . . . Vocational schools which are directed and controlled jointly by the Central Government, local government, and a ministry are many in number. The problem of leadership relations in the Tientsin Industrial School exists in many schools of this type. This school's problem is a general problem.[23]

Problems in Higher Education

Although the complaints dealing with the operation of institutions of higher education include those already mentioned in the previous sections, there are some problems unique to institutes and universities.

As in the lower schools, the race for quantity has resulted in a deterioration of quality, and both the teaching personnel and the students in higher education are below the standards set by the state:

> During the past several years, more than 20,000 new teachers were taken on, and many of the old teachers have raised their ideological, political, and academic qualifications. But all the new teachers taken on were assistant teachers freshly graduated from the regular courses of higher education. As a result, although there are more than 38,000 teachers in the institutions of higher education throughout the country in 1955, over 50 percent of them are instructors. In the case of the engineering courses, over 60 percent of the teaching staff is made up of assistants. . . . Teachers of such quality are bound to affect directly the quality of the students.[24]

Two years later, the situation had not improved:

> The number of qualified teachers has not kept pace with the rapid expansion of enrollment. Although the number of instructors in higher education is over 42,000, most of them are young and with insufficient experience. Instructors account for not less than half of the total, while professors and associate professors constitute slightly over 13 percent.[25]

The deficiencies in the physical plant of the universities and institutes, although not as bad as in the lower schools, are nevertheless serious:

> Capital construction, teaching equipment, libraries, and school finances are still far from requirements, although the state has given institutes of higher learning great support every year; this has also affected the fulfillment of the plans. . . . The estimates of expenditures on teaching equipment and capital construction, in particular, have exceeded actual expenditures on these two items. The principal cause of this was that the presidents of colleges and universities had almost no authority to deal with finances.[26]

[23] *Kuang-ming Jih-pao* [Kuang-ming Daily], Dec. 28, 1956.
[24] *Jen-min Jih-pao* [People's Daily], June 30, 1955.
[25] *Vestnik Vysshey Shkoly* [U.S.S.R. Bulletin of Higher Education], No. 3, 1957.
[26] *Jen-min Jih-pao* [People's Daily], Sept. 4, 1956.

Factors which are often mentioned in connection with the poor quality of college graduates are an overloaded curriculum, insufficient amount of home study time, and overwork. The life of a Chinese student is minutely planned, and virtually no time is left for the student to apportion for himself. Every student is expected to attend an average of 35 hours of classes every week, in addition to regular indoctrination and propaganda sessions and social and extracurricular activities, all of which leaves little time for class preparation. A slower and less capable student does not have the opportunity to spend additional time on home study. Also, students are so conditioned to regulations and group activity that many are unable to perform independent analysis and work—a frequent complaint of industrial enterprises which hire graduates.

The People's Daily strongly attacked overwork in schools:

> Students and teachers became exhausted and their health was weakened year after year. If these conditions are not changed, the consequences will be unthinkable. . . . Work in excess of what one's physical strength or mental powers can bear will only cause irreparable losses and will do harm to the construction enterprises. In the last few years, students and teachers not only have worked and studied for over 10 hours a day and had no rest on Sunday but have also been assigned to do practical work in the field of production or to carry out other activities during the summer and winter holidays.[27]

Overspecialization has been a particularly serious problem in Chinese higher education. The fields of study have been narrowed to such an extent that there is virtually no possibility of interchange among specialists. An example of this tendency was brought out by Sung Ping-tse, Director of the Construction and Operations Pedagogic Laboratory at Tientsin University. At a conference convened by the Ministry of Higher Education he stated:

> Civil engineering is a science, and those studying it should understand both structures and construction operations. Studying structures without understanding operations results in designs that are isolated from practicality; conversely, studying operations without understanding construction results in blind operations. Therefore, the industrial and civil construction specialty should no longer be divided, so students will have a broad and basic knowledge of their fields.[28]

He then pointed out that in the old universities civil engineering required the study of railways, bridges, structures, water conservation, and the like, to provide the students with a broad base, while now overspecialization has produced such majors as construction operations, steel

[27] *Ibid.*
[28] *Kuang–ming Jih-pao* [Kuang-ming Daily], Jan. 17, 1957.

structures, and steel reinforced concrete structures. A student majoring in railroad bridge construction knows nothing of highway bridge construction, or railroad building in general. The Ministry of Higher Education revealed that in some institutes of higher learning mathematics has been divided into as many as 19 specialized branches and physics into 20 specialized branches, whereas 5 to 6 specialized branches would adequately cover the field of mathematics. The institutes of technology established 240 departments and courses.[29] A person graduating from 1 of 19 branches of mathematics cannot be called a mathematician, and a graduate of 1 of the 240 specialties in higher institutes can be little more than a skilled technician in a very narrow field.

For 1 month in the spring of 1957, during the "Hundred Flowers Movement," the professors were given an opportunity to express themselves. Their statements cover a wide range of subjects and are very revealing of the deficiencies in higher education. Although some of these statements pertain specifically to the People's University, they may usually be accepted as reflecting the general situation. The summaries of their statements are presented below.[30]

Professor Hsia Shih-wu said:

> The People's University has been established for 7 years, but it still has no fixed policy. At first, I heard that they wanted it to become a comprehensive university, later they wanted it to become a theoretical university, and now they want it to become a university which stresses finance and economics. No one actually knows what the university is going to be. This has hampered the actual work considerably.

Professor Li Hsi-san:

> The People's University is a university in name only, and it resembles a secondary school in the content of its instruction and a primary school in teaching methods.

Professor Hsu Meng-Hsiung:

> The People's University does not look like a school, but a large beehive of dogmatism. All it has done is to disseminate dogmatism.

Professor Lang Lang-tien:

> While lecturing, many teachers of the People's University have no opinions of their own. They just make wholesale use of the teaching materials translated from the Russian.

Professor Chao Hsi-yu:

> The idea that Marxism-Leninism can replace everything has been prevalent, and that one who understands Marxism-Leninism is qualified to become the principal of a university, a president, a minister, or anything else. This is wrong.

---

[29] *New China News Agency,* June 1, 1957.

[30] *Ibid.,* May 31, 1957.

Professor Li Ching-han, reminiscing on his experience during the period of thought reform, said:

This is not only disrespect for personal rights but an outright insult. If you think now that our opinions are too harsh and that you cannot take them, please remember that we are the dogs trained by you. Actually, we did not learn all that you taught us.

Wang Te-chou:

I am a 60-year-old instructor, although I was a professor before the liberation. However, I know of a number of persons who became assistant department heads immediately after their graduation from the People's University just because they were party members, although their academic level and teaching ability were poor.

Assignment of College Graduates

As mentioned in the preceding chapter, the state draws up detailed enrollment quotas for every specialty offered by institutions of higher education. Because of this and because of the need for college graduates, one would naturally assume that the Communists are making the best possible use of the people who are currently graduating from institutes and universities. However, this is not the case. Many reports indicate that there is a great inefficiency both in the estimates of future manpower requirements and in the placement of college graduates.

One survey by reporter Wang Po-kung of the *New China News Agency,* in 1957, is sufficient to illustrate the prevailing situation:

The number of graduates of the engineering geology and hydrological geology departments needed by the state this year is estimated to exceed 4.9 times the actual number of graduates. There will also be a shortage of graduates specializing in mining survey, land and hydrological survey, welding, mining, metallurgy, mechanical engineering, electrical engineering, civil engineering, civil construction, transportation, post- and tele-communication, food industry, physics, medicine, and philosophy.

On the other hand, the number of graduates specializing in certain subjects has been exceeding the needs of the state. For instance, there will be some difficulty in finding work assignments for 3,000 Russian-language graduates this year. There will also be a surplus of graduates specializing in automobile and tractor engineering, petroleum mining, pharmacy, supply and marketing cooperatives, finance and credit, botany, zoology, history, oriental languages, and "higher education."

Since the departments concerned have been complaining about the shortage of specialized personnel in the building of the state, the question arises, What has caused the surplus of graduates specializing in petroleum mining and other branches of studies? People in educational circles are of the opinion that the present situation has been caused by our country's lack of experience in economic planning and in training of specialized personnel simultaneously, as a result of which the two have not been properly geared to meet each other's needs.[31]

After elaborating further on this problem and the problem of over-specialization, Wang went on to the question of assignment of graduates. Of the total number of university graduates from August 1953 to December 1956, over 5 percent requested reassignment because they were not doing work in their line. Probably as many others were doing work for which they were not trained but did not request transfer. There were some students who asked to be reassigned because of the "selfish desire to work in scientific organizations, universities, designing departments," or for family, financial, or health reasons. However, Wang pointed out the following glaring examples of misassignment of students:

> For instance, mathematics students were assigned to teach Russian in factories, physics students to serve as proofreaders in printing establishments, electrical engineering students to install electric light bulbs and small motors in movie-developing studios, and organic chemistry students to work in inorganic analysis and electroplating in bicycle factories. In one extreme case a student of the Tungchi University who had specialized in structural engineering, after being assigned to an engineering unit, was asked to receive telephone calls, to take care of incoming and outgoing documents, cut stencils, and perform other office drudgeries. . . .
>
> Last summer [1956] a group of medical graduates was assigned to a certain construction and engineering company, only to find out upon their arrival that the company had not yet been established. The departments of physical culture and athletics have even assigned students to teach in physical culture schools which will not be ready until 1958 or 1960, as a result of which the jobs held by these students exist in name only. Some units have treated graduates like balls, kicking them around.
>
> For instance, five Russian-language graduates from Shanghai were assigned to the Second Ministry of Machine Building Industry in Peking, which in turn assigned them to a factory in Szechwan. Finding no work for them, the factory sent them to Nanking. Another instance involved a student of the Chiao-tung University who was assigned to the Ministry of Geology. After being kicked around from one department to another, he was finally given an offer in a repair and assembly plant at Heng-yang. To his dismay, upon his arrival, he found that the construction of the factory would not begin until 1958 and that there would be no job for him until then.[32]

---

[31] *Ibid.*, June 1, 1957.
[32] *Ibid.*

Reporter Wang concludes that at this stage in China's economic development, such problems are inevitable—that the students will have to accept jobs that may not be exactly in their field of study but are not too distant from the general field of interest. He does hope, however, that students will eventually have more freedom of choice and will be informed in advance of their assignments and not on the morning of the day they are to depart, as is often the case.

This problem was also aired at a symposium held by the Ministry of Higher Education for students of 10 Peking universities. They mentioned many of the points covered above. One student pointed out that from 1953 to 1956 only one-tenth of the students who studied mining engineering obtained work in their own profession. They not only complained of the assignment policies but also criticized many of their courses, particularly those dealing with political theories. A specific complaint was that "the intellectual level of teachers of courses in political theories is inadequate." [33]

Education and Planning

All the factors that have contributed to the poor quality of instruction in mainland China may be ascribed to inadequate planning during a period when enrollment was growing at fantastic rates. In striving to fulfill and overfulfill enrollment quotas, not enough attention was paid to personnel and facilities, to quality and requirements, and to adapting the enrollment needs of higher level schools to the future needs of the economy.

A typical example was reported in an educational journal:

> After learning that only 36 percent of their school-age children were attending school, some hsien (counties), under the slogan of "simultaneously survey, plan, and operate the school," achieved compulsory education in several months. Since there was no provision for additional teachers and budgets for expenditures, disorganization arose and many difficulties for future planning were created.[34]

A similar example in vocational education:

> The Canton Wine Industrial School, under the Ministry of Light Industry, fixed the student enrollment at 960 for a 4-year course. Based on this figure, 240 students should be recruited every year, but in 1956, 520 were recruited, increasing total enrollment for the 4-year period to 2,080 students.[35]

Although the specific figures are somewhat confusing, the point of the complaint is clear.

---

[33] *Ibid.*, May 19, 1957.
[34] *Jen-min Chiao-yu* [People's Education], Jan. 9, 1957.
[35] *Chi-hua Ching-chi* [Planned Economy], Sept. 24, 1956.

As a result of this faulty planning, many of the graduates are unable to find jobs in the field in which they were trained, as will surely be the case with the excess of wine specialists.

Under a free system, in the process of gradually developing and expanding the educational facilities and student enrollments, a natural balance is struck between the various levels of education. In other words, of the total graduates from secondary schools, a certain proportion enters the labor force while the rest go into higher educational institutions; the same is true at the other school levels. But in China, the sudden emphasis on education has created many unnatural situations: For example, many children graduating from primary schools have been prevented from continuing their education, while during some years there have not been enough graduates from secondary schools to fill the allotted quotas for entrants at the higher level (see table 3).

TABLE 3.—*Graduates of senior secondary schools compared with the entrants into institutions of higher education, 1950–58* [1]

Year	Graduates from senior secondary schools [2]	Entrants into institutions of higher education [3]	Year	Graduates from senior secondary schools [2]	Entrants into institutions of higher education [3]
1950–51....	44, 300	35, 000	1955–56....	156, 000	165, 600
1951–52....	34, 500	65, 900	1956–57....	202, 600	107, 000
1952–53....	58, 400	71, 400	1957–58....	221, 700	152, 000
1953–54....	72, 100	94, 000	1958–59....	242, 000	270, 000
1954–55....	106, 000	96, 200			

[1] The graduates in this table are only those from secondary general schools, since they comprise the overwhelming majority of the students who go on to higher institutions. Although some students from specialized schools (both normal and vocational) also go on to specialized institutes, their number is relatively small. It must also be noted that not all the senior secondary school graduates can be spared for higher education, since there is a great need for manpower at their level of attainment.

[2] See ch. III, table 4.

[3] See ch. IV, table 1.

In June 1956 the Minister of Education reported:

One of the most outstanding problems with respect to ordinary education is the shortage of secondary school students, which seriously affects national construction [construction of the Communist regime] needs. According to an initial estimate, up to 1958 the number of senior secondary school graduates cannot meet the higher educational institutions' requirements for such graduates. By 1959 the ratio between [entrants into] higher educational institutions and the number of graduates from senior secondary schools will be only 1 to 1.23. Two years ago there was an apparent surplus of junior secondary school graduates. However, this proved not to be the case. In fact, the situation was caused by the erroneous ideas of some junior secondary graduates and the heads of their families. They despised manual labor and manual laborers. They were unwilling to take part in productive labor and demanded that they be allowed to attend schools. However, it was impossible then for all junior secondary school graduates to attend schools. Thus, the situation was tense in the summer and fall of 1954 and 1955. At the beginning of 1956, however, all quarters noticed the shortage of junior secondary school graduates. In 1956 the number of junior secondary school graduates was expected to reach 787,037. Even if all had chosen to attend school, they would not have been able to meet the full requirements of the senior secondary schools and the secondary level vocational schools for new students.

With the graduates of 1956, it is impossible to meet the demand of various productive agencies in industry and agriculture for 300,000 junior secondary school graduates. The 1957 graduates of junior secondary schools can barely meet the demand of senior secondary schools for new students. They will still be unable to meet the demand of the productive agencies of industry and agriculture.[36]

Almost a year later, the Minister of Education spoke again, before the Chinese People's Political Consultative Conference. He maintained that the situation was normal and correct and that youths unable to go on with their schooling should go home and happily participate in agricultural production:

During the summer holiday of this year [1957], there will be a great many advanced primary and junior secondary school graduates who will be unable to go to the next school level. The same condition will exist for senior secondary school graduates. Also, there will be an appropriate number of school-age children who will be unable to enter school. This is a question which worries many people. . . . The situation concerning the inability of all advanced graduates of primary school to be promoted will exist not only this year but it will exist for a long time from now. We should regard it as a normal situation. . . . Whether they take up production work or are promoted to a higher level of education, the fundamental and final objective is to develop socialist production and raise labor productivity. As for admission of school-age children into schools and promotion of students, the question can be solved by relying on the ability of the masses in the rural areas and their initiative in the establishment of private schools by individuals and cooperatives to meet the shortage of public schools. . . . Since schools will still not accommodate all, secondary and primary school graduates whose homes are in rural areas should face their problem and return happily to their homes to take part in agricultural production. . . . We must overcome

[36] *New China News Agency,* June 20, 1956.

such erroneous thinking as "learning is superior to all things" and "ambition should be achieved through study." [37]

He then went on to glorify labor: "Carry out labor education among the young so that they may love and respect labor and erect a new pillar of society."

Actually, a solution (of sorts) was devised much sooner than the Minister anticipated. With the expansion of commune-operated primary schools and secondary agricultural schools, the children of peasants no longer have to be sent back to the country because of a shortage of urban school facilities but can stay in their village, participate in productive labor, and attend both primary and secondary school on a spare-time basis.

From the above quotations, it is clear that the quality of education in China today leaves much to be desired and that one leg is doing considerably more walking that the other. Nevertheless, it is dangerous to ignore the fact that, excluding the literacy classes, there are over 100 million young people attending schools. Undoubtedly among this multitude there are thousands of outstanding individuals who manage to rise above the masses and obtain an education, not so much because of the existing system but despite it. The majority of the primary school graduates have probably acquired, in varying degrees, some knowledge of the "three R's" along with some rudimentary, though often perverted, idea of the world around them. The quality of the secondary school graduates must vary from school to school and particularly between rural areas and the larger cities. The few so-called "key institutions" at all educational levels do cater to the promising student; however, it may be safely predicted that the system cannot produce large numbers of highly qualified scholars.

---

[37] *Chinese Home Service* (News Agency), Mar. 16, 1957.

CHAPTER VI

Science and Technology

Chinese science and technology have a long history; however, the first modern scientific concepts and research methods were introduced with the reorganization of the educational system in the beginning of this century. Even after the establishment of the Academia Sinica in Peking in 1928, however, scientific research remained on a fairly low level and was greatly handicapped by the absence of adequate research facilities and by a shortage of funds for improving conditions. The situation was quite similar even in the better Chinese universities. Because of these conditions, a relatively large number of students went abroad to obtain their education. Those who returned to China were later used to form the nucleus of staffs responsible for scientific and technological developments under the Communist regime.

Any consideration of the controls, organization, and developments in the fields of science and technology in Communist China immediately leads to the names of Kuo Mo-jo and Nieh Jung-chen. Although neither one of these individuals is a scientist, they both play dominant roles in establishing and implementing Communist policies over all aspects of scientific development.

The ubiquitous Kuo Mo-jo is the dean of China's scientific and cultural world. Although his main position is that of the President of the Chinese Academy of Sciences, he is also Chairman of the China Federation of Literary and Art Circles, of the Chinese Historical Society, of the China Peace Committee, and vice chairman of a number of other councils and associations. He made his name primarily in the field of literature but is also considered to be a historian, an archeologist and a paleographer. A skilled speaker, he has participated in numerous missions outside of China, and his propagandistic efforts as a "nonpartisan" occupying an important leadership post in the Communist hierarchy are quite effective, particularly in other Asian nations.

Marshal Nieh Jung-chen is a former Acting Chief of the General Staff of the armed forces and a veteran military leader. In 1954 he made the first step in the transition from army assignments to political duties by becoming a member of the Standing Committee of the First National People's Congress, and in 1956 he became the Vice Premier of the State

Council. In his present post as Chairman of the Scientific and Tech nological Commission, Nieh has broad powers over the future development of science and the professional life of the scientist.

People's Science

The words "science" and "technology" are used daily in the Communist Chinese press and by the masses of workers and peasants. One is just as likely to encounter them in connection with manure collecting or hog raising as with the construction of the much-talked-of atomic reactor. The importance assigned to science in Communist China is illustrated by the fact that the "five loves" being taught to all, starting with primary school, are: Love of the fatherland, love of the people, love of labor, *love of science,* and care of public property.

The slogans and pronouncements emphasizing the scientific method are deceiving. China remains, for the most part, a country where science and technology are in their infancy, where scientists are at a premium, and where the introduction of a metal plow is considered a scientific achievement and a technological advance. In order to rationalize the low level of scientific development in China with Communist plans for rapid technological advance, the propaganda machine has perverted the meaning of these words to such an extent that "scientific and technological" achievements are attainable by virtually all the adults in the country. In 1958 it was announced at a meeting in Szechwan Province reporting the "great leap forward" in science and technology that "no less than 5 million technical innovations had been made since the beginning of the year." [1]

Aware that the level of Western technology can not be achieved by China for many years to come, the Communists have attempted to minimize foreign and emphasize Chinese accomplishments, stressing the fact that prior to Western influence China was among the leading scientific nations of the world: "Superstitiously worshipping foreign countries and valuing everything foreign above things native has left a deep mark on the mentality of the Chinese people, especially the intellectuals." [2] This approach is most vividly illustrated in connection with medicine. Since there are few doctors trained in Western medicine, traditional Chinese medicine has been given new prestige, and doctors trained in Western medicine have been required to adapt many of the procedures and cures utilized by the old herbists.

The disparagement of Western accomplishments and "book learning" in general was emphatically expressed by Chen Po-ta, deputy director of the propaganda department of the Party Central Committee. Although he felt that the education system should be prepared to train large

---

[1] *New China News Agency,* Jan. 22, 1958.

[2] *Hung-ch'i* [Red Flag], No. 9, Oct. 1, 1958. This is an excerpt from a speech by Nieh Jung-chen at the First Congress of the Scientific and Technical Association of the Chinese People's Republic.

numbers of intellectuals, he pointed out that just because a number of people had attended college or had attained a doctor's degree in the past did not necessarily mean that they had gained a proper knowledge.

On the contrary, those who had not been to college or abroad or who had not received a doctor's degree might possess knowledge equivalent to the standard of a college education. At present there is a group of old cadres in various fields of work [composed of] former workers without any formal education who had learned their trade by studying diligently to master scientific techniques in the course of their work.[3]

The drive to popularize science has had the effect of obscuring the facts and figures on scientific development in China. A casual observer could easily come to the conclusion that the new emphasis on science has had widespread and lightninglike effect in converting China into a country of scientists. A few quotations from the Chinese mainland press will illustrate the absurdity of this drive. Referring to Kiangsi Province, one newspaper stated that—

For the sake of truly enabling all the people to take up science and in order to build and strengthen a proletarian army of science, technology, and culture, it was decided at the conference to build up a 1-million-man army of scientists in the province; that is, the number of research workers in the 25,000 agricultural co-ops will be increased to 700,000, and the number in factories, mines, and educational institutions will be increased to 300,000. For the sake of strengthening leadership for scientific, technological, and cultural work, and of developing local activism for participation in such work, the conference demanded that scientific research organs should be universally established. All existing research institutes in the various administrative districts and municipalities shall be changed into branches of the Academy of Sciences, scientific research stations shall be established in hsien [counties], scientific research stations shall be established in ch'u [districts], scientific research laboratories shall be established in hsiang [townships] and chen [towns], and general research groups shall be formed in the agricultural cooperatives.[4]

It was also demanded that these research organizations should begin work at once in accordance with the needs of production.

Of course this means that "scientific" work in China is now performed not only by scientists but also by workers and peasants, many of whom have made "great contributions in science," although admittedly many of them have had "little formal education." Most of China's provinces are making preparation to set up more research institutes and branches of the Academy of Sciences as centers for local scientific work. In Kwangsi Chuang autonomous region—

---

[3] *New China News Agency*, Mar. 10, 1958.

[4] *Kuang-ming Jih-pao* [Kuang-ming Daily], Aug. 2, 1958.

Fifty-one scientific research institutes have been set up by city and county administrations; 35 cities have their own associations for the dissemination of scientific knowledge, and many rural districts, agricultural cooperatives, and factories and schools have their own scientific groups.[5]

The level of these new scientific and technical societies and research associations that are springing up throughout the country may be judged by the fact that many "outstanding workers and model peasants" are admitted as members. The accomplishments and "innovations" of these people are recorded with great precision and number in scores of millions—their nature is difficult to imagine.

The organization established to lead the masses into this new scientific era was the China Association for Dissemination of Scientific and Technical Knowledge, formed in August 1950. Its aims were to propagate scientific and technical knowledge among the broad masses, to explain natural phenomena in terms of Socialist materialism, to dispel traditional superstitions and fears, to publicize scientific achievements, and to educate the masses in hygiene, sanitation, and progressive production methods. In 1956 this association had 27 branches which supervised 600 district committees, 1,300 county units, and 3,000 working teams. The membership numbered 320,000 and was composed of a large number of professional people.[6] In September 1958 this organization was merged with the Chinese Federation of Scientific Societies to form the Scientific and Technical Association of China. In the words of Nieh Jung-chen, the new organization should be a "party-led, Socialist, national, scientific, and technical organization of the masses" to aid the party in conducting a "technical and cultural revolution."

Despite this popularization of science and ridicule of the trained scientist, work on a higher level is being conducted in the institutes of the Chinese Academy of Sciences, at institutions of higher learning, and in the laboratories and workshops of the more important industrial enterprises—once again an illustration of "walking on two legs." The effort to bring science down to the level of the masses may be a form of investment in the future of China's dreams of scientific and technological accomplishments.

The much-discussed 12-year plan for scientific development was drafted in 1956. It was drawn up by scientific workers and discussed and expanded at conferences. Suggestions from the Soviet scientific delegation visiting China were incorporated, and the plan was finalized in 1957. The main function of this plan is to meet the national needs in economic construction, agriculture, health, and the like, and in the process train 10,500 "advanced scientists" by 1967. A total of 582 identified problems in science and technology were grouped into 57

[5] *New China News Agency,* Aug. 11, 1958.
[6] *Ibid.,* Jan. 22, 1958.

aspects of research and finally consolidated into the following 12 categories: (1) Peaceful use of atomic energy; (2) new electronics techniques; (3) jet propulsion; (4) automation in production and precision equipment; (5) surveying and prospecting for petroleum and other scarce materials; (6) exploration of mineral resources; (7) metallurgy studies; (8) study and development of fuels and heavy machines; (9) technical problems associated with exploration of the Yellow and Yangtze Rivers; (10) study of agriculture, with emphasis on mechanization, electrification, and the use of chemicals; (11) study of important diseases; and (12) basic theoretical problems in natural sciences.

Only 1 year after the final version of the plan was adopted, Nieh Jung-chen issued the following statement:

> Judging by present conditions, generally speaking, the plan can be accomplished 5 years ahead of schedule—a certain portion can even be fulfilled 7 years ahead of schedule. As a matter of fact, certain parts of the plan have already been completed.[7]

The national local scientific and technological work conference, held in Shanghai from December 22, 1958, to January 4, 1959, discussed the scientific accomplishments of the past several years—achieved under the leadership of the Party and through the participation of all the people in the scientific and technological revolution. At the conference it was maintained that the work during the past 3 years showed that China had taken preliminary steps on the road to scientific and technological progress. The conference also decided on a number of general tasks similar to the categories of the 12-year plan, to be carried out in the following six fields of work during 1959: (1) Study of the newest and most advanced scientific and technological knowledge; (2) the development of industry and transportation; (3) the development of agriculture; (4) the development of medical science and public health; (5) "renovation of mother nature"; and (6) the study of basic theories.[8] This, they said, requires "more tremendous forward leaps."

The above goals are broad enough to include almost any type of scientific or technological research. It may be assumed that with their practical approach, the Chinese Communists will for the most part concentrate on developments which will produce immediate results. The essence of their hopes in connection with scientific progress may once again be summarized in the words of Nieh Jung-chen:

> We should try to master the scientific achievements of the Soviet Union and other countries within the shortest possible time and to carry out research in line with the actual situation of the country.[9]

---

[7] *Hung-ch'i* [Red Flag], No. 9, Oct. 1, 1958.
[8] *New China News Agency,* Jan. 15, 1959.
[9] *Ibid.,* Mar. 12, 1958.

The most reasonable interpretation would seem to be that Chinese leaders realize that the gap in the level of scientific and technological development between China and the West is so great that it would be folly to pursue advanced research while this chasm exists—that the quickest and most practical way to raise China's level is to borrow and copy from the advanced nations and adapt what is borrowed to the country's own needs, for "the basic tasks of our scientific research is development of production and building of socialism." [10]

Control of Research and Development in Science and Technology

Whereas the Scientific and Technical Association of China directs all the activities in what may be referred to as popular science, scientific research and development at the higher level is now controlled by the Scientific and Technological Commission, under the chairmanship of Nieh Jung-chen. This Commission was created in November 1958 through the merger of the State Technological Commission and the Science Planning Commission and was made directly responsible to the State Council. This unification of the leadership in scientific studies has made it possible to keep scientific developments and planning under closer Party surveillance.

From 1956 until this latest reorganization in 1958, control over science in China was exercised by the Science Planning Commission (which had also been under the chairmanship of Nieh Jung-chen). In his report to the Second Political Consultative Council in 1956, Kuo Mo-jo (as President of the Academy of Sciences) stressed the waste, inefficiency, and lack of overall planning, coordination, and dissemination of scientific information and the inadequacy in the results of scientific research during the past several years. Partly to rectify this situation and also to manage the development of the 12-year plan for scientific research, the Science Planning Commission was established as a temporary body in the same year. However, in 1957, following a reorganization, it was made permanent, with the following specific responsibilities: (1) Both long-term and short-term planning of scientific work; (2) coordination of research work; (3) responsibility for libraries and laboratories; (4) international cooperation; (5) training of high-grade scientists; and (6) the financing of the main scientific research projects.[11] At the same time, the number of members in the SPC was raised from 35 to 106, most of them prominent scientists, university leaders, and representatives of ministries concerned with research.

There seems to be considerable friction between the Academy of Sciences and the agencies for the control of research and development in science and technology—first the Science Planning Commission and now the Scientific and Technological Commission. The members of

[10] *Jen-min Jih-pao* [People's Daily], Dec. 19, 1957.
[11] *China News Analysis* (Hong Kong), No. 263, Feb. 6, 1959.

the Academy still feel that as scientists they are more capable of carrying out the listed responsibilities. Their arguments are not likely to find receptive ears, for the Chinese Communist Party will hardly return the responsibility for research to the scientists themselves after the disastrous experiences during the period of "blooming and contending." (See section on *Problems of the Working Scientist,* below.)

Through the Scientific and Technological Commission the Party maintains complete and absolute control over all matters dealing with science and technology in China. By means of detailed planning, the state outlines the direction of scientific research and development and determines who will work where and on what. Research projects originating in the institutes of the Academy of Sciences, in the industrial ministries, and at higher educational institutions also have to be approved by the Scientific and Technological Commission. The transition from relative freedom of research to complete Party domination was not an easy one, and firm control over the scientist was not established until the "rectification" campaign, following the period of "blooming and contending" in 1957. The natural inclination of scientists for individuality and freedom found fluent expression during the spring of 1957 when they were permitted to express their opinions—to "bloom and contend." During this brief period, Kuo mo-jo stated that the Party's administrative leadership for the sciences was being carried out with the support and cooperation of the scientists themselves; with regard to academic leadership, the Party was to rely all the more on the scientists themselves and to allow them to develop their own scientific research.[12]

The new approach described by Kuo Mo-jo in 1957 was never effected. Party control over the scientists was only intensified by placing all the authority in the Science Planning Commission, later merged into the Scientific and Technological Commission. Nieh Jung-chen made the following statement in October 1958, just prior to the merging of the Science Planning Commission into the new commission:

> After more than a year's rectification and antirightist struggle, Party leadership in scientific work has been greatly strengthened. What actually happened after the rectification and the antirightist struggle has eloquently proved that, under Party leadership and with politics in command, the scientific enterprises of our country can develop at an unprecedentedly high speed. It is obvious now that the Party is a genuine expert not only in establishing the direction, principles, and policies for scientific work but also in leading scientific operations forward in a much better way than [did the] bourgeois experts.[13]

---

[12] *Jen-min Jih-pao* [People's Daily], May 24, 1957 (report of an opening address at the Second Plenary Meeting of the Academic Department Committee of the Chinese Academy of Sciences).

[13] *Hung-ch'i* [Red Flag], No. 9, Oct. 1, 1958.

In addition to general control over scientific activities, the Party's main aim has been to limit theoretical research and to make sure that science concentrates on the practical problems which face China in its industrial race. Although this emphasis on the practical has been the theme ever since 1949, it was greatly intensified since the "leap forward" of 1958. This emphasis upon the practical was also contained in Nieh Jung-chen's statement in October of that year:

> Experiences in the development of science in our country during the past few years have proved that only by starting from the standpoint of production and socialist construction can the scientific institutions of this country develop rapidly. . . . Bourgeois scholars maintain that scientific research is exploratory in nature and thus cannot be planned because planning will fetter "free creations." We consider this viewpoint utterly incorrect. In a socialist society scientific studies must be and can be developed in a planned manner.[14]

A similar approach to China's scientific needs was expressed more than a year earlier by Kuo Mo-jo. However, he was speaking to an audience of scientists during a more relaxed period when he described the aspects of scientific research in these words:

> Scientific research generally takes two directions. One is a lineal upward breakthrough, and the other is a spreading out on certain planes. To spread out on certain planes means to apply scientific theories, already known, to practical production and practical living. This is a gigantic task that requires the services of a large number of scientists and technicians of different branches and different levels. The upward breakthrough, on the other hand, takes scientific theories to higher levels on the basis of practical experience—that is to say, prepares ground for science in as yet unknown realms. This requires scientists and technicians of the highest possible quality but their number need not be so large.[15]

Carrying the integration of science and production to its extreme, Peking has obliterated many of the existing demarcations between science, education, and production. Not only are schools being run in factories, conducting research in close coordination with production, but numerous experimental factories have been established in schools and research institutes so that the results of the research can be readily applied to production. As a result of complete Party domination and the policy of close integration of science with production, true and unfettered research and development is seldom found, while the work performed by an overwhelming majority of the scientists is little more than the adaptation of established scientific methods and techniques to current needs.

---

[14] *Ibid.*

[15] *Jen-min Jih-pao* [People's Daily], May 24, 1957.

The Chinese Academy of Sciences

The importance assigned to science is evident in the fact that only one month after the establishment of the Communist regime in 1949, the Chinese Academy of Sciences was created through the reorganization of the 12 institutes of Academia Sinica, located in Peking, Nanking, and Shanghai, and the 8 institutes of the Peking National Academy of Sciences. During its first 3 years the Academy concentrated on revising objectives, readjusting scientific organs, and reorganizing scientific workers in order to integrate scientific activity with national development. A Soviet journal stated that:

> For the rapid growth of science and its fruitful service to the practical side of Socialist construction it was important for the Chinese scientist to master Marxist-Lenin methodology as the basis of scientific research; for this it was necessary to accomplish an ideological reeducation of the old bourgeois scientists and the education of young scientific cadres in the spirit of Marxism-Leninism. This all became a subject of daily care and the most fixed attention of the Communist Party and the People's Government.[16]

The Academy was set up to direct scientific research, to train and distribute scientific manpower, to reorganize, intensify and solidify scientific development, and in general to control all phases of science. Actually, to assure the implementation of its policies over all scientific and technological activity, the Communist Party never relinquished its controls, and the authority of the Academy did not extend to the policy level. The subordination of the Academy to the Science Planning Commission in 1956 and later to the Scientific and Technological Commission removed it from the immediate control of the State Council (with its numerous responsibilities), thus strengthening the Party's direct control over all scientific endeavors.

The Academy of Sciences is divided into five departments: (1) Physics, mathematics, and chemistry; (2) technical sciences; (3) philosophy and social sciences; (4) geology and geography; and (5) biological sciences. Until May 1957 the last two departments were combined under the Department of Earth Sciences.[17] In addition to these departments, the Academy controls the regional or provincial branch academies. Both at the national level and at the regional level, the respective academies direct the work in the research institutes under them through the five departments. Each department is headed by a board and a standing committee. In 1955 the number of board members ranged from 40 in the Department of Technical Sciences to 84 in the Department of Earth Sciences; the number of standing committees ranged from

---

[16] *Vestnik Akademii Nauk SSSR* [Bulletin of the Academy of Sciences of the USSR], October 1957.

[17] *K'o-hsueh T'ung-pao* [Scientific Bulletin], May 1957.

PROBABLE ORGANIZATION OF THE CHINESE ACADEMY OF SCIENCES

STATE COUNCIL

SCIENCE PLANNING COMMISSION

CHINESE ACADEMY OF SCIENCES

COUNCIL OF THE ACADEMY

ADMINISTRATIVE SECRETARIAT

CENTRAL LIBRARY

SCIENCE PUBLISHING HOUSE

DEPARTMENTS

BIOLOGICAL SCIENCES

INSTITUTES

PHYSICS, MATHEMATICS, CHEMISTRY

INSTITUTES

GEOLOGY AND GEOGRAPHY

INSTITUTES

TECHNICAL SCIENCES

INSTITUTES

PHILOSOPHY AND SOCIAL SCIENCES

INSTITUTES

REGIONAL AND PROVINCIAL BRANCHES

DEPARTMENTS and/or INDIVIDUAL INSTITUTES

110

15 in philosophy and social sciences to 22 in the earth sciences.[18] There is also an academic committee, for academic supervision, and an overall inspection committee attached to each of the five departments. The latter committee is responsible for carrying out inspection missions in institutes of the Academy, universities and colleges, and industrial establishments conducting research.

Although there is a considerable variation in the reported number of scientific research institutes attached to the Academy, the most frequently encountered figures indicate that their number increased from 31 in 1952 to 68 in 1957, and then to 170 in 1958 during the "leap forward" (table 1). The greatest concentration of institutes is in Peking (with over 30 in the western suburbs of the city) and in Shanghai. Each institute has a Communist Party branch office whose secretary has authority over its finances and personnel. A list of 166 institutes, by name, appears in appendix I.

TABLE 1.—*The Chinese Academy of Sciences: personnel and institutes*

	1952 [1]	1955 [2]	1957 [1]	1958 [3]
Number of research institutes...............	31	....	68	170
Total staff...............................	5, 239	....	17, 335	28, 300
Research personnel.....................	1, 292	2, 483	5, 506	5, 900
Senior research workers..............	317	428	746	....
Assistant research workers............	314	421	755	....
Assistants, trainees, and technical personnel.........................	661	1, 634	4, 005	....

Blanks indicate figures are not available.

[1] *Peking Review*, No. 5, Apr. 1, 1958.
[2] *New China News Agency*, Jan. 31, 1956.
[3] *Ten Great Years* (Peking: State Statistical Bureau, 1960).

Although most of the serious scientific work in China is being conducted in the institutes of the Academy, it would seem that not all the institutes do work of the same level of competence and that both the growth in the number of institutes and the popularization of science have adversely affected the standing of the institutes. Most of the pseudoscientific institutes, however, have been set up under the regional branch academies. For example, about one-fifth of the membership in the Szechwan branch of the academy (set up in Chengtu in November 1958) is composed of "innovators and inventors who made their mark in agriculture and industry despite little formal education.[19]

[18] *Jen-min Shou-ts'e* [People's Handbook] (Peking: 1956).
[19] *New China News Agency*, Nov. 15, 1958.

Although a uniformly high level of scientific proficiency does not exist for the staff of the Academy (considering all of its branches), still, it does have on its staff some of the most highly qualified scientists in China. However, the rapid growth in the Academy's personnel (so proudly proclaimed by the Communists) has been concentrated in the total staff and not in the research personnel. Even between 1957 and 1958, when "everything was leaping forward" and the total staff of the Academy increased by 63 percent, the increase in the research personnel was only 7 percent. Table 1 presents data concerning the Academy for the years 1952–58. A breakdown of research personnel into levels for 1958 is not available, but using the 1957 breakdown (with the total only 7 percent below that for 1958), the senior research workers (representing the most qualified personnel) and the assistant research workers each constituted only slightly more than 4 percent of the Academy staff. Within the total research personnel, these two top-level groups of research workers each constituted less than 14 percent of the total; and the total research staff comprised only 31.7 percent of the Academy staff. But even more important is the fact that between 1952 and 1957 the proportion that the senior and assistant research workers constituted of the total research personnel had been steadily declining. In other words, whereas there had been a fairly rapid expansion in the lower ranks of the research personnel, relatively few were admitted to the higher positions.

The Academy of Sciences plays an important role in the training of scientists. An advanced study program was authorized by the State Council in 1955 and the first 65 candidates were examined and selected in March 1956.[20] The program made full use of established scientists by assigning small groups of students to one individual for intensive training. In addition to studying compulsory subjects appropriate to the field of training, each student had to take Russian and one other foreign language and had to study dialectical and historical materialism; he also had to take oral examinations and defend a thesis. The intention to keep this program at a high level is evident from the fact that in 1957 the quota of 361 graduate students was not met because of the poor quality of the candidates. Although it is not known whether this program is still in effect, the "great leap" undoubtedly left its mark on it, and the program has probably been reconsidered and revised. It is possible that the new University of Science and Technology will eventually supply most of the candidates for advanced study at the Academy. The 12-year program for scientific development envisages the training of 10,500 scientists by 1967.

The Academy of Sciences maintains some of the most advanced laboratories and other research facilities in China, and its libraries contain 4 million books.[21] The Central Science Library, which is maintained by

[20] *Ibid.,* Aug. 20, 1956.
[21] *Druzhba* [Friendship] (Peking), Jan. 15, 1958.

the Academy in Peking (with branches in Shanghai and Nanking), is reported to have 2.5 million books and 1.7 million periodicals.[22]

Another important function of the Academy is the control and operation of the Science Publishing House. In addition to publishing a large number of scientific journals, it has issued 1,106 books during the period 1953–57, totaling some 4 million copies.[23] The academy has also organized a Scientific Translation Committee responsible for making foreign scientific literature available in Chinese. Scientific dictionaries have been compiled giving the Chinese equivalents of foreign terms in 40 fields of research.[24] Both the Science Publishing House and the Scientific Translation Committee are directed by the Translation and Publication Department of the Academy of Sciences.

Other Institutions Engaged in Scientific Research

In addition to the Academy of Sciences, scientific research is also being conducted in institutions of higher education and by the institutions of industrial and other state ministries. Despite claims of much activity, it is believed that, for the most part, research in higher educational institutions is not extensive and is of a low order. It has been reported that in 1957, 157 institutions of higher education had research programs, with 20,000 faculty members working on 17,000 projects of both scientific-research and technical-application nature.[25] Various universities proudly announce the number of specific research projects that will be undertaken during the coming year. For example, Northeast People's University listed 223 subjects for scientific research; Nanking University listed 327; Futan University listed more than 200. No matter what the exact nature of these projects (and many of them certainly do not belong in a university), these institutions do maintain a fairly large share of the laboratories and equipment necessary for scientific research and, more importantly, a large proportion of scientific personnel. Despite the fact that the numbers race extends even to science, some serious work is undoubtedly being done at the universities, although most of it is in the realm of practical science rather than fundamental science, many universities contracting with industrial enterprises for research in various fields. For example, Tsing-hua University had contracts with 66 industrial enterprises for research on such problems as welding at An-shan Steel Works; casting graphite iron for ball bearings; sand analysis for the new Pao-t'ou Steel Works; generating equipment for Hsin-an-chiang and Liu-chia-hsia hydroelectric power projects.[26]

One assignment that institutions of higher education are presently

[22] *Jen-min Jih-pao* [People's Daily], Jan. 3, 1958.
[23] *Ibid.*
[24] *Ibid.,* Feb. 16, 1956.
[25] *Druzhba* [Friendship] (Peking), Jan. 15, 1958.
[26] *New China News Agency,* Nov. 23, 1957.

working on is in the field of native science and technology and on methods of integrating native science with "foreign experience":

> Native methods are not merely simple, poor, elementary ones; they represent Chinese practical inventions based on the ability to adapt to local circumstances. Therefore, Tsinghua University on the one hand is learning advanced world science and technology and on the other hand is doing research on Chinese native methods in production and scientific method. For instance, in such cooperation a compound powerplant has been designed to burn various fuels available in counties and villages.[27]

In some measure the relative importance of research done at institutions of higher education versus research at the institutes of the Academy of Sciences may be gleaned from the budget figures—even though the data are not altogether comparable. Whereas the 1957 budget of the Academy was 90 million yuan, only 10 million yuan was set aside for research at universities and colleges.[28] Considering that research involves considerable expenditures for equipment and facilities, that scientists are comparatively well paid, and that overall administrative costs of the Academy should be apportioned to its various endeavors, it would nevertheless appear safe to conclude that the academy's total expenditures for research are several times greater than the combined research budgets at institutions of higher education.

The ministries direct scientific industrial research both in specially established institutes and at the larger plants and factories. They maintain a number of designing and planning offices to make economic surveys and to study sources of raw materials and transportation capabilities as the basis for the location of new industries; from scattered reports it is apparent that many of the laboratories and research offices of individual plants are also doing more than routine testing. Scientific research in the fuel, metallurgical, machine building, chemical, and building industries reportedly is to be greatly developed.

In June 1957 Nieh Jung-chen had expected research organs of the Central Government ministries to be widely extended in the provinces, but—

> . . . in 1958 the expansion took the form of the establishment of branches of the Academy of Sciences and not of the ministries. The reason for this was that in the meantime, during the anti-rightist campaign, the Communist Party itself had taken direct control of all administration and of scientific organization as well, so that scientific work both in the cities and in the provinces was directed by the Party organizations.[29]

[27] *Hsin-hua Pan-yueh K'an* [New China News Agency Biweekly], No. 23, Dec. 10, 1958.
[28] *Vestnik Akademii Nauk SSSR* [Bulletin of the Academy of Sciences of the USSR], October 1957.
[29] *China News Analysis* (Hong Kong), No. 263, Feb. 6, 1959.

The total number of persons engaged in scientific and technical research under the ministries in 1958 was approximately 25,000, although the figure obviously is maximal and includes junior personnel and assistants. In 1955 Kuo Mo-jo reported that there were 60 research institutes under the various ministries, with more than 3,000 workers. It would appear that the 3,000 in 1955 and the 25,000 in 1958 do not refer to the same category and the latter figure represents broader inclusion rather than growth alone. Of the total of 25,000 reported for 1958, 14,700 were doing work in the fields of industry and communications; 1,200 were in agriculture, forestry, animal husbandry and fishing; and 2,200 were working in medicine and health.[30]

Soviet Cooperation

The Soviet Union has been playing an important role in China's recent achievements, and there is hardly any field of activity where Soviet influence has not left an imprint. A major contribution has been in the field of scientific and, particularly, technical cooperation. The showpiece of Sino-Soviet cooperation was the construction of a heavy water-type atomic reactor with a capacity of 10,000 kilowatts and a cyclotron producing alpha particles with a 25-million-volt energy. This experimental reactor was dedicated in Peking on September 27, 1958, in the presence of Soviet nuclear scientists who worked on it. However, this cooperation extended also to a lower and more practical level.

The Sino-Soviet Agreement on Scientific and Technical Cooperation, concluded in October 1954, marked the beginning of planned, long-term cooperation in this field. The close scientific cooperation between the two countries has been evidenced by the following factors: (1) Soviet scientists and technicians have been sent to China; (2) Chinese scientists have been spending time in the Soviet Union to study both theory and practice; (3) students have been sent to the Soviet Union for advanced study; and (4) Russian scientific theory and practices have been overwhelmingly adopted by the Chinese, and Soviet scientific books are rapidly being translated into Chinese.

The Chinese are the first to admit the Soviet contribution to their scientific development. Kuo Mo-jo has expressed his thanks to Soviet scientists on many occasions. For example, in May 1957, he said:

> In the several years since the liberation, our science, like other branches of the national economy, has been making rapid progress. This is chiefly attributable, apart from the devoted efforts of our own scientists and technicians, to aid given us by the scientists of the Soviet Union. . . . Again, in the formulation of long-term plans for scientific development, the Soviet Academy of Sciences has sent us more than 10 of the finest scientists of the Soviet Union to assist us. Large numbers of Soviet experts in China, and experts of other fraternal countries, too, have taken part in the task.[31]

---

[30] *Ten Great Years* (Peking: State Statistical Bureau, 1960).

[31] *Jen-min Jih-pao* [People's Daily], May 24, 1957.

During the period 1949–56, over 100 delegations with 1,900 Chinese scholars visited the Soviet Union. Scientists participating in this exchange attended meetings, toured scientific installations, and studied scientific theory. For example, at the end of 1956, the Chinese Academy of Sciences sent a mission to the Soviet Union to study the conditions of research work in titanium metallurgy, semiconductors, automation, electronics, electrical engineering, machinery, and dynamics. This was done to facilitate preparations for establishing institutes in these fields in China.[32]

On January 8, 1958, the Scientific Cooperation Agreement was signed between the Governments of China and the Soviet Union concerning joint efforts and Soviet assistance to China in major scientific and technological research. The main contents of the agreement, as outlined by Kuo Mo-jo, were as follows: (1) To carry out full cooperation in scientific research with the Soviet Union, with more planning and with stress in certain fields; (2) to consolidate and develop direct contact between the scientific research organs of the two countries; (3) to sponsor trips enabling the scientists to visit each other's country for the purpose of study; and (4) to solve the question of supply of noncommercial scientific equipment, machinery, instruments, samples, materials, testing solutions, and a small quantity of miscellaneous equipment.[33] During the 5-year duration of the agreement, the Soviet Union will assist China in undertaking 122 important scientific and technical research programs. She has agreed to aid China in such varied fields as the theoretical study of physical chemistry, biophysics, and electrophysics; techniques to prevent corrosion of metals and prolong the life of machinery; and techniques of water conservation and soil amelioration.

A distinction, which probably reflects an important trend, can be made between the Scientific and Technical Cooperation Agreement of 1954 and the Scientific Cooperation Agreement signed in January 1958. The first had to do mostly with technological aid for construction and operation of industrial plants and other technical operations. The second had to do with cooperation in the field of research and development.

There has been some speculation that perhaps Soviet scientific and technical aid to China has reached its peak and is on the decline. For example, Gerald Clark, of the North American Newspaper Alliance, wrote after a visit to China:

> There is little doubt about the diminishing number of Soviet technicians inside China. As recently as 2 years ago they were estimated in the tens of thousands. Today [1958], according to one Western estimate, they total no more than 4,000 and their families.[34]

[32] *Ibid.,* May 28, 1957.
[33] *New China News Agency,* Mar. 5, 1958.
[34] Reprinted in *The Evening Star,* Washington, D.C., Nov. 24, 1958.

Although exact data on the trends in the number of Soviet technicians in Communist China are not available, both the "tens of thousands" and the 4,000 referred to above may be opposite extremes. The *People's Daily* reported that by the end of 1958 there were 7,000 Soviet technicians in China,[35] while a Russian source stated that "about 10,830 specialists in all fields of economics, culture, and education were sent from the Soviet Union to the Chinese People's Republic" during the decade of the Communist regime.[36] The fairly prevalent opinion in the West that perhaps the Soviet Union is becoming somewhat concerned over the rapid development of its giant ally is to some extent negated by the continuing scientific cooperation. In 1958, 288 senior Soviet specialists worked in China under the auspices of the Chinese Academy of Sciences.[37] As late as spring of 1959, the Soviet and Chinese Academies of Sciences signed an executive plan for scientific cooperation between the two academies. This plan "provides for concrete measures in cooperation between the two countries both in the fields of natural and social science.[38] Even more important in this connection is the agreement signed in Moscow on February 7, 1959, as a result of which the Soviet Union agreed to help build 78 large industrial enterprises and power stations in China between 1959 and 1967.

Although most of the exchange of technical documents and literature between the Soviet Union and China is carried out by the Commission for Scientific and Technical Cooperation, there is also direct exchange between libraries and publishers and by personal correspondence of specialists. At the same time, there is great emphasis being placed on the translation and publication of Soviet scientific-technical literature: "From 1949 to 1955, there were translated and published 3,000 titles of Soviet technical books having a total circulation of more than 20 million copies." [39] In 1956 the Soviet Academy of Sciences sent to China about 70,000 books,[40] while additional scientific and technical books were sent for temporary use by the Lenin Library in Moscow and the Saltykov-Shchedrin Library in Leningrad.

It is of course obvious that the Chinese rely heavily on their cooperation with the Soviet Union in the field of science and technology, although they hope gradually to decrease their dependence on their neigh-

---

[35] *Jen-min Jih-pao* [People's Daily], Oct. 4, 1959.

[36] *Kommunist* [The Communist], vol. XXXVI, No. 3, February 1960.

As of this writing, persistent reports are beginning to appear to the effect that virtually all the Soviet technicians and specialists have been withdrawn. It is, of course, too early to judge either the validity of such reports, or the full impact that such a move might have on the economy of China.

[37] *Peking Review,* No. 5, Apr. 1, 1958.

[38] *New China News Agency,* June 1, 1959.

[39] *Uchenyye Zapiski Kafedry Geografii i Ekonomiki Stan Vostoka* vypusk vtoroy [Learned Notes of the Geographical and Economic Faculty on the Eastern Countries] (Moskva: 1958).

[40] *Druzhba* [Friendship] (Peking), Nov. 9, 1956.

bor to the north.   However, they have carried their aping of everything Russian to absurd lengths, and frequent complaints are heard with regard to indiscriminate copying and imitation.

Although the overwhelming proportion of its scientific contacts are with the Soviet Union, Chinese scholars also maintain contacts with the Soviet-bloc countries.   For example:

> During the past 2 years [1956–58] China had organized at different times visits and study tours to more than 20 countries by 290 scientists of all branches and departments, and had also taken part in 78 academic conferences held by individual countries and international academic conferences.   In the meantime we had received 268 scientists from over 20 countries who came to our country in connection with various scientific activities.[41]

It is not known how many of the 268 scientists came for brief tours of inspection and how many spent time in China in connection with certain projects.

Problems of the Working Scientists

It is not surprising to find data on scientific policies and accomplishments and on some of the formal arrangements of scientific research, but it is unusual to be able to get some insight into the actual everyday problems and complaints of the working scientist.   Yet these reveal more clearly the actual status of science and of scientific work in a country than all the official proclamations put together.   It is therefore most fortunate that the Second Plenum of the Department Committee of the Chinese Academy of Sciences met in Peking during the brief period in the spring of 1957 when the theme throughout China was, "let a hundred flowers bloom, let the diverse schools of thought contend"—the period of "blooming and contending."   During the month of May the Communists allowed almost unlimited criticism, and the members of the Academy of Sciences took advantage of this opportunity to pour out some of their complaints.   Although this period of "blooming and contending" was short lived, latent dissatisfactions undoubtedly continue and there are some indications that they are perhaps intensified.

In general, the criticisms voiced during that brief period may be divided into three categories: Those dealing with leadership, with organization, and with working conditions.   Most of them were summarized in the May 27 and 28 issues of the *People's Daily,* and quotations and discussion below are therefrom unless otherwise cited.

The complaints dealing with leadership centered primarily about the Chinese Academy of Sciences, the theme being that the Academy was "not yet ready to assume national academic leadership."   While some of those present criticized the organizational system of the Academy as undemocratic, others went so far as to score "some

---

[41] *New China News Agency,* Sept. 3, 1958.

of the harsh and brutal acts of the scientific leadership." Also directed at the leadership were complaints about centralization of assignments of scientists. Economist Ch'ien Chia-chu compared the centralization of assignments to a compulsory marriage where there was absolutely no freedom of divorce, and urged that a "free market" for scientific personnel be set up to supplement socialist centralization of assignment.[42] Another economist, Shen Chih-yuan, went ever further, suggesting that—

> . . . the government should conduct a general survey of the scientific research workers who were scattered all over the country and who had been assigned to unsuitable jobs, so that they might be reassigned.[43]

One of the most frequent complaints has been that too much of the scientists' time must be spent on administrative and other nonprofessional activities. For example, historian Lu Chin-yu suggested in his speech before the gathering in Peking that the Academic Council of the Academy of Sciences should gradually assume academic leadership, distinguishing itself from the Academy's Administrative Council, so that the relationship between administrative leadership and academic leadership, and between administrative work and scientific research, might be "gradually clearly defined and made normal." Along the same line, one scientist asked whether—

> . . . it was possible for the State Council to issue a nationwide order permitting scientists capable of assuming leadership in scientific research to excuse themselves indefinitely from administrative work and social activities, so that they might devote themselves entirely to scientific research and training of cadres.

Having listened to these and other statements on the same subject for almost a week, Kuo Mo-jo declared:

> Here I wish to salute those of our comrades engaged in administrative and office work. . . . There work is valuable, but their task is thankless. . . . Thanks particularly to those who are scientists themselves but who, because of the needs of the state, are compelled to take up administrative or office work. They are in truth demonstrating self-sacrifice.[44]

He then assured the gathered scientists that the "Party and the government will relieve us scientists of much of our administrative work." However, only a few days later the blooming flowers faded and died, as did the promises of Kuo Mo-jo.

But so long as "contending" was permitted, a major complaint concentrated on lack of freedom for research: That there was "too much administrative interference with academic work and too little freedom

---

[42] *Jen-min Jih-pao* [People's Daily], May 29, 1957.
[43] *Ibid.*
[44] *Ibid.*, May 31, 1957.

for academic thought"; that there was "no guarantee that there will be adequate time for research"; and, because of the overwhelming emphasis on the practical aspects of scientific research, that there was "lack of support or insufficient support for research that is not included in state plans." In other words, the initiative of the individual scientist was stifled and he was required to work only on assigned tasks integrated with requirements as prescribed by the overall plan.

As far as the social sciences were concerned, there was complaint that the relevant data were "not accessible, making the scientists' work exceedingly difficult and making it impossible for them to base their work on reality." It was rightly asserted that the Academy "gave preference to the physical sciences at the expense of the humanities."

Other complaints dealt with the lack of an adequate plant for scientific work. Perhaps in line with an old Chinese saying that "it is better to have no books than to believe entirely in books," the scientist in China does not have a sound scientific library, especially if he is located outside the two major centers of Peking and Shanghai. Scientific equipment is both inadequate and inferior. Although China is dependent on the Soviet Union and other outside sources for much scientific equipment, she is making many types herself. Much of this equipment is made by the scientific institutes themselves. For example, the Institute of Applied Physics makes optical and refractory instruments, the Geological Institute has begun turning out seismographs, gravity meters, and the like—again, the integration of the practical with the theoretical.

Despite the fact that personal gains and personal prestige were presumably no longer considerations, and that collectivism had taken over in every activity, there were numerous complaints that scientists were too interested in their own advancement, that there was too much competition among them, and that they were reluctant to "pass on their knowledge and techniques to others—even their own assistants." There was further criticism that science was departmentalized and that the various departments and sections were unwilling to cooperate with one another.

The outburst of criticism during that brief period of "blooming and contending" had rather severe aftereffects. During the period of rectification that followed, the scientists were expected to express their remorse and confess their ignorance. Typical of many statements was one reporting on a scientific and technical "leap forward" conference held in Szechwan:

> Many Western-trained scientists who attended the conference criticized their own blind worship of the sciences of foreign countries as well as their wrong ideas that the Party committees knew nothing about science and technology.[45]

Professors at universities started writing hundreds of statements for the bulletin boards and articles for the daily press, and they appeared at

[45] *New China News Agency,* Nov. 16, 1958.

mass meetings to criticize themselves and assure the audiences of the benefits of ideological reeducation. Hu Chen-sian, professor of medicine at Peking University, for example, was quoted as saying: "Earlier during the movement for ideological reform I thought that it was carried out too violently and that it offended my personal dignity. I am now aware that it was destroying my service to interests of American imperialism." [46]

The atmosphere became tense and there was a general tightening up in the little freedom of initiative that was left. The most notable effect was the uprooting of thousands of intellectuals for either a temporary or a permanent stay in the "country." The purpose of this transfer was to rehabilitate these individuals, who were branded as rightists, reactionaries or—almost as bad—neutrals, and to make them better teachers, technicians, and scientists through physical labor performed side by side with the peasants:

> Over a million intellectuals in government offices, enterprises, and schools went to the farms and factories for a year's work. . . . To carry further forward the Communist Party's tradition of tempering its cadres through physical labor, it was decided last September [1958] that, with the exception of those who are getting on in years or are physically weak, all government functionaries should do manual labor for at least 1 month every year.[47]

When this policy was at its height, it seems to have been just as ruthlessly applied to the top-ranking scientists as to any other group—there are no indications that exceptions were allowed. For example:

> Similar wholesale transfers to the villages are being carried out among students and professors in the universities. At the prototype of Marxist schools, the Peking People's University, 300 professors and lecturers are on the move.[48]

Also: "Research workers of the Chinese Academy of Agricultural Science have left the capital for the countryside for 1 year to bring their research work closely in unison with actual production.[49] This whole scheme was closely integrated with the policies designed to detract from the importance of persons with a higher education and to popularize science among the masses. The general atmosphere during this period is illustrated by a poem published in the *Peking Review* in 1959 and presumably written by an intellectual who had just returned from a stay in a village:

> After ten months I wasn't the same;
> I left with much more than I came;

---

[46] *Borba* (Belgrade), July 6, 1958.
[47] *Peking Review*, Feb. 10, 1959.
[48] *China News Analysis* (Hong Kong), Nov. 29, 1957.
[49] *New China News Agency*, Apr. 7, 1958.

I filled in the gaps of my school education;
Learnt that labor makes the nation.
Today it's back to the city once more—
An intellectual who knows the score.[50]

There is some possibility that the severity of the attacks against intellectuals was eased to some extent, although some of the attitudes expressed have certainly persisted.   In 1959 an article in the Chinese Communist Party's theoretical journal departed from the dominant propaganda line which prevailed during 1958 and took a markedly solicitous attitude toward the role that could still be played by veteran teachers and specialists.[51]   Adopting a position reminiscent of Chou En-lai's January 1956 report on intellectuals—which called for greater support and utilization of the existing intelligentsia—the article said that young students should "humbly learn" from their elders, absorbing needed "specialized knowledge" from even those who still adhere to "bourgeois academic viewpoints."   It also conceded that some criticisms of bourgeois academic ideas have been one-sided and oversimplified.   Although it praised the achievements of young scientists and technicians, the article warned them against "arrogance" and repeatedly stressed that really important scientific achievements are not quickly or easily attained.   This sober view of realities in meeting the problems of scientific advancements and the solicitous attitude toward older intelectuals are in contrast with prevailing themes adopted in 1958 during the "leap forward."

Incentives for the Working Scientists

The seemingly unattractive position of the scientist in Communist China nevertheless has its compensations.   It is true that by Western standards there seems to be a surprising disregard for the precious commodity represented by top-level scientists.   However, standards are relative and there are compensatory factors; despite being a suspect group, the scientists are accorded a fairly high priority in the Communists society.

Scientists at the academy, professors at universities, and other research personnel are well paid.   They are also provided with free or nominal-rent quarters, pay no income taxes, and collect fees for writing papers and textbooks.

In 1955 the State Council adopted a system of awards and prizes for scientific research "relating to practical advances in science and technology as applicable to building socialism." [52]   The Academy of Sciences is the awarding body, and any citizen of Communist China or foreign scientist whose work has contributed significantly to the development of science in China is eligible for the awards.   The first group so honored

---

[50] *Peking Review,* Feb. 10, 1959.

[51] *Hung-ch'i* [Red Flag], No. 5, Mar. 1, 1959.

[52] *New China News Agency,* Aug. 31, 1955.

received their awards in January 1957. Of a total of 34 prizes, there were 3 first-class awards, 5 second-class awards, and 26 third-class awards. The first prize carries with it a cash grant of 10,000 yuan; the second, 5,000 yuan; and the third, 2,000 yuan. Each prize is accompanied by a medal.

The recipients of the first-class awards were: (1) Hua Lo-keng, director of the Institute of Mathematics of the Academy of Sciences, for his work on "Theory of Polyfunctions of a Complex Variable in the Classical Field," published in 1956; (2) Wu Wen-chun, also in the Institute of Mathematics, where he heads research in topology, for his work on "The Rational Group and Insertion Group in Geometric Spaces"; (3) Ch'ien Hsueh-sen, director of the Institute of Mechanics of the Academy of Sciences, for his "Theory of Engineering Control" (on fundamentals and problems of automation).

CHAPTER VII

Professional Manpower

Number and Distribution of University Graduates in China

The Chinese journal *Planned Economy,* referring to the year 1957, reported that there were then "only over half a million college graduates in China." [1] By breaking this figure down into its components and combining the university graduates as reported by the Nationalist Ministry of Education with the number of graduates reported by the Communists, it is possible to judge the validity of the figure in the above statement. Although precision in such an analysis is obviously impossible, it is important to determine whether this figure is reliable enough to be used as a base and as a point of departure. The reasoning in this analysis is presented in table 1 on the following page.

It becomes apparent from table 1 that, although the utilized data are of varying reliability, the figures seem to be fairly reasonable. Theoretically, the difference of 26,000 might be considered to be the excess of persons with college degrees who left China over those who obtained their education abroad and are now living in China. Actually, there are too many variables in the figures utilized for this residual to have a strict interpretation. For example, if the number of persons with higher degrees is increased to 515,000 (an increase of 3 percent), the residual drops to 11,000 (a decrease of 58 percent).

Some esitmates have been made of the total population movement in and out of China since 1949; however, one may only guess as to the extent to which persons with higher education are represented among either group. Although the number who left China is greater than the number who returned, the net effect is probably negligible. One clue to the total under consideration was reported in 1956 by Kuo Mo-jo, president of the Academy of Sciences. He stated that "nearly 10,000 Chinese scientists and students are working in the United States, Great

---

[1] *Chi-hua Ching-chi* [Planned Economy], No. 5, May 5, 1958.

TABLE 1.—*University graduates in China, 1957*

Number of persons with higher education in China_____ [1] 500, 000
Graduates, 1948–49 through 1956–57 _____ [2] 352, 000

Difference (implied number of surviving pre-1949 graduates in China
as of 1957) _____ [3] 148, 000
Pre-1949 survivors (as projected) _____ [4] 174, 000

Difference _____ [5] 26, 000

[1] *Chi-hua Ching-chi* [Planned Economy], No. 5, May 9, 1958. Although the wording of the statement suggests that this figure may be slightly higher, in Communist statistical practices, "over half a million" is not likely to be significantly above the stated figure. If it were 526,000, the report would probable read "over 525,000" or "almost 550,000."

[2] The actual reported number of graduates was 359,000 (see ch. IV, table 1). This total was reduced by 2 percent to account for mortality.

[3] Since the total number of persons with higher education may be slightly higher than 500,000, this figure is minimal.

[4] The numbers of pre-Communist graduates were reported in *Chung-kuo Chiao-yu Nien-chien* [Chinese Educational Yearbook] (Shanghai: Ministry of Education, 1948) ; see appendix table A–4. Their survivors have been obtained as follows:

Year	Graduates	Survival rate to 1960	Number of survivors	Age in 1960
1913–17............	6, 013	0. 487	2, 928	65–69
1918–22............	6, 653	. 598	3, 978	60–64
1923–27............	12, 229	. 689	8, 426	55–59
1928–32............	26, 345	. 762	20, 075	50–54
1933–37............	41, 251	. 820	33, 826	45–49
1938–42............	35, 508	. 866	30, 750	40–44
1943–47............	82, 311	. 904	74, 409	35–39
Total.........	210, 310		174, 392	

Graduates: The graduates were combined into 5-year groups and the assumption was made that most of the graduates would be between 20 and 24 years of age. Thus, average years of graduation were 1915, 1920, etc., and the average age at graduation was 22½ years. The number of graduates for 1948–49 is not available. The total is slightly lower than the one appearing in appendix table A–4, because about 4,000 persons who have graduated prior to 1913 have been excluded from this calculation.

Survival rate: Calculated from model life tables in *Methods for Population Projections by Sex and Age*, Population Studies, No. 25 (New York: United Nations, 1956), by assuming a male life expectancy of 50 years. This relatively high life expectancy was chosen because, as a rule, university graduates in China would have the highest standard of living in terms of food, housing, and medical services. Virtually all of them would be located in urban areas and they would be the group least affected by floods, famines, etc. Also, it is important to note that over 75 percent of the total number of graduates completed schooling after 1932.

Number of survivors: Obtained by multiplying the graduates by the survival rate.

[5] The difference between the implied and projected number of surviving pre-1949 graduates. See text for a discussion of this residual.

Britain, France, Japan, and other countries." [2]   However, this number seems minimal and may include only scientists and technical personnel but not all persons with completed higher education.

There are two other points that should be kept in mind in assessing the figure of 500,000 college graduates: A substantial number of individuals completed their education abroad and returned to live and work in China; others attended higher level institutions in Manchukuo and were excluded from the Nationalist statistics—the latter category amounting to perhaps 6,000 persons.[3]   However, it must be presumed that all of them were included in the reported total.

Although the figure of 500,000 persons with completed higher education as of 1957 may not be precise, it must nevertheless be concluded that it is a reasonable and usable total.   Once this premise is accepted, it is relatively simple to project it to January 1960 by adding the 72,000 graduates for 1957–58 and 62,200 graduates for 1958–59 (ch. IV, table 5).   Because the new total of 634,200 has not been adjusted for attrition for the 2 years since 1957, it is somewhat arbitrarily rounded down to 625,000 (table 2)—the figure utilized in this report as one most closely representing the population with completed higher education as of January 1960.

The estimated distribution of college population by field of specialization and the method utilized in obtaining this distribution are presented in table 2, while the discussion that follows covers some additional data pertaining to engineers, scientists, and medical personnel.

Engineers

One of the problems facing Red China on her road to industrialization is the shortage of trained engineers.   To fill this gap as quickly as possible, the Communists have placed increasing emphasis on this profession.   Among graduates from institutions of higher education, engineers comprised an average of only 17.1 percent for the period 1928 through 1947; this average rose to 30.1 percent for the period 1949 through 1958.   In absolute numbers, the graduates from engineering faculties reached a peak of 22,000 in 1956.   Since then their number has not exceeded 20,000 (see table 3).   As of January 1960, it is esti-

---

[2] *New China News Agency,* June 6, 1956.

[3] One Japanese source gives the total enrollment in Manchukuo institutions of higher education between 1932 and 1942 as 31,461: 1932, 171; 1933, 160; 1934, 544; 1935, 1,203; 1936, 1,842; 1937, 2,240; 1938, 2,927; 1939, 4,372; 1940, 4,819; 1941, 6,176; 1942, 7,007 (*Dai-Manshu Teikoku Nenkan* [Yearbook of Manchurian Empire], Dairen: 1944).   Assuming that 20 percent of these received degrees, there would be approximately 6,000 graduates.

TABLE 2.—*Estimated distribution of population with completed higher education, by field of specialization,*[1] *January 1960*

[Numbers in thousands]

(1) Field of specialization	(2) Number of graduates 1928 through 1947	(3) Adjusted to estimated number of living pre-1949 graduates		(4) Reported graduates from 1948–49 through 1957–58	(5) Adjusted to total graduates from 1948–49 through 1958–59		(6) Distribution of college population as of January 1960	
		Number	Percent		Number	Percent	Number	Percent
Engineering..........................	31.7	21.4	17.1	129.6	150.3	30.1	171.7	27.5
Natural sciences.....................	15.8	10.7	8.5	23.5	27.3	5.4	38.0	6.1
Medical sciences.....................	9.5	6.4	5.1	39.0	45.2	9.1	51.6	8.3
Education (pedagogy).................	21.1	14.2	11.4	103.9	120.5	24.1	134.7	21.5
Agriculture..........................	13.1	8.8	7.0	26.0	30.2	6.0	39.0	6.2
Finance and economics...............	18.9	12.7	10.2	49.1	57.0	11.4	69.7	11.2
Law and social sciences..............	50.8	34.3	27.4	28.1	32.6	6.5	66.9	10.7
Liberal arts.........................	24.5	16.5	13.3	31.8	36.9	7.4	53.4	8.5
	185.4	125.0	100.0	431.0	500.0	100.0	625.0	100.0

[1] Not by present occupation.

Col. 1.—Several of the categories as reported by both the Nationalist Ministry of Education and the Communist State Statistical Bureau have had to be combined to make the data comparable. The engineering category includes all technical specialties; medical sciences include dentistry, pharmacology and public health; agriculture includes forestry.

Col. 2.—Source: *Chung-kuo Chiao-yu Nien-chien, 1948* [Chinese Educational Yearbook] (Shanghai: Ministry of Education, 1948). See appendix table A–4. Data on the total number of graduates are available for the period prior to 1928, but they are not distributed by field of specialization. The period covered, however, includes more than 85 percent of the total number of graduates during the pre-Communist period.

Col. 3.—The reported figures in col. 2 are adjusted proportionately to the estimated number of persons with higher education who had received their degrees prior to 1949 and are still living in China. Although for 1957 the data implied 148,000 survivors with higher degrees (table 1), it is believed that by 1960 their number could have decreased to 125,000 (a somewhat sharper decline than may be expected through normal mortality). Actually, however, the figure of 125,000 is independently obtained as a residual and its accuracy depends upon the validity of the 500,000 college graduates reported for the past 10 years. The method automatically adjusts for most of the effects of migration, because the 500,000 purports to be a net figure, and also assumes that mortality would affect all graduates uniformly, regardless of profession. Because the distribution by field of specialization is based only on the graduates from Chinese higher educational institutions, there is a slight bias that decreases the proportion of medical doctors, scientists, and engineers (more frequently the majors of Chinese students studying abroad) and increases the numbers in other categories. This becomes apparent in the discussion dealing with medical doctors.

Col. 4.—Source: *Ten Great Years* (Peking: State Statistical Bureau, 1960). See ch. IV, table 5.

Col. 5.—Although the total number of graduates 1948–49 through 1958–59 was 493,000 (see ch. IV, table 11), the distribution by field is available for only 1948–49 through 1957–58 (col. 4). The assumption is made that the graduates in 1958–59 (62,200) will follow the distribution reported for the previous 10 years. For convenience the total was increased by 7,000 to 500,000, and mortality (minimal for the post-1948 graduates) was not taken into consideration. To avoid confusion, it must be pointed out that the 500,000 graduates in this column is not identical with the 500,000 in table 1—simply a coincidence.

Col. 6.—Sum of cols. 3 and 5.

DISTRIBUTION OF POPULATION WITH COMPLETED HIGHER EDUCATION

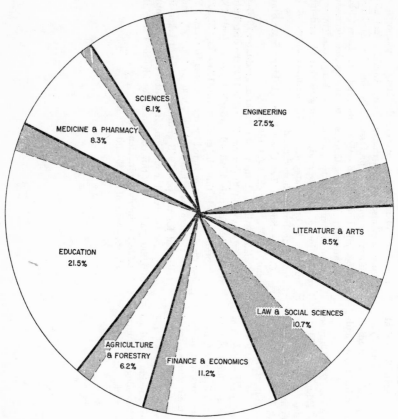

Completed education before 1949

SCIENCES
6.1%

ENGINEERING
27.5%

MEDICINE & PHARMACY
8.3%

LITERATURE & ARTS
8.5%

EDUCATION
21.5%

LAW & SOCIAL SCIENCES
10.7%

AGRICULTURE
& FORESTRY
6.2%

FINANCE & ECONOMICS
11.2%

SOURCE: TABLE 2

mated that there were approximately 170,000 persons in Communist China with completed higher education in engineering (table 2). Although an estimate, this figure cannot be radically off the mark in terms of magnitude; it can be deceiving, however, if the qualifications of these persons as engineers are not considered at the same time.

The overall quality of the present-day graduates of institutions of higher education is discussed in chapter V. The conclusions presented and implied in that section are just as valid for the graduates of engineering courses. One possibly inadvertent comment by Chou En-lai stresses the overall impression of relatively inferior training. In a speech to the Central Committee in January 1956, he stated that "though there are little more than 31,000 engineers of different grades in China, many of the 63,600 technicians who have graduated from the universities and colleges are now doing the work of engineers" [4]—a total of 94,600.

[4] *New China News Agency,* Jan. 29, 1956.

Year	Entrants	Enrollment	Graduates [1]
1948–49............................	....	....	4, 752
1949–50............................	....	[3] 30, 300	4, 711
1950–51............................	[2] (12, 911)	[3] 38, 500	4, 416
1951–52............................	[2] (14, 416)	[3] 48, 500	10, 213
1952–53............................	[2] (28, 313)	[3] 66, 600	14, 565
1953–54............................	[2] (28, 065)	[3] 80, 100	15, 596
1954–55............................	[4] 33, 800	[5] 95, 000	18, 614
1955–56............................	[6] 35, 000	[5] 109, 600	22, 047
1956–57............................	[7] 62, 200	[8] 150, 000	17, 162
1957–58............................	[9] 37, 200	[10] 163, 000	17, 499
1958–59............................	[11] 46, 000	[12] (190, 000)	....

Blanks indicate figures are not available.

[1] *Ten Great Years* (Peking: State Statistical Bureau, 1960).

[2] Estimated by combining data on enrollment and graduates. For example: From the 1952–53 enrollment of 66,600 are subtracted the 14,565 graduates; the resulting 52,035 is subtracted from 80,100, the 1953–54 enrollment, to obtain the theoretical number of 28,065 entrants for 1953–54. Actually, because withdrawals are not accounted for, the method produces a minimal number, and the true number of entrants is probably at least 10 percent higher.

[3] *New China News Agency*, Dec. 2, 1954.

[4] *Ibid.*, May 20, 1954.

[5] *Current Background*, Nov. 26, 1956 (Hong Kong: U.S. consulate general).

[6] *Kuang-ming Jih-pao* [Kuang-ming Daily], June 29, 1955.

[7] *New China News Agency*, Mar. 16, 1956.

[8] *Jen-min Jih-pao* [People's Daily], Mar. 18, 1957.

[9] *Kuang-chou Jih-pao* [Kuang-chou Daily], May 29, 1957.

[10] *Peking Review*, No. 27, Sept. 2, 1958.

[11] *New China News Agency*, July 2, 1958.

[12] The graduates in 1958 (17,500) are subtracted from the 1957–58 enrollment (163,000). Then the new entrants in 1958 are added (46,000). This is a maximal figure, since it does not take into account the withdrawals. Assuming that withdrawals constitute 10 percent of the graduates, total 1958–59 enrollment in engineering is estimated at about 190,000.

The distinction between "engineers" and "technicians who have graduated from the universities and colleges," leads to the speculation—even if farfetched—that Chou was distinguishing between pre- and post-Communist regime graduates. His 31,000 "engineers" is almost identical with the number of engineering graduates from 1928 through 1947 (table 2, col. 2—unadjusted total); his 63,600 "technicians" compares with a figure of 63,404 as the total number of engineering graduates during the academic years 1950–51 through 1954–55 (the last closing academic year before his speech). Coincidence or not, Chou's choice of words was appropriate for, in the strictest sense, few of China's so-called engineers may be referred to as anything but "technicians who have graduated from the universities and colleges." Whether the new crop of "engineers" meets the current needs of China is a separate question. It may be argued that at present China has a greater need for skilled technicians with narrow specialties than for highly qualified engineers of the Western variety.

It is also important to mention briefly the distinction between persons educated as engineers and those performing engineering functions. Of course a precise estimate of the quantitative effect of this distinction is impossible; however, several generally compensatory factors can be mentioned. On the one hand, there are certainly individuals working as engineers and having the rank of engineer despite the absense of formal higher education. For example, during the first 5-year plan, 770,000 skilled workers were trained on the job, and 30,000 of them have been "promoted to technician or engineering positions." [5] On the other hand, there are engineers who are working outside their profession. It seems likely that, as in the Soviet Union, a substantial number of engineers are employed as administrators and in other nontechnical capacities, although due to the special need for their services in China, their proportion is probably lower than in the Soviet Union. Only seldom does the context make it possible to deduce whether the reference is to working engineers or graduates of engineering courses.

Further comment on the type of training received by students in higher engineering and technical schools is presented in the example below with reference to Tsing-hua University. However, three points must be kept in mind: In the first place, this particular university is one of the leading engineering schools in China and graduates the most highly trained engineers in the country. In the second place, since there is often a wide chasm between theory and reality, there is no way to determine how closely a student follows the prescribed curriculum. In the third place, the cited report precedes the most recent developments in Chinese education, such as the increased emphasis on productive work performed simultaneously with regular study.

Tsing-hua Polytechnical University near Peking was founded in 1911 on Boxer War indemnity funds. The Communists converted it into a polytechnical institute; with the help of Soviet experts, they reorganized the curriculum, introducing Soviet texts and methods. In 1956 it had 1,000 professors and 9,000 students.[6]

In 1957, Chien Wei-chang, the Vice President of Tsing-hua, made a speech in which he discussed the university's curriculum and compared it with similar schools in the Soviet Union and with the California Institute of Technology.[7] Table 4, in effect, summarizes a large part of his speech.

---

[5] Chen Ta-lun, "Changes in Our Industrial Controls," *Ching-chi Yen-chiu* [Economic Research], No. 3, March 1958.

[6] N. V. Fedyushov, *V Gostyakh u Velikogo Druga* [Visiting a Great Friend] (Vladivostok: 1957).

[7] *Jen-min Jih-pao* [People's Daily], Feb. 12, 1957.

TABLE 4.—*Comparison of curriculums of Tsing-hua Polytechnical University, a Soviet university, and California Institute of Technology*

[In hours]

	Tsing-hua Polytechnical University			Soviet University, 1955	California Institute of Technology, 1956
	1957 (plan)	1955	Pre-1950		
Degree..............	Engineer	Engineer	B.S.	Engineer	B.S.
Basic courses [1].........	1,177	1,330	976	1,376	1,167
Technical courses [2]......	821	893	960	1,082	921
Specialized courses [3].....	930	1,069	1,072	1,096	367
Average study time per week..............	26	31	28.5	33	26
Average lecture time per week..............	17	17.4	18.1	18.7	16

[1] Include mathematics, physics, chemistry, mechanics, and drafting.

[2] Include principles of electrical engineering, thermodynamics, hydraulics, etc.

[3] Include lathe designs, principles of lathe operations, factory organization and management, economics, organization, planning of enterprises, etc.

Source: *Jen-min Jih-pao* [People's Daily], Feb. 26, 1957.

He also said that the content of many of the subjects and the quality of the lectures were low at Tsing-hua, but then went on to point out its advantages over American schools. He said that at the California Institute of Technology, civil, mechanical, electrical, and chemical engineering students all have the same required courses in the first year, resulting in civil and mechanical engineers having to spend 199 hours on organic and inorganic chemistry. He regarded this as superfluous. At Cornell University, he continued, students in mechanical engineering have to take such courses as public speaking, price control, market reports, and industrial engineering. Irrespective of the accuracy of his facts with regard to American universities, his contention that Communist China's curriculum is "more to the point" cannot be debated, once the respective goals of the two educational systems are defined. At Tsing-hua, the first year and a half is spent on basic courses, and the second year and a half, mainly on technical courses. Starting with the third year, there is little classwork.

Natural Scientists

When the Communists took over the control of mainland China, they inherited more than 10,000 persons with higher degrees in the field of the natural sciences (table 2). There seems to be no way to determine the distribution of these individuals by field of specialization, and of course no way to estimate how many of them continued to work in their field. Those who continued to work in their chosen profession were located primarily in the large urban centers of the country—teaching and doing research at universities, working in the few privately supported laboratories and scientific organizations, or employed by some of the large industrial enterprises.

In the field of the natural sciences, the enrollment in higher educational institutions increased from 7,000 in 1949–50 to 25,000 in 1956–57, and the total number of graduates in this field has been reported at 23,472 for the period 1948–49 through 1957–58 (table 5). The distribution of these students by specific field is also not reported.

Although the growth in scientific education is impressive, it has not been as rapid as was the growth in engineering and technical education. The reason for this is probably found in the overall Party policies toward science and scientists. Previously, the spirit of scientific education and research in China was one of freedom, or "science for science's sake." After 1949 there was a notable change in emphasis. Not only was scientific thinking made to conform to political thinking, but the emphasis on immediate and practical results greatly limited the freedom for pure scientific research. Thus, whereas an engineering graduate could almost immediately start "repaying" the state for expenditures on his education, the return from a physics graduate, for example, would, in most cases, not be as prompt or as apparent under present conditions in China.

This does not mean that the Chinese Communists are not interested in pursuing scientific research and development. It does mean that, with their practical approach, they feel that in order to modernize and industrialize their country as rapidly as possible, it is expedient to borrow and copy from the more advanced nations of the world. The immediate problem is not to rush forward leaving a gaping hole between the double-shared plow and an atomic reactor but to fill this gap as quickly as feasible within the country's immediate goals.

It would seem safe to say that most of the present crop of 4-year graduates in science have received inferior training and are incapable of original scientific achievements, even if they were given the opportunity and the freedom to pursue their interests. A large proportion of the more qualified students who are going into laboratories and research institutes have probably done graduate work in the Soviet Union, while most of the senior research workers are foreign-trained scientists who have managed to survive the purge of the rightists and the demand for self-criticism and mutual accusations and were sufficiently "rectified" to retain their positions.

Some additional discussion on scientists may be found in chapter VI.

Medical Scientists

As in the case of all other professions, medical personnel, and particularly physicians, have always been in short supply in China; but there

Year	Entrants	Enrollment	Graduates
1928–29		1,910	285
1929–30		2,191	280
1930–31		2,872	308
1931–32		3,530	435
1932–33		4,159	512
1933–34		4,722	698
1934–35		5,324	924
1935–36		6,272	996
1936–37		5,485	935
1937–38		4,458	794
1938–39		4,802	737
1939–40		5,828	799
1940–41		6,090	881
1941–42		6,202	856
1942–43		5,852	735
1943–44		6,099	723
1944–45		6,177	903
1945–46		6,480	829
1946–47		9,091	1,419
1947–48		10,060	1,701

NOTE.—1928–48 data are from *Chung-kuo Chiao-yu Nien-chien* [Chinese Educational Year Book] (Shanghai: Ministry of Education, 1948).

Year	Entrants	Enrollment	Graduates
1948–49			[1] 1,584
1949–50		[2] 7,000	[1] 1,468
1950–51			[1] 1,488
1951–52			[1] 2,215
1952–53		[2] 9,600	[1] 1,753
1953–54	[3] (4,600)	[2] 12,400	[1] 802
1954–55	[4] 5,740	[2] 17,100	[1] 2,015
1955–56	[5] 5,000	[2] 20,000	[1] 3,978
1956–57	[3] (9,000)	[6] 25,000	[1] 3,524
1957–58	[7] 7,790	[8] 27,100	[1] 4,645

Blanks indicate figures are not available.

[1] *Ten Great Years* (Peking: State Statistical Bureau, 1960).

[2] *Current Background*, Nov. 26, 1956 (Hong Kong: U.S. consulate general).

[3] Estimated by combining reported data on enrollment and graduates. Because dropouts are not accounted for, entrants in 1953–54 and 1956–57 are underestimated by roughly 10 percent.

[4] *New China News Agency*, May 20, 1954.

[5] *Kuang-ming Jih-pao* [Kuang-ming Daily], June 29, 1955.

[6] *Jen-min Jih-jao* [People's Daily], Mar. 18, 1957.

[7] *Kuang-chou Jih-pao* [Kuang-chou Daily], May 29, 1957.

[8] *Jen-min Chiao-yu* [People's Education], Oct. 9, 1957.

has been no such unusual acceleration in the training of doctors as there has been for engineers and other technical personnel. While the number of engineering students increased by 438 percent from 1949–50 to 1957–58, the number of medical students increased only 223 percent (table 6), or barely kept up with the increase in the total university enrollment (ch. IV, table 1). The explanation may be only in the nature of a conjecture. Realizing that there are definite limitations set by the budget, by the number of qualified students, and by requirements for other specialists, the Communists may have relegated medical training to a lower priority. Also, in rural areas, where previously there were virtually no medical facilities or personnel except for an occasional herbist, the government relies on subprofessional personnel to make any possible improvements in the field of health and sanitation.

TABLE 6.—*Higher education: students and graduates in medical sciences, 1928–58*

[Rounded to nearest hundred]

Year	Entrants	Enrollment	Graduates
1928–47			[1] 9, 499
1948–49			[2] 1, 314
1949–50		[3] 15, 200	[2] 1, 391
1950–51	[4] (3, 600)	[3] 17, 400	[2] 2, 366
1951–52	[4] (6, 400)	[3] 21, 400	[2] 2, 636
1952–53	[4] (5, 400)	[3] 24, 200	[2] 2, 948
1953–54	[4] (7, 700)	[3] 29, 000	[2] 4, 527
1954–55	[5] 9, 300	[6] 33, 900	[2] 6, 840
1955–56	[7] 9, 000	[6] 36, 500	[2] 5, 403
1956–57	[8] 3, 200	[4] (44, 300)	[2] 6, 200
1957–58	[9] 18, 500	[10] 49, 100	[2] 5, 393

Blanks indicate figures are not available.

[1] *Chung-kuo Chiao-yu Nien-chien* [Chinese Educational Yearbook] (Shanghai: Ministry of Education, 1948).

[2] *Ten Great Years* (Peking: State Statistical Bureau, 1960).

[3] *New China News Agency*, December 2, 1954.

[4] Estimated by combining reported data on enrollment, entrants and graduates. Because drop-outs are not accounted for, enrollment in 1956–57 is overestimated and entrants in 1950–51 through 1953–54 are underestimated by roughly 10 percent.

[5] *New China News Agency*, May 20, 1954.

[6] *Ibid.*, November 26, 1956.

[7] *Kuang-ming Jih-pao* [Kuang-ming Daily], June 29, 1955.

[8] *New China News Agency*, March 16, 1956.

[9] *Kuang-chou Jih-pao* [Kuang-chou Daily], May 29, 1957.

[10] I. G. Kochergin, *Zdravookhraneniye i Meditsina v Kitayskoy Narodnoy Respublike* [Public Health and Medicine in the Chinese People's Republic] (Moskva: 1960).

Native Medicine

In 1958 the Communists adopted a policy that appeared to increase the number of doctors sevenfold, while actually not improving the existing situation. In the past, the great majority of the Chinese population depended on Chinese traditional doctors, or herbists, to provide them with cures and potions in case of illness. In 1955 the number of such herbists was reportedly close to half a million. In November 1958 the Central Committee of the Chinese Communist Party decreed that from then on the traditional Chinese medicine would be given a place equal or even superior to that of Western medicine. As a result of this new status for herb medicine, the Party ordered all physicians trained in Western medicine to study traditional Chinese methods. Medical students must now attend lectures on traditional medical usages and are trained in acapuncture and herbology. Conversely, dozens of medical schools have been set up where herb doctors are instructed in short study courses and are acquainted with the principles of anatomy, physiology, and pathology. Thus, although the herb doctors are being elevated in overall level, they are in no sense comparable to the Western-type doctor.

The details of the new status for native medicine, the propaganda efforts that followed the decree establishing it, and the practical effects of the order make an interesting tale and a subject for a separate study. An editorial in the official Communist newspaper summarized the new line.[8] The main points of the editorial were that traditional Chinese medicine is the crystallization of the people's experience over the past several thousand years and that in many instances it is more effective than Western medicine; by concentrating on research in the field of traditional medicine, China might create a new medical science.

A national conference on traditional medicine which was concluded on December 2, 1958, pointed out the following necessary steps to be taken:

> Vigorously initiate a movement for medical doctors to study Chinese pathology; collect millions of good Chinese prescriptions; conduct research on Chinese medicine; launch a mass movement for producing herbs; and struggle to develop a new medical science for the motherland.[9]

In addition to elevating the status of the traditional doctors, the decree was consonant with the overall policy of deemphasizing Western learning in general, in elevating the status of whatever springs from the masses, and in putting intellectuals "in the proper place." At the end of 1958 there were 68,000 apprentices learning to be herb practitioners.[10]

---

[8] *Ibid.,* Dec. 14, 1958.

[9] *Chinese Home Service* (News Agency), Dec. 5, 1958.

[10] *New China News Agency,* Dec. 5, 1958.

Medical education in China has undergone a number of reorganizations since 1950, including the integration and division of various medical institutions and departments. Most medical schools are divided into medical (therapeutic), public health, oral medicine (dentistry), and pharmacology departments. Following a 1954 conference of personnel of the higher medical educational establishments, a 5-year course of study was established for the first two categories and a 4-year course for the last two categories. At present, it is reported that all higher medical curriculums have a 6-year duration.

Although some of the counts differ, in 1957 one source reported 38 medical institutes in China.[11] The enrollment in these colleges has increased from 15,200 in 1949–50 to 49,100 in 1957–58 (table 6), and during the period 1948–49 through 1957–58, over 39,000 persons graduated from medical institutes. Almost 40 percent of the students in the medical colleges are women.

The conditions in medical colleges are no better than in other institutions of higher education. Attached to most of these colleges is some type of hospital or clinic, and the students get more practical experience than "book learning." The *Health Daily* complained:

> Owing to the lack of resident physicians in the wards, students are substituting for them. This reduces the time spent by medical students in studying clinical medicine, which is essential in the training of a good doctor.[12]

The same newspaper also complained that too many subjects were covered in the 5-year course as compared to the 6-year course in the U.S.S.R. The course includes the study of Chinese traditional medicine and the principles of Marxism-Leninism in addition to the basic medical sciences. It seems that many of the basic facts of medicine are unknown by the students and that "many medical students are being taught by subprofessional personnel."

Contrary to the trend in all other fields of specialization, the Ministry of Health has canceled specialization in medicine, with few exceptions, and proclaimed that general practitioners are needed much more urgently than specialists.[13]

The data on the number of physicians in China today—physicians trained in Western medicine—is confusing and inconsistent with the reported number of graduates. Whereas the number of physicians increased from 41,400 in 1950 to 75,000 by 1956, the total number of reported graduates from medical institutions was only 19,300. On the other hand, during the years 1956, 1957, and 1958, the number of physi-

---

[11] I. G. Kochergin, *Zdravookhraneniye i Meditsina v Kitayskoy Narodnoy Respublike* [Public Health and Medicine in the Chinese People's Republic] (Moskva: 1959).

[12] *Chien-k'ang Pao* [Health Daily], Feb. 19, 1957.

[13] *Ibid.*, Feb. 1, 1957.

cians remained virtually unchanged, while 17,000 graduated from medical institutions (table 6).

TABLE 7.—*Comparison between implied and actual number of graduates from medical institutes, 1951–58*

[Rounded to nearest hundred]

Year	Doctors trained in Western medicine [1]	Less 2 per-cent attrition applied to former year [2]	Implied number of graduates [3]	Reported number of graduates [4]	Difference [5]
1950........	41,400	....	....	....	....
1951........	(46,500)	40,600	5,900	1,400	−4,500
1952........	51,700	45,600	6,100	2,400	−3,700
1953........	56,400	50,700	5,700	2,600	−3,100
1954........	63,000	55,300	7,700	2,900	−4,800
1955........	70,500	61,700	8,800	4,500	−4,300
1956........	75,000	69,100	5,900	6,800	900
1957........	74.000	73,500	500	5,400	4,900
1958........	75,000	72,500	2,500	6,200	3,700
			43,100	32,200	−10,900

Blanks indicate figures are not available.

[1] See table 8 for sources. The number of doctors for 1951 was estimated through interpolation.

[2] The 2-percent rate of attrition may be minimal because of the relatively advanced age of many of the doctors.

[3] Derived by subtracting the estimated number of doctors who have survived from the preceding year from the reported number of doctors.

[4] *Ten Great Years* (Peking: State Statistical Bureau, 1960). It is not known whether the reported number of doctors is for the beginning of the year, the end of the year, or an annual average. Since Chinese data are seldom given for the beginning of the year, the reported number of graduates was moved up 1 year, on the assumption that their effect on the reported number of doctors in the country would not be apparent until 1 year following graduation. In other words, the 1,400 persons who graduated in 1949–50 are assumed to have entered the profession in 1951 and are rounded to the nearest hundred to correspond with the other data in the table.

[5] Excess or deficit reported to implied annual increment of doctors.

Thus, whereas it would require 43,100 graduates (deducting annual attrition) to account for the reported increase in the number of doctors between 1950 and 1958, the number of graduates was only 32,200, leaving a discrepancy of 10,900 (table 7). There is an additional factor here that would tend further to accentuate the discrepancy. As mentioned above, the medical institutes include not only therapeutic medicine but also public health, dentistry, and pharmacology. Therefore these specializations are also reflected in the reported number of graduates from medical institutions, although to an undetermined degree, since no breakdown of the graduates is available. In the Peking Medical School, which may or may not be typical of other institutions, approximately 75 percent of the student body is studying therapeutic medicine.[14] Assuming that this is typical of the country as a whole, the discrepancy between graduates and reported number of doctors rises to 19,000. This may not be an appropriate distinction, however, since it is very likely that dentists and even pharmacists with higher degrees are included under the general category of doctors. Also, there seems to be no apparent explanation for the stability in the number of reported doctors for 1956, 1957, and 1958, years in which an average of 5,700 persons graduated from medical schools annually (table 6).

It must be noted that the number of persons with higher medical education was estimated at 51,600 for 1960 in table 2, or 23,400 below the 75,000 reported for 1958. Although the discrepancy is increased if the graduates for 1959 are added to the figure of 75,000, there are several observations that should be made with regard to both figures.

Although 75,000 doctors is perhaps the most frequently quoted figure, there are references to lower totals. For example, one source reported 50,000 doctors for 1957.[15] On the other hand, the 51,600 doctors estimated for 1960 in table 2 may be minimal, primarily because this figure is based on graduates of Chinese universities and does not take into consideration the relatively large number of physicians trained outside China. This becomes apparent when the estimated and reported numbers of doctors from the pre-Communist era are compared. Table 2 estimated 6,400 doctors living in China in 1960 who had received their degrees in Chinese universities prior to the Communist takeover; perhaps there were 8,000 alive in the late 1940's. It was reported that in 1947 there was a total of 13,447 doctors in China trained in Western medicine.[16] Because the latter figure includes all doctors, while the former is limited to doctors educated in China, it may be inferred that the difference between the 2 figures approximately represents the number of doctors in China who had received their education abroad.

In effect, these efforts to arrive at an acceptable figure for the number of doctors in China trained in Western medicine is nothing but an attempt to apply some logic to data that does not lend itself to definitive

---

[14] *Soren Chugoku Gakujutsu Shisatsu Hokoku* [Report on the Inspection of Science and Technology in the Soviet Union and China], Feb. 25, 1956 (selected translations by U.S. Joint Publications Research Service, in Rept. No. DC–356, Nov. 14, 1958).

[15] *Chien-k'ang Pao* [Health Daily], Feb. 1, 1957; translated by U.S. Joint Publications Research Service, in Rept. No. 225, Feb. 11, 1958: *Health and Sanitation in Communist China.*

[16] I. G. Kochergin, *Zdravookhraneniye i Meditsina v Kitayskoy Narodnoy Respublike* [Public Health and Medicine in the Chinese People's Republic] (Moskva: 1959), p. 22.

analysis. The most that can be said is that their number falls somewhere within the 50,000 to 75,000 range.

Although the Communists have been making efforts to distribute some of the medical personnel into the rural areas, most of those sent to such areas have been subprofessional; at least 75 percent of all qualified doctors, and probably more, are in the cities, which contain some 15 percent of the total population. Although there is no information on the urban-rural distribution of the medical personnel, there are such data on hospital beds, indicating that between 1952 and 1958 there was virtual stability in the proportion of hospital beds located in urban areas, fluctuating from 62 to 66 percent over the 7 years.

TABLE 8.—*Medical personnel and hospital beds, 1948–58*

[Rounded to nearest hundred]

Year	Doctors trained in Western medicine[1]	Medical assistants	Nurses	Mid-wives	Hospital beds[2]	Number of persons[3]	
						Per doctor	Per bed
1949......	....	....	....	....	[4]84,000	....	6,500
1950......	[5]41,400	[4]53,000	[4]38,000	[4]16,000	[4]106,000	13,300	5,200
1951......	....	....	....	....	[4]134,000	....	4,200
1952......	[5]51,700	[4]67,000	[4]61,000	[4]22,000	[4]180,000	11,000	3.200
1953......	[5]56,400	....	....	....	[4]215,000	10,400	2,700
1954......	[5]63,000	[6]86,000	[5]93,800	[5]32,000	[4]250,000	9,600	2,400
1955......	[5]70,500	....	....	....	[4]279,000	8,700	2,200
1956......	[7]75,000	....	....	....	[4]328,000	8,400	1,900
1957......	[4]74,000	[4]136,000	[4]128,000	36,000	[4]364,000	8,700	1,800
1958......	[4]75,000	[4]131,000	[4]138,000	35,000	[4]440,000	8,700	1,500

Blanks indicate figures are not available.

[1] Some of the seeming inconsistencies in this series are discussed in the text.

[2] The number of hospital beds in this series is considerably higher than reported in other sources. For example, one Russian source reports the following figures: 1950, 99,800; 1951, 124,100; 1952, 160,300; 1953, 181,100; 1954, 204,835; 1955, 220,968; 1956, 261,745; 1957, 194,733; 1958, 371,453 (note 6, below). Still other figures may be found for any one year. In addition to the simple inadequacy of statistics, there may be a difficulty in defining a hospital bed. The series here is explained by the following footnote: "Figures in this table do not include simply constructed beds. There was a big increase in the number of this type bed in 1958. There are more than 992,000 simple beds in various health organizations throughout the country; this is a 900-percent increase over the corresponding figure for 1957."

[3] The population figures for this calculation are from table 1, chap. VIII. Alternate population estimates would have no appreciable effect on the significance of this ratio.

[4] *Ten Great Years* (Peking: State Statistical Bureau, 1960).

[5] *Razvitiye Narodnogo Khozyaystva Kitayskoy Narodnoy Respublika* [Economic Development of the Chinese People's Republic] (Moskva: 1956).

[6] I. G. Kochergin, *Zdravookhraneniye i Meditsina v Kitayskoy Narodnoy Respublike* [Public Health and Medicine in the Chinese People's Republic] (Moskva: 1959).

[7] *Jen-min Shou-ts'e* [People's Handbook] (Peking: 1958).

Table 8 also presents the latest figures on the number of subprofessional medical personnel. Although there has been an overall increase in the number of medical assistants, nurses, and midwives, the shortage of personnel at this level seems to be as acute as that of physicians. The slight decline in the number of medical assistants and midwives between 1957 and 1958 may possibly reflect the new emphasis on Chinese traditional medicine.

Available Manpower With Completed Secondary Education, January 1960

At this point it may also be well to consider briefly the segment of the population with completed secondary education; that is the group that may be loosely categorized as semiprofessional. Because of the shortage of graduates of higher educational institutions, the Chinese economy relies on this middle echelon of the labor force to a much greater degree than is the case in the more advanced nations. They are the teachers, the skilled workers, foremen, "middle specialists" in the fields of health, science, and industry, and often occupy important posts in both the Party and the state governments. Of course, the number of persons who could be categorized as semiprofessionals cannot be determined simply by equating the size of this group with the number of graduates of secondary schools because persons are omitted who attain this level through experience and advancement within employment channels.

The number of persons with completed senior secondary education as of 1960 is difficult to estimate, and the figures that follow should be taken only as representing something of the magnitude of this group. They are also presented with a greater degree of rounding than has been the practice in other sections of the study. It is estimated that as of 1960 there were roughly 700,000 graduates of senior secondary schools (all types) surviving from the pre-Communist period.[17] However, an error of 10 or even 20 percent in this figure would not be surprising. Somewhat more reliable is the estimate of 2.6 million senior secondary graduates for the period 1949 through 1959. Actually, some of the normal-school graduates and, especially, vocational-school graduates may not have the equivalent of a senior secondary education. Nevertheless, the sum of these 2 groups of graduates comes to 3.3 million. This figure is maximal because almost all the graduates of higher educational institutions have completed secondary education, are accounted for separately, and theoretically should be subtracted from the 3.3 million. To do this by period and by type of education is hazardous and unnecessary,

---

[17] The basic projection is in appendix table A–1 and results in 640,620 survivors. Because the graduates of 1948 are excluded from this calculation, the total is rounded up to 700,000 and distributed approximately in proportion to the survivors of the 3 types of schools as follows: Senior general, 400,000; senior normal, 200,000; senior vocational, 100,000.

so table 9 distributes the full 3.3 million. However, a rough estimate of the number of persons in China with only a secondary school education would probably fall somewhere between 2.6 and 2.8 million.

TABLE 9.—*Number of persons with completed secondary education, January 1960*

Type of school	Pre-1949 [1]	1949–59 [2]	Total
Senior general............................	400, 000	1, 200, 000	1, 600, 000
Senior normal............................	200, 000	700, 000	900, 000
Senior vocational........................	100, 000	700, 000	800, 000
	700, 000	2, 600, 000	3, 300, 000

1. See appendix table A-1 for projection and footnote 4 thereof for the upward adjustment of the figures.

2. These figures are rounded from tables 4 and 6 in ch. III. See text for evaluation of these data.

Distribution of Population With Completed Secondary and Completed Higher Education, by Age and Sex, January 1960

China is a nation of young specialists. It is estimated that in 1960 over half of the persons with completed higher education and over three-quarters of the persons with only completed secondary education are under 30 years of age (table 10). This, of course, is due to the very

TABLE 10.—*Rough distribution of university and secondary school graduates, by age, 1960*

Age	University graduates [1]		Secondary school graduates [2]	
	Number	Percent	Number	Percent
Under 30................	325, 000	52	2, 600, 000	79
30–49....................	265, 000	42	630, 000	19
50 and over..............	35, 000	6	70, 000	2
	625, 000	100	3, 300, 000	100

[1] It is assumed that the average age of graduates from higher educational institutions is 22½ years. Thus, almost all the graduates since 1953 would fall in the "under 30" bracket. The graduates between 1949 and 1953 were combined with the survivors of the earlier graduates as calculated in table 1 of this chapter to estimate the other two age groups.

[2] It is assumed that the average age of graduates from senior secondary institutions is 17½ years. Thus, all the graduates since 1948 fall in the "under 30" bracket. The surviving graduates of the pre-Communist period were combined from data developed in appendix table A-1. Since these figures are not based on an actual count but are based on data on graduates, to translate these figures to population with a maximum of secondary education, 625,000 has to be subtracted from 3,300,000 for a total of 2,675,000 (see text in preceding section for discussion of this point).

large numbers graduating since 1949 compared to the extremely small number of graduates in the previous period. Because of the continually increasing numbers of fresh graduates, the proportion of persons over 30 years of age in this group will remain low for a considerable time.

There are no detailed data on the distribution by sex of graduates from higher and from secondary educational institutions. However, under the assumption that there is a close correlation between the number of women enrolled and graduated, it is possible to make some valid judgments on the proportion of women among the graduates during the pre-Communist period.

The proportion of females in the total enrollment in institutions of higher education between 1932 and 1946 is presented in appendix table A–5. The most rapid increase in enrollment of women occurred between 1932 and 1937; there was virtual stability in the percent that women constituted of the total student body between 1937 and 1946. Over the whole period covered by the statistics (1932–46), the proportion of women increased from 12 to 18 percent. The greatest increase took place in the field of agriculture and forestry, followed by the fields of medical science, engineering, finance and economics, political science and law, natural sciences, and literature and arts—in descending order of increase. Surprisingly, only in the field of education was there a decrease in the proportion of women.

An 18-percent proportion of women among the living college graduates who received their training prior to 1949 has been assumed. This seems to be justified by the fact that reported data indicate almost no change in the enrollment of females in higher education over the last 10 years of the period covered by statistics (1932–46), and because only in this period did their number become significant. Applying this percentage to the estimated 125,000 survivors with higher degrees received during the old regime (see table 2), a figure of 22,500 (rounded to 23,000 in table 12) is obtained.

In 1939 girls constituted 19 percent of the total enrollment in secondary schools;[18] in 1946 there was virtually no change—20.2 percent.[19] In senior secondary schools alone, the percentages were 21.6 in 1939 and 19.5 in 1946. Assuming that girls constituted 18 percent of the graduates of senior secondary schools prior to 1949 (see table 9), their present number would be 126,000.

Table 11 shows the proportion of women at the various educational levels since 1948. After an almost 4-percent rise between 1949 and

---

[18] *Chung-hua Min-kuo Chiao-yu T'ung-chi* [Republic of China Educational Statistics], 1941, p. 101.

[19] *Chung-hua Nien-chien* [China Yearbook], vol. 2, 1948, p. 1633.

1952, their proportion in institutions of higher education remained virtually unchanged during the next 6 years. It is assumed that women have constituted 23 percent of the graduates from institutions of higher education for the whole period since 1949. As reported in 1958, the highest proportion of women to men appeared in enrollment in the fields of medicine and pharmacy, where they constituted 40.2 percent of the student body, while in literature, art, and education they constituted 22.2 percent.[20] The first group represents a large increase over that of the pre-Communist period; the latter, a small decrease.

TABLE 11.—*Number of female students in educational institutions, various levels, as percent of enrollment, intervals 1949–58*

Year	Higher educational institutions		Secondary specialized schools		Secondary general schools		Primary schools	
	Number	Percent	Number	Percent	Number	Percent	Number	Percent
1949....	23,000	19.8	158,000	......	....	......	....	......
1952....	45,000	23.4	158,000	24.9	585,000	23.5	16,812,000	32.9
1957....	103,000	23.3	206,000	26.5	1,935,000	30.8	22,176,000	34.5
1958....	154,000	23.3	397,000	27.0	2,667,000	31.3	33,264,000	38.5

Blanks indicate figures are not available.

Source: *Ten Great Years* (Peking: State Statistical Bureau, 1960).

The increase in the proportion of women to men in secondary education has been somewhat more rapid, particularly in the general schools where in a period of 6 years their proportion increased from 23.5 percent to 31.5 percent. It is assumed that women have constituted 28 percent of the graduates from all types of secondary schools during the Communist period.

Table 12 summarizes these estimates in relation to the estimated population with completed higher and secondary educations.

---

[20] *Peking Review,* No. 27, Sept. 3, 1958.

TABLE 12.—*Summary of estimated population with completed higher and secondary education, by sex, January 1960*

| | Higher educational institutions | | | | |
	Male	Percent	Female	Percent	Total
Pre–1949...............	102, 000	82	23, 000	18	125, 000
Post–1949..............	385, 000	77	115, 000	23	500, 000
Total.............	487, 000	78	138, 000	22	625, 000

| | Secondary educational institutions | | | | |
	Male	Percent	Female	Percent	Total
Pre–1949...............	574, 000	82	126, 000	18	700, 000
Post–1949..............	1, 872, 000	72	728, 000	28	2, 600, 000
Total.............	2, 446, 000	74	854, 000	26	[1] 3, 300, 000

[1] Includes the 625,000 who went on to higher educational institutions.

CHAPTER VIII

Survey of the Population and Labor Force

This chapter attempts briefly to cover the most important factors relating to the population and labor force of Communist China. Even though in the present context a detailed treatment of these subjects is inappropriate, the size and rate of growth of the total population, the distribution of the population between urban and rural areas, the age and sex structure of the population, and a notion about the size and basic characteristics of the urban labor force should be reviewed to place the discussions of education and professional manpower into better perspective. These factors, in China, will play a major role in determining the speed with which the Communists attain their stated objectives.

More specifically, how does population enter into the discussions of education and manpower? Of course there is the conspicuous relationship: The larger the population, the more children must be sent to school and the more people will be available for the labor force. This oversimplification is deceiving. It is true that in absolute numbers China has an immense number of people within the main working ages, but their proportion to the total population is considerably lower than in the more advanced countries. During the demographic transition period, in which China now finds itself, the proportion of children to adults has a tendency to increase even further. Lower death rates, and particularly lower infant mortality, in combination with a continuing high birth rate result in a higher probability of survival for babies and children; on the other hand, the older cohorts are the product of a period of high mortality rates. Thus, whereas in more advanced countries about one-quarter of the population is under the age of 15, in a country such as China children under 15 constitute at least 40 percent of the total population. In other words, China has about 15 percent fewer inhabitants who are old enough to produce and to provide for a much larger nonproductive population than does a more advanced nation. This factor becomes even more striking when one considers that 15 percent of China's population represents about 100 million persons.

Also, the resources that are used in rearing and training children do not produce as great a return in China as they do in the United States, for example. In the United States, a person who has completed high school may have as many as 50 years of productive work ahead; in

China, a student who has completed secondary education has perhaps only 30 years, in terms of productiveness, in which to reimburse the State for the outlay of educating him and to leave a certain "residual" before passing on. This point may be taken a step further. Because of greater efficiency and productivity and the technical basis of our economy, it takes an American worker a much shorter time to repay the initial outlay that was necessary to raise and educate him than it does a Chinese worker, whose productivity is much lower. In the final analysis, all these factors reflect on the rate of capital accumulation and on the speed with which the stated goals of economic and social development are met.

POPULATION

Total Population

Usually, a census answers most of the questions dealing with the size and characteristics of the population of a country, ending all speculation, theories, and guesswork. The 1953 census registration of Communist China had an opposite effect, precipitating heated discussions as to the size and the rate of growth of the mainland population. Not only demographers but also historians, economists, political scientists— persons who have seldom been concerned with the validity of Chinese population data—have been motivated to expound their views on the number of persons living in China today. Prior to 1950 any figure in the vicinity of 450 million was considered to be sufficiently representative of the size of the population, especially since there was no way either to prove or disprove its validity. With the release of the 1953 data, including some details on procedures followed in obtaining and assembling this material,[1] and with the availability of scattered information on recent rates of population growth, persons working with China's population statistics have become much more sensitive about the validity of their estimates and their basic assumptions.

The 1953 Count

Because every estimate of the present population of China is based on the 1953 reported figure of 582.6 million as the point of departure, the first step must be a judgment of this figure. The evaluations of the 1953 count label it everything from "a scientific and accurate modern census" to "pure and simple fabrication." It is safe to say that the truth lies somewhere between these two extremes. Because of efficient centralized controls, the Communists were able to take a count that was probably more accurate than any previously attempted.[2] At the

---

[1] The most detailed discussion of the results and procedures utilized in the 1953 census registration is contained in S. Krotevich, "Vsekitayskaya perepis naseleniya, 1953 g," *Vestnik Statistiki,* No. 5, September-October 1955.

[2] See L. Orleans, "The 1953 Chinese Census in Perspective," *Journal of Asian Studies,* August 1957.

same time, there were many technical, cultural, political, geographic, and other factors that complicated the task of enumeration, leading either to overstatement or understatement of the population of China. Because there is no conclusive way to prove the relative effects of these tendencies and therefore no reasonable method of adjusting the 1953 data (assuming that an adjustment is necessary), and since some of the errors probably would tend to compensate each other, the total population reported for 1953 is accepted as an adequate and usable base for subsequent projections of the Chinese population.

Post-1953 Reports

The figures for the total population of the mainland reported in Communist sources since 1953 have shown little regularity and appear to be little more than guesses by the various individuals citing them. For example, the Minister of Food, in a speech before the People's Congress, reported a 1956 population of 603,230,000; for the same year, the journal *Liang Shih* [Food] [3] reported 616,500,000; yet the journal *T'ung-chi Kung-tso* [Statistical Work] [4] stated that the population of mainland China at the end of 1956 was 627,800,000. The figure of 640 million may be encountered in any number of sources dated from 1956 through 1958, while the figure of 650 million has been the most popular since then. While the *New China News Agency* on May 3, 1959, was reporting a population of 649,900,000, one recent visitor to China, presumably on the basis of direct data given him by Communist officials, reported a total of 673 million for the end of 1958. [5] The only reason for bringing out these inconsistencies is to suggest the possibility that the Communists themselves have only a vague idea of the size of the present population of mainland China.

In lieu of a full-fledged census, there are two possible ways in which the current population of a nation may be estimated, and both of them depend on the establishment of an effective and accurate registration system. The first method is an actual registration of the country's *de facto* population. The second is a registration of the births and the deaths in order to project a base population on the basis of the derived vital-statistics rates. Although detailed provisions for a registration system have been set up by the state, [6] the implementation of these regulations has not been rapid, and the completeness and accuracy of the data procured by the system are, to say the least, problematical.

Reflecting on the registration system and therefore on the precision of Chinese population data is the fact that reported figures for provincial populations in the postcensus years have been extremely sparse and

---

[3] *Liang Shih* [Food], No. 11, Jan. 25, 1957.

[4] *T'ung-chi Kung-tso* [Statistical Work], No. 11, June 14, 1957.

[5] S. Chandrasekhar, *Population of China* (Hong Kong: 1959).

[6] The complete text of the regulations was reported by the *New China News Agency,* Jan. 9, 1958.

have usually been confined to rounded approximations. Even in the recently published Soviet short encyclopedia of China, where an obvious attempt was made to include the latest provincial populations, only 6 of the 26 provinces and autonomous regions listed had populations for a date later than 1953 (4 for 1958 and 2 for 1957).[7] Each of the six more current provincial figures (in sum representing over one-third of the total population) shows a rate of growth over the 4- or 5-year period that is considerably below the rate of growth implied by the various reports of the total population; none of the implied rates in those six provinces exceeds 2 percent a year. Since the Chinese are not attempting to suppress provincial population figures, the most obvious explanation of the limited reporting is that these were the only provinces for which current estimates were available. It is therefore surprising that in late 1959, in a statistical volume which reports Communist China's achievements over the past 10 years, a complete listing of provincial populations for the end of 1957 (three provinces for the end of 1958) was reported.[8] Although the differential growth of the various provinces, as reported in 1953 and in this series, seems to be internally reasonable, the sudden appearance of these data after a 6-year interval raises certain suspicions. If these data were available for 1957 and for other years, why were they suppressed? If they were not available and the registration system did not produce usable provincial statistics, how were the reported year-by-year figures for the total population of China derived?

Several factors account for the fact that population data in Communist China have been negligible in quantity and questionable in reliability. The Chinese Communists have explicitly stated that statistics should not blindly follow "reactionary texts," but should serve the political and economic objectives of the nation. Furthermore, although China has a planned economy that presumably requires accurate population and manpower data, her policies and goals are largely independent of demographic statistics and would not change if the population of the country were found to be 25 or even 50 million more or less than the figure which may be currently used by the Communists. Not all Chinese population and manpower statistics are uniformally unreliable. For example, it is very probable that the population figures dealing with the urban population are more accurate than those for the rural segment of the population, and that the data on workers and employees, particularly on the personnel with higher education and with special skills, faithfully reflect the actual situation. On the other hand, it makes little difference to the planners if the rural population of a particular province is 47 or 49 million, for example.

This laxity, of course, seems to contradict everything we know about the tight controls imposed on every individual in the land. How, one

---

[7] *Nash Drug Kitay* [Our Friend China] (Moskva: 1959).

[8] *Ten Great Years* (Peking: State Statistical Bureau, 1960).

might ask, can this authority be implemented if the number of persons involved is not known. Actually, every person *is* closely supervised and accounted for, but only at the commune level in the countryside and at the block or enterprise level in the city. The system breaks down, however, during the process of transmitting the entries from the registration books at the local levels to the hsien, province, and national administrative levels. In the first place, there is simply the physical problem of assembling the figures from some 26,000 communes, 2,000 hsien, and thousands of towns and cities. A shortage of professional statisticians exists even at the national level; at the local levels this work is done by persons with little statistical training. In the second place, the traditionally careless attitude toward statistics in China may have been bolstered by the proclamation that, in effect, statistics must show what the state wants them to show. Because every administrative unit has a more or less established "population quota," it would indeed be a courageous official who would present figures that digress from those accepted during the previous years. Undoubtedly, figures are adjusted at every level to produce predictable results which will not have to be justified and defended. Furthermore, even in the event that the Chinese Communists were to discover that their published figures have been faulty, they are not likely to change them and thereby reflect on the accuracy of their previous statistics and their registration system as a whole.

Validity of Reported Vital-Statistics Rates

Since the population figures reported by the Communists are inconsistent and questionable, the next question is: Do we have reliable vital-statistics rates for all of China as a basis for estimating the rate of natural increase since 1953?

The most often quoted rates refer to 1953, when a sample check revealed a birth rate of 37 per 1,000 and a death rate of 17 per 1,000, or a 2-percent annual rate of increase. Other rates reported by the Communists and implied by reported population figures show even more rapid growth. All these rates seem at odds with most of the previous estimates for China and are incompatible with those for comparable countries which are or were overwhelmingly rural and at a stage of economic development similar to that of China. Higher birth rates, and especially higher death rates, would be easier to reconcile with the probabilities. At best, the discrepancies may be due to the very widespread phenomenon of underregistration of births and deaths, a problem particularly cogent in less-developed countries. For example, a United Nations report [9] quotes for India a birth rate of 25.8 and a death rate of 13.1 on the basis of registered births and deaths. A footnote explains, however, that rates estimated on the basis of the 1941 and 1951 censuses

---

[9] *Population and Vital Statistics Reports,* series A, vol. IX, No. 3 (New York: United Nations).

are 39.9 for births and 27.4 for deaths; thus, the utilization of rates based on registered births and deaths reveals an underregistration of 35 percent and 52 percent, respectively.

Although the above rates of underenumeration are excessive and not necessarily applicable to China, the problem is a serious one which is prevalent in most of the nations attempting to register births and deaths. In a country such as China, one in which there are no controls on fertility, the birth rate could be expected to be in the vicinity of 45 per 1,000. The attempt to introduce birth control in China between 1955 and 1957 was abandoned as a national policy in 1958, presumably because it was a failure.[10] Thus, while the reported birth rate of 37 per 1,000 is at least plausible, most authorities tend to accept a somewhat higher figure within the 40 to 45 per 1,000 range.

The limits for a possible birth rate are considerably more narrow than for the death rate. Since precise statistics for China have never been available, most estimates in the pre-Communist period were either derived from small sample studies or were guesses based on analogy. The general concensus seems to be that, although the death rate varied from year to year depending on the extent of natural and political calamities, its usual level was in the low 30's. In fact, in years in which disasters and adversities were particularly severe and widespread, actual net deficits of population occurred. It would seem most unlikely, therefore, that in a period of some 3 to 4 years (1949–53) the Communists would have been able to lower the mortality rate to 17 per 1,000—below the rate reported for the Soviet Union in 1939. The improvements in the health conditions of the population are undeniable. Through intensive propaganda, some semblance of sanitation has been introduced even in the rural areas of China. However, certain factors would tend to inhibit a significant and rapid reduction of the death rate. Although diseases and epidemics are fewer, they still exist; famines are less widespread, but they are still reported, and there are reliable reports of serious food shortages in many parts of the country; living conditions at construction projects engaging millions of people are, to say the least, extremely poor; medical care is inadequate, with only 1 doctor trained in Western medicine for every 10,000 inhabitants and with medical supplies in short supply; infant mortality must still be very high, probably approaching 200 per 1,000, a rate compatible with a life-table death rate of about 28 per 1,000 (in the Soviet Union infant mortality was 200 per 1,000 in the European part of the country in 1926; in 1939 it was 181 for the country as a whole).

---

[10] See L. Orleans, "Birth Control: Reversal or Postponement?" *China Quarterly*, July–September 1960.

Estimated Rate of Population Growth

In view of the above discussion, it should be apparent that neither the figures reported for the total population since 1953 nor the reported vital-statistics rates correspond to reasonable expectations. Estimates of the present population of China on the basis of assumptions that would seem to be more reasonable and more compatible with the present evaluation of conditions within the country are presented in table 1.

TABLE 1.—*Estimated size of population and its growth, 1953–60*

Year [1]	Population (millions)	Rate of increase during year (percent)	Year [1]	Population (millions)	Rate of increase during year (percent)
1953.......	582. 6	0. 75	1957.......	617. 4	1. 9
1954.......	587. 0	1. 6	1958.......	629. 2	2. 0
1955.......	596. 4	1. 7	1959.......	641. 7	2. 1
1956.......	606. 5	1. 8	1960.......	655. 2	

[1] The 1953 figure is as of June 30; estimates for other years are as of Jan. 1.

Starting with the reported June 30, 1953, population of 582.6 million, a slowly rising rate of natural increase is assumed in table 1. Obviously the rates are somewhat arbitrary. They presuppose a more or less constant birth rate of about 42 per 1,000 for the whole period covered and a death rate that decreases from 27 per 1,000 in 1953 to 20 per 1,000 in 1959. It is very likely that, because of a continuing drop in the death rate, the rate of natural increase will also continue to rise. By 1965 it may approach 2.5 percent, while the population of China will rise to 730–740 million, representing an increase of about 23 percent, or an absolute growth of some 130–140 million over a 10-year period.

In view of the quality of the raw statistics and because all estimates are based on assumptions and to some extent impressions, the size and the rate of growth of the Chinese population are open to contention. It must be kept in mind that an error of only 3 percent can vary the final estimate by plus or minus 20 million—a range large enough to swallow the combined populations of the Netherlands, Norway, Sweden, Belgium, and Greece.

What are the more specific implications of this discussion in relation to China's educational and manpower problems? Extreme assumptions with regard to the present population and birth rate may vary the number of children entering school 7 years hence by as much as 5 million. If the assumptions utilized above are valid, however, it may be concluded that the present primary school facilities will be adequate to handle primary school children for at least a decade and that enrollment in these schools will not exceed the 100-million mark during this period. This prediction is dependent on a continuing decrease in the number of overaged children in primary schools as the participation rate increases. Since enrollment will not increase, this also suggests that there may be some improvement in the type of education provided by primary schools. This, of course, is not the case with secondary and higher schools, where the rate of participation is relatively low, and enrollment will be determined by capabilities and policies which are not as closely tied to size and rate of growth of the population. As for the labor force, if the current policies of manpower utilization continue, it would make little difference if the labor force were to expand by a few million more or less people. It is suggested, however, that the present emphasis on mass labor utilization cannot continue indefinitely, that there are limits to the numbers that can be usefully absorbed by the rural communes, and that in the long run the population problem will become more acute and more difficult to handle.

Urban-Rural Population Distribution

Prior to 1953 the range of estimates for China's urban population was as great as that for the total population. The 1953 census registration reported 77.3 million persons (13.3 percent of the total population) in the urban areas of China, a figure considerably lower than most previous estimates. On the basis of this figure, it is estimated that the 1960 urban population is about 100 million. Although China is an overwhelming rural nation, in a sense this low urban proportion is deceptive, for there are as many persons living in China's cities, towns, and urban-type settlements as there are in such areas in the Soviet Union.

Table 2 includes the only integrated series on urban population so far reported by the Communists. Although there are certain inconsistencies in the data, they are generally judged to be adequate and usable, and their projection follows, as much as possible, the known trends in urbanization during the past few years.[11] The slowing of growth in the urban population during the last few years occurred by design. After the infiltration of millions of peasants into the cities during the middle 1950's and the subsequent attempt at forced evacuation of many of these migrants, the state instituted strict controls over unauthorized movements of the Chinese people. Although several years were required for the effective implementation of these new regulations, there is reason to believe that at present they are strictly enforced and relatively effective.

---

[11] For a discussion of this series of figures and for a more comprehensive analysis of the urban population, see L. Orleans, "The Recent Growth of China's Urban Population," *Geographical Review*, January 1959.

TABLE 2.—*Estimated urban population, 1953–60*

[Numbers in Millions]

Year	Total population [1]	Urban population	Percent urban
1953...............................	582. 0	[2] 77. 3	13. 3
1954...............................	587. 0	[3] 77. 7	13. 2
1955...............................	596. 4	[3] 81. 6	13. 7
1956...............................	606. 5	[3] 82. 9	13. 7
1957...............................	617. 4	[3] 89. 2	14. 4
1958...............................	629. 2	[4] 92. 3	14. 7
1959...............................	641. 7	[4] 95. 7	14. 9
1960...............................	655. 2	[4] 100. 0	15. 3

[1] See text and table 1 in the preceeding section.

[2] S. Krotevich, "Vsekitayakaya perepis naseleniya, 1953 g" [All-China Census of Population, 1953], in *Vestnik Statistiki* [Statistical Journal], No. 5, September–October 1955.

[3] *T'ung-chi Kung-tso* [Statistical Work], No. 11, June 14, 1957. This source also reports 71,600,000 for 1952; 66,320,000 for 1951; 61,690,000 for 1950; and 57,650,000 for 1949 (end-of-year figures).

[4] Estimates assume urban natural increase identical with the natural increase of the total population (see table 1) and an annual rural-to-urban migration of approximately 1.5 million.

In general, there are a number of unanswered questions which handicap a lucid analysis of the urban segment of the population. The most serious problem is that of definition. Several attempts have been made by the Communists to introduce an acceptable and practical delineation of criteria for an "urban area." It is unlikely that any set of criteria is strictly adhered to at the present. One set of criteria for urban population, patterned after the definition utilized in the Soviet Union, is briefly the following: (1) Seat of the municipal People's Committee above the hsien [county] level; (2) a resident population of 2,000 or more of whom 50 percent or more are not engaged in agriculture; (3) a resident population between 1,000 and 2,000 of whom 75 percent are not engaged in agriculture.[12] It seems highly doubtful whether the Chinese have the necessary statistical data to determine for every place with more than 1,000 people the proportion of the population not engaged in agriculture, particularly since data on occupations are presumably not collected as part of the registration system. The difficulty is intensified by the recent tendency for municipalities to incorporate large rural areas under their jurisdiction. Data on cities are not uniform—sometimes including and sometimes excluding the rural population subordinate to a particular city. Nevertheless, it is assumed

---

[12] *T'ung-chi Kung-tso T'ung-hsin* [Statistical Work Bulletin], No. 12, 1955.

that the post-1957 estimates in table 2 are identical in coverage because they are a projection of a series of figures that for the most part exclude the rural population. In this way an attempt was made to maintain consistency, regardless of the precise definition of "urban." The inclusion of rural areas directly subordinated to the large cities would, of course, increase the size of the urban population by several million.

Although the Communists have not published an urban-rural distribution of the school enrollment, this proportion has definite implications with regard to the quality of the education received. There is no doubt that the urban schools generally provide a much better overall education and in that sense play a much more important role in supplying candidates for the bona fide institutions of higher education, all of which are located in the cities. It would be useful to know the number of graduates from urban secondary schools, to be able to judge the selection that is available to institutes and universities, but such data are not available. As for the distribution of primary school enrollment, it is probably fairly closely correlated with the size of the urban and rural segments of the population, and it would seem safe to say that between 15 and 20 percent of all primary school children are attending urban schools.

Age and Sex Structure of the Mainland Population

The age composition of a population has a direct bearing on the rate of population growth, and conversely is itself a product of the levels of births and deaths in the past. It is also an important guide to the size of the working population, the number of children of school age, etc. Data for only a few broad age groups were released with the final tabulation of the 1953 census. It was several years before additional data were reported at two international statistical meetings.[13] Even then, however, there was no integrated data on the age and sex structure of the population of China. In 1959 a health journal published an article entitled "Population Growth and Planned Births," which contained a graphical presentation of a 5-year age-sex pyramid.[14] The cohorts derived by measuring the pyramid were found to be consistent with most of the age and sex data previously released and are presented in table 3.

Whereas there is wide disagreement among demographers with regard to the size and rate of growth of the mainland population, there is general agreement in the rejection of the reported 1953 age and sex structure of

---

[13] Tai Shih-kuang presented sex ratios for irregular age groups (*1953 Population Census of China,* Calcutta: Indian Statistical Institute, December 1956); Ch'en Ta presented an age distribution for ages 0 to 4, 5 to 14, 15 to 24, 25 to 34, etc. (*New China's Population Census of 1953 and Its Relations to National Reconstruction and Demographic Research,* Stockholm: International Statistical Institute, August 1957).

[14] *Jen-min Pao-chien* [People's Health], No. 5, May 1, 1959.

TABLE 3.—*Age and sex structure of the population, 1953*

[Numbers in millions]

Age	Number males	Number females	Total	Age group as percent of population
0–4....................	46. 5	44. 3	90. 8	15. 6
5–9....................	33. 7	30. 0	63. 7	10. 9
10–14..................	29. 9	25. 4	55. 3	9. 5
15–19..................	28. 2	25. 4	53. 6	9. 2
20–24..................	25. 0	23. 0	48. 0	8. 2
25–29..................	24. 1	21. 3	45. 4	7. 8
30–34..................	21. 2	19. 0	40. 2	6. 9
35–39..................	19. 4	17. 8	37. 2	6. 4
40–44..................	16. 5	15. 5	32. 0	5. 5
45–49..................	14. 8	14. 3	29. 1	5. 0
50–54..................	12. 8	12. 3	25. 1	4. 3
55–59..................	10. 7	10. 2	20. 9	3. 6
60–64.................	8. 4	8. 8	17. 2	3. 0
65–69..................	5. 8	6. 7	12. 5	2. 1
70 plus................	4. 9	6. 7	11. 6	2. 0
Total.............	301. 9	280. 7	582. 6	100. 0

Source: The 5-year age groups were measured from a population pyramid graphically presented in *Jen-min Pao-chien* [People's Health], No. 5, May 1, 1959. These measurements were then adjusted to the reported total number of males and females.

the population. The problems that faced the Communists in their effort to obtain an accurate age distribution of the population were numerous and the results indicate that they were either not overcome or were ignored in order to present a picture favorable for propaganda purposes. Much of the 1953 age and sex distribution is internally inconsistent, it does not correspond with the reported vital-statistics rates, and the magnitude of the excess of males in certain age groups raises suspicions. The difficulties in collecting these controversial data and the technical inconsistencies of their final tabulation, however, do not require detailed analysis. Adjustments that would make the reported data more palatable would make little difference in the broad implications of the data. Similarly, a propection of the age and sex structure of this population to 1958 or 1960 would require a thorough analysis, which would be beyond the scope and this study.[15] Thus, although the data are inadequate, their

[15] A series of alternative projections were prepared by the United Nations and may be found in *The Population of Asia and the Far East, 1950–80,* Population studies No. 31 (New York: United Nations, 1959). A detailed study of the age and sex data also appears in John S. Aird, *The Size, Composition, and Growth of the Population of Mainland China* (Washington: U.S. Department of Commerce, Bureau of the Census, Foreign Manpower Research Office, 1960).

significance as discussed in the beginning of this chapter is quite apparent and would change little as a result of adjustments and projections.

The high proportion of the population under 15 years of age is probably even greater now than it was in 1953. Every year roughly 16 to 17 million children reach the schol age. Conversely, although the number of persons in the main working ages will continue to increase, their proportion to the total population will, at least temporarily, diminish slightly.

THE URBAN LABOR FORCE

Estimating the size of the Chinese labor force has always been a hazardous venture, impeded by problems of definition and statistical measurement. Nevertheless, despite the tenuous nature of some of the estimates, a brief discussion of the size and characteristics of the urban labor force is presented below, to place the professional segment of the working population in better perspective.

The character of China's economy was never conducive to the evolution of Western-type concepts of "labor force" or "gainfully occupied," and a suitable body of statistical data has not been assembled. Since 1949 there has been a somewhat greater flow of statistical data on some segments of the labor force, but many gaps still exist and the problem of definitions is at least as acute as it has been in the past. Nevertheless, until recently, by applying some of the basic demographic techniques and concepts, it has been possible to derive from the age and sex structure of the population some idea of the size of the working population. Since the introduction of communes in the summer of 1958, the "great leap forward," and the policy combining education with production, the structure of the labor force in China has become even more amorphous. Presumably everyone who is able to hold a hoe or pick up a piece of scrap metal is in the labor force—and childbearing, attendance at school, or partial invalidism no longer excuses one from productive work for the motherland.

For the purpose of this study, the size of the total labor force is of only marginal interest and will only be touched upon: It may be noted in passing that as of the middle of 1958 there were approximately 180 million males and 165 million females between the ages of 15 and 59, the main age group of workers, comprising about 55 percent of the total population of China. Of greater importance for comparative purposes is the size of the urban labor force—the workers and employees—and especially those in that segment of this group who are engaged in industry, construction, and transportation, and communications.

In most countries the urban labor force constitutes between 45 and 55 percent of the total urban population. Little difference is observed from country to country in the proportion of males in the prime age group of workers who are actually engaged in productive activity; the extent of female participation, on the other hand, does vary extensively from one economy and one culture to another.

If an acceptable age and sex composition of the urban population were available, it would be possible to set up certain hypothetical limits for the size of the urban labor force. Despite the absence of such data, however, it is possible to make a few general observations and point out some of the more important distinctions between the urban and rural structure of the population that would have an effect on the size of the labor force. Sample studies on Chinese population confirm the fact that, for the most part, the observed characteristics were identical to those discernible in other urban populations: The cities of China had the larger portion of their total populations in the prime working ages—and, conversely, a smaller portion of children and old people. Also, the high proportion of the population in that group was due to the large number of men with permanent jobs or occupations in the cities who kept their families in the native villages, and to the temporary inmigration of males during the slack agricultural seasons. This, of course, resulted in an extremely high male sex ratio among the urban population. It would seem reasonable to assume that such characteristics (not necessarily for the same reasons) are still apparent in the cities of China today, although women probably constitute a somewhat larger share of the new urban migrants.

As mentioned above, it is difficult to draw a sharp line between the working and nonworking population in China today. With the creation of urban communes, women were "liberated" from their household chores, old men and women and young children were absorbed into productive activities—if not in the established plants and offices, then in the block production and service teams. The exact extent of their participation is not always clear, and although the press and radio make much of the fact that everyone works, many of these people contribute only in a marginal capacity. Because the nature and degree of the productive contribution would vary with each person and would depend on the criteria adopted, an individual may or may not be included in the labor force. Because the Communists apparently do not provide these criteria, the demarcations between the working and the nonworking population remain obscure. An estimate—one that would include all the full-time workers as well as some marginal workers—would place the urban labor force at about 55 to 60 percent of the urban population.

Workers and Employees

Until 1958 the data on workers and employees were more complete and more usable than on any other segment of the labor force. Although many unanswered questions remain about specific figures and about some of the concepts utilized in defining this category, it was nevertheless possible to regard the workers and employees as the nucleus of the urban labor force, and to some extent the country's economic growth could be measured by the increase in their numbers. As in other quantitative data, there were discrepancies of various degrees in the figures for any specific year. In some instances the differences were due to the fact that one figure may have been an annual average while another may have been an end-of-year figure. In other instances the differences were so large that an explanation was more difficult to find. Table 4 presents one of the integrated series of statistics on workers and employees and compares their growth with that of the urban population.

TABLE 4.—*Growth in the number of workers and employees, 1949–58*
[End-of-year figures]

Year	Number of workers and employees (millions) [1]	Urban population (millions) [2]	Workers and employees as percent of urban population
1949...............................	8.0	57.7	13.9
1950...............................	10.2	61.7	16.6
1951...............................	12.8	66.3	19.3
1952...............................	15.8	71.6	22.1
1953...............................	18.3	77.7	23.5
1954...............................	18.8	81.6	23.1
1955...............................	19.1	82.9	23.0
1956...............................	24.2	89.2	27.2
1957...............................	24.5	92.3	26.6
1958...............................	45.3	95.7	47.4
1959...............................	44.2	100.0	44.2

[1] *Ten Great Years* (State Statistical Bureau, 1960). All figures include a small proportion of workers and employees in agriculture (including forestry and fishing): 1950, 43,000; 1952, 97,000; 1953, 111,000; 1954, 137,000; 1955, 134,000 (V. A. Zhamin, *Selskoye Khozyaystvo Kitaya* [Agriculture in China], Moskva; 1959). See text for a discussion of the 1958 figure of 45.3 million. The figure for 1959 is based on a report that the number of workers and employees increased by 19,650,000 between the end of 1957 and the end of 1959 (*New China News Agency*, Jan. 28, 1960). There have also been several textual reports indicating a slight decrease in the number of workers and employees between 1958 and 1959.

[2] See table 2. Figures therefrom as of Jan. 1 of each year are shown here as representing end-of-year figures of each prior year.

To a large extent the tripling in the number of workers and employees between 1949 and 1957 was the result of reclassification of persons who, although part of the labor force, were not included in the worker-and-employee category. This divergency between the size of the urban labor force and the number of workers and employees may be contrasted with the situation in the Soviet Union where workers and employees constitute virtually all of the urban labor force. The millions of persons outside of this category were engaged in such occupations as private and quasi-private trade, unorganized handicrafts, military personnel, domestics and other service personnel, casual laborers, and coolies. To some extent the relative effect of reclassification as opposed to outright growth in numbers may be seen from the almost steady increase in the percent that workers and employees constituted of the urban population (table 4).

The almost doubling of the number of workers and employees between the end of 1957 and the end of 1958 obviously reflects a policy change and requires some comment. This was the period of the "great leap forward" when great efforts were made to get as many persons into the labor force as possible, and millions of women were forced to leave their homes and children in order to engage in some form of productive or service activity. Table 5 presents figures on the growth of women among the workers and employees. Despite this growth, women constituted only 3.7 million of the 20.8-million increase in workers and employees during 1958. The theory that the Chinese concept of workers and employees now approximates more closely the Soviet definition, since the figure of 45.3 million begins to approach the estimated size of the urban labor force, is not precisely correct because certain segments of the rural labor force are undoubtedly included in this total. Specifically: "The number of workers and employees for 1958 includes those employed in the newly opened industrial establishments at the county [hsien] level and below and the workers and employees in those industrial and commercial enterprises, grain agencies, and cultural and educational organizations which the state transferred to the people's communes." [16] The inclusion of the rural population seems to be further confirmed by the fact that four-fifths of the total increase during this one year has been assigned to the growth of workers in industry.[17] Since it is obvious that the existing and new urban industrial enterprises could not possibly have absorbed 16.6 million workers in only 12 months, the figure must include the workers engaged in the "industrial" enterprises set up not only in the urban but also in the rural communes. Although workers in the average commune industries are probably excluded from the 45.3 million, it is reported that those factories that proved to be above average in amount and quality of production were transferred by the state from commune ownership to the ownership by the "whole people," under the management of the responsible industrial ministry. The laborers in such enterprises, by definition, became workers and employees. How widespread this practice has been is difficult to say; however, it may have involved several million people.

---

[16] *Ten Great Years* (Peking: State Statistical Bureau, 1960).

[17] The series of workers in industry referred to here is presented in table 7. The totals are somewhat larger than in the series presented in table 6. The reason for the discrepancy between the two series is not immediately apparent.

TABLE 5.—*Growth of women among the workers and employees, 1949–58*

Year	Number of women	Percent of total workers and employees (from table 4)	Year	Number of women	Percent of total workers and employees (from table 4)
1949.......	600,000	7.5	1955.......	2,473,000	13.0
1952.......	1,848,000	11.7	1956.......	3,266,000	13.5
1953.......	2,132,000	11.7	1957.......	3,286,000	13.4
1954.......	2,435,000	12.9	1958.......	7,000,000	15.4

Source: *Ten Great Years* (Peking: State Statistical Bureau, 1960).

Because of the difficulty introduced by the 1958 data, there are at least two approaches open to an analysis of the urban labor force. The first is the acceptance of the 45.3-million figure for workers and employees as of the end of 1958, despite the fact that the exact components of this figure are not known. The other approach would be to estimate the size of this group on the basis of past growth trends and to postpone the use of the larger figure until it is more fully explained by the Peking regime. In this analysis the second approach is selected, and an average rate of growth between 1951 and 1957 is applied to the number of workers and employees in 1957 to derive an estimated 28.2 million by the end of 1958 and 32.3 million by the end of 1959. Both figures are within the frame of reference utilized by the pre-1958 definition of workers and employees.[18]

A complete distribution of the workers and employees by specific categories is not available, and for the most part only scattered figures are reported. The distribution within the so-called production categories is more complete (table 6). Although the proportion of workers and employees in industry, construction, and transportation and communications has remained virtually constant, there have been significant internal shifts. The only proportional growth is observed in the construction category, while transportation and communications, and particularly industry, have shown relative decline. Within the production categories subtotal, the proportion of the labor force in industry has dropped from 78.5 percent in 1949, to 70.7 percent in 1952, to 61.4 percent in 1956, and to an estimated 58.7 percent by the end of 1959. It must be stressed, however, that in absolute numbers this category has shown an average annual increase of about 600,000.

---

[18] A detailed study with a somewhat different interpretation of the labor force data will become available in a projected publication: John Philip Emerson, *Industry Employment in Mainland China, 1952–57, and Its Relation to Nonagricultural Employment* (Washington: U.S. Department of Commerce, Bureau of the Census, Foreign Manpower Research Office).

TABLE 6.—*Occupational distribution of urban workers and employees between production and "other" categories*

[Numbers in thousands]

Category group	1949[1]		1952[1]		1956[1]		1959[2]	
	Number	Percent	Number	Percent	Number	Percent	Number	Percent
Total of production categories............	3,900	48.7	7,440	47.1	11,680	48.1	15,500	48.0
Industry..........................	3,060	(78.5)	5,260	(70.7)	7,170	(61.4)	9,100	(58.7)
Construction......................	200	(5.1)	1,050	(14.1)	2,950	(25.3)	4,400	(28.4)
Transportation and communications......	640	(16.4)	1,130	(15.2)	1,560	(13.3)	2,000	(12.9)
Total of "other" categories (health, education, commerce, etc.)...............	4,100	51.3	8,360	52.9	12,600	51.9	16,800	52.0
Total, all categories.................	8,000	100.0	15,800	100.0	24,280	100.0	32,300	100.0

[1] *T'ung-chi Kung-tso* [Statistical Work], No. 14, 1957. Some of the totals differ slightly from those reported in the *Ten Great Years*.

[2] The total of 32.3 million workers and employees refers to the urban segment of the labor force and was estimated by assuming a continuation of the average rate of growth reported between 1951 and 1957 (see text). Because of the stability in the percent that the production categories comprised of the total workers and employees for the reported years, an average of 48 percent was applied to derive the 15.5-million estimate for those categories as of the end of 1959. The same rates of growth that were observed for industry and for transportation and communications between 1952 and 1956 were applied to each category, respectively, to project it to the end of 1959. The number of persons in the construction category was then derived as a residual after subtracting the sum of industry and of transportation and communications from the production categories. The more modest growth represented by the figure of 4.4 million for construction is realistic in view of the extremely rapid expansion that this category has undergone between 1952 and 1956, a rate of expansion probably not sustained on a continuing basis.

Comparison of the Number of Professionals and Semiprofessionals With the Total Workers and Employees

It would be ideally desirable to determine the percentage of workers and employees in each branch of the Chinese economy who are professionals and semiprofessionals. However, it is only possible to present rough ratios between persons with certain educational attainments and some broad categories of the workers and employees.

It is estimated that after graduations in 1959 there were a total of 170,000 persons with college degrees in engineering in China (ch. VI, table 2). The number of workers and employees in the overall production categories—industry, construction, and transportation and communications—has been estimated at 15,500,000 as of the end of 1959 (table 6). Thus, holders of degrees in engineering comprise only a fraction over 1 percent of these categories. If only the workers and employees in industry are compared, this percentage goes up to 1.9 percent. Of course not all the graduates in engineering work in industry, construction, and transportation and communications; some of them may be in univerisities, in the Academy of Sciences, or in some unrelated field. On the other hand, persons who may have received their degrees in some other field of specialization may now be working as technicians in industrial plants. But regardless of these factors, the ratio of nearly 100 workers in the production categories to every engineer in the country with a completed higher education, wherever he may be working, is worth noting in gaging the level of China's industrial economy. About 2½ percent of the workers and employees outside the production categories have completed higher education.

A comparison between workers and employees and persons with a secondary technical education would be still more tenuous, particularly since a person at this level may attain certain skills and knowledge through experience and on-the-job training that would place him on at least an equal level with a graduate of a secondary vocational school. However, table 7, below, does bring together two series of figures, both of which were reported in the same source and which make it possible to compare workers in industry with the engineering and technical personnel (both professional and semiprofessional). Although the source does not say specifically who is included under the heading "engineering and technical personnel," the numbers would suggest that the size of this category approximately equates with the technical graduates from higher and secondary schools. The slow increase in the proportion of such personnel to the total number of workers in industry took a sudden dip from 5.5 percent to 2.4 percent between 1957 and 1958. It must be remembered, however, that the 1958 figure for "industrial" workers probably includes those in urban and rural commune industries; therefore the ratio of 1 professional or semiprofessional technician to every

20 workers in industry (1955 through 1957) is more realistic when applied to the established urban industrial enterprises of China.

TABLE 7.—*Engineering and technical personnel as percent of total workers in industry, 1952–58*

[Numbers in thousands]

Year	Total workers in industry	Engineering and technical personnel	Percent
1952	4,939	164	3.3
1953	6,188	210	3.4
1954	6,408	262	4.1
1955	6,477	344	5.3
1956	8,626	449	5.2
1957	9,008	496	5.5
1958	25,623	618	2.4

Source: *Ten Great Years* (Peking: State Statistical Bureau, 1960). Although the source states that the figures pertain to "workers in industry," they differ from those reported in table 6. The industrial workers in this table cover the 3 production categories (industry, construction, and transportation and communications), but include only personnel directly engaged in production for the years 1952 through 1957. In all probability the 1958 figure of 25,623,000 includes both the personnel engaged in production and in administrative, service, and other activities within the production sector of the economy. The latter figure also includes persons engaged in "industrial" enterprises in the urban and rural communes (see text). The number of engineering and technical personnel approximately equates with the number of persons with technical secondary and higher education.

It may also be appropriate at this point to mention a broader category which in certain respects represents the top echelon of the Chinese labor force even more accurately than the persons who have attained certain educational qualifications. This is the group that is repeatedly referred to in the Communist press as "intellectuals." Millions of words have been written in China over the past several years, particularly during the rectification campaign, on scores of problems pertaining to intellectuals, but a precise definition of this group has never been given. From the descriptive and quantitative data, however, it is clear that among the intellectuals are included virtually all the persons with university and college degrees and most of those who have completed secondary schools. Also included in this group are people with little formal education who have attained a certain status by virtue of practical experience or political conformity, such as Government employees, shop foremen in plants and factories, Communist Party officials, or officers in the Red army. Loosely defined, they are the middle and higher echelons of the white-collar workers and all others who do not claim some form of physical labor as their main occupation.

The "about 5-odd million" intellectuals reported to be in existence in 1958 [19] were located primarily in the urban areas; it is extremely unlikely that many of them were in the rural areas, especially since it has been reported that a peasant-intellectual is anyone who has had 5 years of primary education. They comprised approximately 10 percent of the urban labor force, forming the backbone of the Chinese economic aand political system.[20]

[19] *Chi-hua Ching-chi* [Planned Economy], May 1958.

[20] For a detailed description and analysis of the trials and tribulations of intellectuals in Communist China, see Theodore H. E. Chen, *Thought Reform of the Chinese Intellectuals,* Hong Kong: University Press, 1960.

APPENDICES

APPENDICES

APPENDIX A
Tables on Education

TABLE A-1.—*Estimated number of 1913-47 graduates of senior secondary schools surviving to 1960*

Year	Enrollment [1]			Graduates [2]				Surviving graduates, 1960 [4]			
	Senior general	Senior normal	Senior vocational	Senior general	Senior normal	Senior vocational	Survival rate [3]	Senior general	Senior normal	Senior vocational	Total
1913–17	73,066	56,475	23,921	14,029	12,763	4,952	0.451	6,327	5,756	2,233	14,316
1918–22	88,884	68,657	34,640	17,066	15,516	7,170	.546	9,318	8,472	3,915	21,705
1923–27	120,876	69,433	38,265	23,208	15,691	7,921	.630	14,621	9,885	4,990	29,496
1928–32	264,152	207,898	46,044	50,717	46,985	9,531	.703	35,654	33,030	6,700	75,384
1933–37	357,236	164,279	83,881	58,884	41,570	20,771	.766	45,105	31,843	15,911	92,859
1938–42	528,101	120,256	104,973	91,381	27,362	20,017	.821	75,024	22,464	16,434	113,922
1943–47	1,115,928	330,060	231,208	214,258	74,593	47,860	.870	186,404	64,896	41,638	292,938
Total	....	....	....	469,543	234,480	118,222	....	372,453	176,346	91,821	640,620

1 Total enrollment in general, normal and vocational secondary schools was reported for all but 9 years (*Chung-kuo Chiao-yu Nien-chien* [Chinese Educational Yearbook], Shanghai: Ministry of Education, 1948). The missing years were derived by interpolation. The enrollment in the senior levels of these schools was given in the same source, but only for the years 1931 through 1945. Since there was a fairly consistent correlation between senior school students and total enrollment within the 3 types of scoools ((e.g., in 1932 senior secondary school students constituted 15 percent of total secondary school students; in 1933, 16 percent; in 1934, 17 percent; in 1935, 19 percent; in 1936, 18 percent; in 1937, 16 percent; in 1938, 16 percent), a proportion of 16 percent over a period of 15 years was utilized to estimate senior school enrollment for the missing years. This enrollment was then combined into 5-year groups, to minimize the possible error.

2 The number of graduates from the 3 types of secondary schools is reported for the years 1931 through 1945 (*Chung-kuo Chiao-yu Nien-chien* [Chinese Educational Yearbook], Shanghai; Ministry of Education, 1948). To estimate graduates for the missing years, correlations between enrollment and graduates was derived on the basis of reported years: 19.2 percent for general secondary schools, 22.6 percent for normal schools, and 20.7 percent for vocational schools.

3 Survival rates were calculated from United Nations model life tables (*Methods for Population Projections by Sex and Age*, Population Studies, No. 25, New York: United Nations, Department of Economic and Social Affairs, 1956), assuming a male life expectancy of 40 and the average age of graduation as 17%. Of course, strictly speaking, a life expectancy of 40 is not appropriate for the whole period covered.

4 Because the total of 640,620 excludes the graduates of 1948, it is arbitrarily adjusted upward to 700,000 in the text. This figure represents an estimate of all living persons who completed secondary education prior to the Communist regime.

169

TABLE A-2.—*Enrollment in secondary schools, most years, both levels, 1912–46*

School year	General	Normal	Vocational	Total
1912–13................	59, 971	28, 525	9, 469	97, 965
1913–14................	72, 251	34, 826	10, 256	117, 333
1914–15................	82, 778	26, 679	9, 600	119, 057
1915–16................	87, 929	27, 975	10, 551	126, 455
1916–17................	75, 595	24, 959	10, 524	111, 078
1922–23................	118, 658	43, 846	20, 300	182, 804
1925–26................	129, 978	37, 992	18, 011	185, 981
1928–29................	188, 700	29, 470	16, 641	234, 811
1929–30................	248, 668	65, 695	26, 659	341, 022
1930–31................	396, 948	82, 809	34, 852	514, 609
1931–32................	401, 772	94, 683	40, 393	536, 848
1932–33................	409, 586	99, 606	38, 015	547, 207
1933–34................	415, 948	100, 840	42, 532	559, 320
1934–35................	401, 449	93, 675	46, 355	541, 479
1935–36................	438, 113	84, 512	50, 637	573, 262
1936–37................	482, 522	87, 902	56, 822	627, 246
1937–38................	309, 563	48, 793	31, 592	389, 948
1938–39................	389, 009	56, 679	31, 897	477, 585
1939–40................	524, 395	59, 431	38, 977	622, 803
1940–41................	642, 688	78, 342	47, 503	768, 533
1941–42................	703, 756	91, 239	51, 557	846, 552
1942–43................	831, 716	109, 009	61, 009	1, 001, 734
1943–44................	902, 163	130, 995	67, 929	1, 101, 087
1944–45................	929, 297	157, 806	76, 010	1, 163, 113
1945–46................	1, 262, 199	202, 163	102, 030	1, 566, 392
1946–47................	1, 495, 874	245, 609	137, 040	1, 878, 523

Source: *Chung-kuo Chiao-yu Nien-chien* [Chinese Educational Yearbook] (Shanghai: Ministry of Education, 1948).

TABLE A-3.—*Senior secondary school graduates, 1931–45*

Year	General	Normal	Vocational	Total
1931.....................	10, 761	15, 984	....	26, 745
1932.....................	12, 240	13, 625	2, 988	28, 853
1933.....................	9, 591	10, 717	3, 272	23, 580
1934.....................	13, 161	7, 617	4, 779	25, 557
1935.....................	13, 161	7, 617	4, 779	25, 557
1936.....................	13, 270	11, 225	4, 447	28, 942
1937.....................	9, 701	4, 394	3, 494	17, 589
1938.....................	10, 188	4, 594	3, 111	17, 893
1939.....................	11, 763	5, 511	2, 411	19, 685
1940.....................	15, 279	4, 437	3, 438	23, 154
1941.....................	22, 833	6, 107	5, 014	33, 954
1942.....................	31, 318	6, 713	6, 043	44, 074
1943.....................	37, 257	7, 491	6, 393	51, 141
1944.....................	41, 667	9, 438	6, 612	57, 717
1945.....................	53, 125	13, 069	8, 705	74, 899
Total.............	305, 315	128, 539	65, 486	499, 340

Source: *Chung-kuo Chiao-yu Nien-chien* [Chinese Educational Yearbook] (Shanghai: Ministry of Education, 1948).

TABLE A-4.—*Distribution of graduates from higher educational establishments, by field, 1928–47*

Year	Total	Engineering	Sciences	Agriculture and forestry	Health	Political science and law	Education	Finance and economics	Literature and arts
Prior to 1927	28,569	.....	.....	.....	.....	.....	.....	.....	.....
1928	3,253	302	285	73	79	1,420	398	219	477
1929	4,164	434	280	98	122	1,681	446	276	827
1930	4,583	412	308	153	137	1,898	561	234	883
1931	7,034	932	435	361	232	2,560	519	454	1,541
1932	7,311	897	512	375	259	2,713	625	516	1,404
1933	8,665	1,008	698	473	383	3,175	1,189	583	1,156
1934	9,622	1,163	924	410	309	3,478	1,374	697	1,267
1935	8,673	1,037	996	416	388	2,596	792	707	1,741
1936	9,154	1,322	935	361	418	2,667	718	719	2,014
1937	5,137	969	794	282	400	1,059	512	324	797
1938	5,085	1,083	737	303	350	1,182	460	387	583
1939	5,622	1,208	799	435	336	1,312	418	389	725
1940	7,710	1,773	881	632	546	1,685	585	753	855
1941	8,035	1,783	856	820	649	1,831	517	798	781
1942	9,056	1,949	735	840	621	1,913	1,231	1,051	716
1943	10,514	1,886	723	1,016	669	2,511	1,317	1,471	921
1944	12,078	2,197	903	1,064	582	2,579	1,739	1,743	1,311
1945	14,436	2,643	892	1,263	748	3,403	1,905	2,027	1,582
1946	20,185	3,900	1,419	1,663	1,035	4,769	2,539	2,630	2,230
1947	25,098	4,792	1,701	2,064	1,236	6,350	3,250	2,969	2,736
Total	213,984	31,690	15,813	13,102	9,499	50,782	21,095	18,947	24,547

Blanks indicate figures are not available.

Source: *Chung-kuo Chiao-yu Nien-chien* [China Educational Yearbook] (Shanghai: Ministry of Education, 1948).

TABLE A–5.—*Proportion of women among students in institutions of higher education, 1932–46; distributed by field of specialization, 1934–46*

[In percent]

Year	Total	Engineering	Sciences	Agriculture and forestry	Health	Political science and law	Education	Finance and economics	Literature and arts
1932	12.1								
1933	13.7								
1934	15.0	1.7	18.4	4.5	17.9	7.8	32.1	14.6	25.7
1935	15.5	2.3	12.1	3.7	17.1	8.7	43.6	16.5	21.5
1936	15.2	2.0	19.6	4.3	20.3	8.9	34.2	15.3	22.5
1937	17.2	2.4	23.2	7.4	22.4	11.4	34.0	19.6	29.7
1938	18.4	3.9	23.7	10.3	30.0	13.4	35.3	17.4	28.7
1939	17.6	2.9	23.5	10.9	24.8	14.5	33.5	21.9	26.6
1940	19.5	3.5	24.7	12.7	28.4	14.4	35.7	24.7	33.9
1941	19.8	4.8	25.2	14.4	30.9	15.5	34.1	23.7	30.9
1942	19.1	4.7	24.7	14.5	32.2	13.5	32.8	21.7	27.9
1943	18.6	4.1	24.9	14.8	31.4	12.7	31.8	22.4	25.9
1944	18.8	4.1	24.7	15.3	32.1	12.4	31.4	20.5	27.2
1945	19.0	3.7	26.4	17.4	35.2	11.3	31.1	20.1	26.8
1946	18.3	2.6	26.4	13.5	27.8	11.5	31.3	22.2	28.2

Blanks indicate figures are not available.

Source: Calculated from data reported in *Chung-kuo Chiao-yu Nien-chien* [China Educational Yearbook] (Shanghai: Ministry of Education, 1948).

APPENDIX B

Sample Curriculums

TABLE B–1.—*Instruction program for elementary schools for the 1957–58 school year*

[Hours per week]

Subjects	Grades						Total annual hours
	1	2	3	4	5	6	
Chinese language and literature.	12	12	12	12	10	10	2, 312
Arithmetic...................	6	6	6	6	6	6	1, 224
Nature study...............	.....	.....	.....	.....	2	2	136
Geography..................	.....	.....	.....	.....	2	2	136
History....................	.....	.....	.....	.....	2	2	136
Basic agriculture (village schools)...................	.....	.....	.....	.....	1	1	204
Handiwork..................	1	1	1	1	.....	.....	....
Physical education...........	2	2	2	2	2	2	408
Singing....................	1	1	1	1	1	1	204
Drawing...................	1	1	1	1	1	1	204
Weekly students' meetings.....	1	1	1	1	1	1	204
Total hours.............	24	24	24	24	28	28	....

Source: U.S. Joint Publications Research Service, *A Few Notes on Chinese Elementary Education*, Mar. 9, 1959. Translated from *Komonsky* (Comonius), vol. 82, No. 4, Prague, April 1958.

TABLE B–2.—*Curriculum for secondary schools, 1957–58*

[Hours per week [1]]

Subjects	Junior secondary school			Senior secondary school		
	1st year	2d year	3d year	1st year	2d year	3d year
Chinese:						
Language........	3	2	2	....	....	....
Literature........	5	5	5	5	5	5
Mathematics:						
Arithmetic.......	6	....	....	....	....	....
Algebra..........	....	4 or 3	2	4/3	2	2
Geometry........	....	4 or 3	3	2/3	2	2
Trigonometry.....	....	....	....	....	2	2
History:						
Chinese..........	3	3	....	....	3	3
World...........	....	....	3	....	....	....
Contemporary....	....	....	....	3	....	....
Political Education....	2	1	1	2	2	2
Geography:						
Physical.........	3	....	....	....	....	....
Natural..........	....	2/3	....	....	....	....
Chinese..........	....	....	3/2	....	....	....
Economic........	....	....	....	....	2	....
Biology:						
Botany..........	3	2	....	....	....	....
Zoology.........	....	2/4	2	....	....	....
Human anatomy..	....	....	....	....	2	....
Physics................	....	3/2	2	3	3	5
Chemistry.............	....	....	2/3	2	2	3
Foreign language......	3	....	....	4	4	4
Physical training......	2	2	2	2	2	2
Music................	1	1	1	....	....	....
Drawing.............	1	1	1	....	....	....
Agriculture...........	....	....	2	....	....	....
Total [1]........	32/32	32 or 30/34 or 32.	31/31	27/27	31/31	30/30

[1] The figure on the left side of the stroke is the number of hours for the 1st semester, and to the right side, the number of hours for the 2d semester; otherwise, hours are the same for each semester. The sum of the hours in each column did not add to the total stated in the source, which was not explained; they have been changed hereon.

Source: U.S. Joint Publications Research Service, *Education in Communist China*, Rept. No. 753, Oct. 16, 1958.

TABLE B–3.—*Curriculum for secondary normal schools, 1957–58*

[Hours per week [1]]

Subjects	1st year	2d year	3d year
Language and instruction methods of language in primary schools:			
Chinese	2	2	2
Literature	4	4	5
Instruction methods of language in primary schools	....	....	2
Mathematics and instruction methods for mathematics in primary schools:			
Mathematics	....	2	....
Algebra	3	....	....
Geometry	2	2	2/–
Instruction methods	....	....	2/3
Physics	2	3	2/–
Chemistry	3	....	....
Human anatomy	2	....	....
Geography:			
Physical	2/–	....	....
Chinese	–/2	2/–	....
World	....	–/2	....
History:			
World contemporary	2	....	....
Chinese	....	3	3
Politics	2	2	2
Psychology	....	2/1	....
Education	....	2	3
Physical education	2	1/2	1/2
Art	2	2/1	1/2
Practice teaching	....	1	3/4
Total hours per week [1]	28/28	28/27	28/28
Total weeks per term	18/17	18/17	18/13

[1] The figure on the left side of the stroke is the number of hours for the 1st semester, and to the right side, the number of hours for the 2d semester; otherwise, hours are the same for each semester. The sum of the hours in each column did not add to the total stated in the source, which was not explained; they have been changed hereon.

Source: U.S. Joint Publications Research Service, *Education in Communist China*, Rept. No. 753, Oct. 16, 1958.

APPENDIX C

Institutions of Higher Education

AUTHOR'S NOTE.—The basic list of institutions of higher education, their departments, and fields of specialization were taken from Current Background, No. 462, July 1, 1957 (Hong Kong: U.S. consulate general). It is a translation of a brochure issued by the Ministry of Higher Education entitled "Guide to Institutions of Higher Education." Although it was published over 3 years ago (March 1957), it appears to be the most current and the most comprehensive list released by the Chinese Communists. It must be pointed out, however, that a comparison of this listing with almost any other will reveal numerous discrepancies, not only in the institutions that may be included or excluded, but also in the names and even locations of some of the schools. One possible advantage in a 1957 listing is that it includes only the bona fide institutions of higher education and excludes the "red and expert" colleges and other institutions representing the era of the "great leap forward." Minor revisions and additions have been incorporated into the listing to make it reflect some of the known changes that have occurred during the past several years. The number appearing in parenthesis following the name of the institution represents the number of years in the regular course. Exceptions appear in parenthesis following the names of departments or specific courses.

Types of Institutions

COMPREHENSIVE UNIVERSITIES

1. *Amoy University* (4), Amoy:
   Arts:
   > Departments of Chinese Language and Literature (5); Foreign Languages and Literature (5); History.
   Science:
   > Departments of Mathematics; Physics; Chemistry; Biology (including zoology and botany).

Finance and Economics:
    Department of Economics (political economics, money and credit, trade economics, statistics, and accountancy).
2. *Anhwei University* (5), Wuhu:
    Departments of Chemistry; Physics; History; and Geography.
3. *Chengchow University* (5), Chengchow:
    Science:
    Departments of Mathematics; Physics; and Chemistry.
4. *China People's University* (5), Peking:
    Arts:
        Departments of History; Philosophy; Historical Archives (4); Journalism.
    Finance and economics:
        Departments of Economics (political economics); Planning and Statistics (planning of national economy and statistics); Industrial Economics; Agricultural Economics; Trade Economics; Finance.
    Political science and law:
        Department of Law.
5. *Chinan University,* Canton:
    Departments of Mathematics; Preindustrial; Mining and Geology; and Marine Products.
6. *Chungshan University* (4), Kuangchow:
    Arts:
        Departments of Chinese Language and Literature; Western Languages and Literature (English Language and literature, French language and literature); History; Philosophy.
    Science:
        Departments of Mathematics; Physics; Chemistry; Biology (zoology and botany); Geography (natural geography and economic geography).
6. *Futan University* (5), Shanghai:
    Arts:
        Departments of Chinese Language and Literature; Western Languages and Literature; History; Journalism; and Philosophy.
    Science:
        Departments of Mathematics; Physics; Chemistry; Biology (zoology, botany, human and animal physiology, vegetable physiology, and anthropology).
    Finance and economics:
        Department of Economics (political economics).
    Political science and law:
        Department of Law.

8. *Inner Mongolia University* (4), Huhehot:
    Arts:
        Departments of Chinese Language and Literature (including Mongolian language and literature); History.
    Science:
        Departments of Mathematics; Physics; Chemistry; and Biology (including zoology and botany).
9. *Kirin University* (5), Changchun:
    Arts:
        Departments of Chinese Language and Literature; History.
    Science:
        Departments of Mathematics; Physics; and Chemistry.
    Finance and economics:
        Department of Economics (political economics).
    Political science and law:
        Department of Law.
10. *Lanchow University* (5), Lanchow:
    Arts:
        Departments of Chinese Language and Literature; History.
    Science:
        Departments of Mathematics; Physics; Chemistry; Biology (zoology and botany); Geography (natural geography).
    Finance and economics (4):
        Department of Economics (accountancy).
11. *Nankai University* (5), Tientsin:
    Arts:
        Departments of Chinese Language and Literature; Western Languages and Literature; History.
    Science:
        Departments of Mathematics; Physics; Chemistry; Biology (zoology and botany).
    Finance and economics:
        Department of Economics (political economics, statistics (4), and accountancy (4).
12. *Nanking University* (5), Nanking:
    Arts:
        Departments of Chinese Language and Literature; Foreign Languages and Literature (Russian, English, German and and French); History.
    Science:
        Departments of Mathematics and Astronomy; Physics; Chemistry; Biology (zoology and botany); Geography; Geology (geology and geochemistry); Meteorology (meteorology and climatology).
13. *Northwest University* (4), Sian:
    Arts:
        Departments of Chinese Language and Literature; History.

Science:
> Departments of Mathematics; Physics; Chemistry; Biology (zoology and botany); Geography (natural geography); Geology.

Finance and economics:
> Department of Economics (industrial economics, statistics and accountancy).

Political science and law:
> Department of Law.

14. *Peking University* (5), Peking:

Arts:
> Departments of Chinese Language and Literature; Russian Language and Literature; Western Languages and Literature (English language and literature, Germany language and literature, and French language and literature); History; Philosophy (philosophy and psychology); Eastern Languages (Japanese language, Vietnamese language, and Arabic languages) (4)); Library Science.

Science:
> Departments of Mathematics and Mechanics (mathematics, mechanics, and mathematical calculations); Physics (physics and meteorology); Chemistry; Biology (zoology, botany, human and animal physiology; vegetable physiology and biological chemistry); Geology and Geography.

Finance and economics:
> Department of Economics.

Political science and law:
> Department of Law.

15. *Shantung University* (4), Tsingtao:

Arts:
> Departments of Chinese Language and Literature; History.

Science:
> Departments of Mathematics; Physics (Chemistry); Chemistry; Biology (zoology and botany); Oceanography.

16. *Szechwan University,* Chungking:

Arts:
> Departments of Chinese Language and Literature; History.

Science:
> Departments of Mathematics; Physics; Chemistry; Biology (zoology and botany).

Finance and economics:
> Department of Economics.

17. *Wuhan University* (5), Wuchang:

Arts:
> Departments of Chinese Language and Literature; Russian Language and Literature (4); History; Philosophy; Library Science (4).

17. *Wuhan University* (5), Wuchang—Continued
   Science:
   >Departments of Mathematics; Physics; Chemistry; Biology (zoology and botany).

   Finance and economics:
   >Department of Economics.

   Political science and law:
   >Department of Law.

18. *Yunnan University* (4), Kunming:
   Arts:
   >Departments of Chinese Language and Literature; History.

   Science:
   >Departments of Mathematics; Physics; Chemistry; Biology (zoology and botany).

   Agriculture:
   >Department of Agriculture and Forestry.

INSTITUTIONS OF TECHNOLOGY

1. *Central China Engineering Institute* (5), Wuchang:
   Department of Dynamics (thermal energy dynamic equipment; hydraulic and dynamic equipment; industrial thermal engineering).

   Department of Electric Power (electric power stations, networks and systems; electrification of industrial enterprises; electrical machines and appliances; automation and kinematics; radio techniques).

   Department of Machine Building (technology of machine building and lathes and tools for metal cutting; technology of and machinery for casting; pressure processing of metals and machinery for the purpose; metallography and heat treatment workshop equipment; machinery and equipment for metal refineries).

2. *Central South Institute of Civil Engineering* (5), Changsha:
   Department of Building Construction (industrial and civil building construction; water supply and drainage).

   Department of Railway Construction (including railway management).

   Department of Bridges and Tunnels (railway bridges and tunnels).

   Department of Road Construction (highways and roads in cities).

3. *Central South Institute of Mining and Metallurgy* (5), Changsha:
   Department of Geological Mineral Prospecting (mineral geology and surveying; mineral prospecting engineering; geological surveying and mineral prospecting).

   Department of Mining (mining of mineral deposits; electromechanical mining; surveying of mines).

   Department of Metallurgy (refining and processing on nonferrous metals; metallography and heat treatment of nonferrous metals and their alloys; pressure processing of nonferrous metals and their alloys).

4. *Changchun Institute of Automobiles and Tractors* (5), Changchun:

Department of Automobiles and Tractors.

Department of Machine Building (technology of machine building and lathes and tools for metal cuttings; technology of and machinery for casting; agricultural machines; economy and organization of machine building industry).

5. *Changchun Institute of Geological Survey* (4), Changchun:

Department of Mineral Geology and Survey (geological surveying and mineral prospecting; mineral geology and survey).

Department of Geophysical Survey (geophysical survey of metals and nonmetals; geophysical survey of petroleum and natural gases).

Department of Hydrographic and Engineering Geology (hydrographic geology and engineering geology).

6. *Chekiang University* (5) Hangchow:

Department of Electrical Engineering (electrical machines and appliances; electric power stations, networks and systems; electrification of industrial enterprises; radio techniques; thermal energy dynamic equipment).

Department of Mechanical Engineering (technology of machine building and lathes and tools for metal cutting; technology of and machinery for casting; optical machines and instruments).

Department of Chemical Engineering (fuel chemical engineering; machinery and equipment for production of chemicals; automation and conditioning of technological process for production of chemicals).

Department of Civil Engineering (industrial and civil building construction).

Department of Water Conservancy (structure of rivers and water conservancy engineering construction for hydroelectric power stations).

Mathematics (department not yet determined).

Physics (department not yet determined).

7. *Chengtu Engineering Institute* (4), Chengtu:

Department of Mechanical Engineering (technology of machine building).

Department of Electrical Engineering (electric power stations, networks and systems).

Department of Chemical Engineering (inorganic matter engineering; machinery and equipment for production of chemicals; plastic engineering; basic organic compounds; sugar produce engineering).

Department of Water Conservancy (structure of rivers and water conservancy engineering construction for hydroelectric power stations; land hydrography).

Department of Civil Engineering (highways and roads in cities; roads, bridges and tunnels).

8. *Chengtu Institute of Geological Survey* (4), Chengtu:

Department of Mineral Geology and Survey (geological surveying and mineral prospecting; mineral geology and survey).

Department of Hydrographic and Engineering Geology (hydrographic geology and engineering geology).

Department of Geology and Survey of Petroleum and Natural Gases (geology and survey of petroleum and natural gases).

9. *Chengtu Institute of Tele-Communications Engineering* (5), Chengtu:

Department of Radio Equipment Designing and Manufacturing.

Department of Telegraphic Equipment Designing and Manufacturing.

Department of Radio Spare Parts Manufacturing.

Department of Electronic Appliances and Equipment Designing and Manufacturing.

10. *Chiaotung University* (5), Sian:

Department of Machine Building (technology of machine building and lathes and tools for metal cutting; pressure processing of metals and machinery for the purpose; metallography and heat treatment workshop equipment; technology of and machinery for casting; welding technology and equipment).

Department of Dynamic Machine Building (internal combustion engines; turbine building; boilermaking; thermal energy dynamic equipment; cooling machines and compressors and their installation).

Department of Transportation Machine and Crane Building (cranes and transportation machines and their equipment; steam engine building; internal combustion engine building; electric engine building; wagon building).

Department of Electrical Appliances Manufacturing (dynamics and electrical appliances; electrical insulation and telegraph cable techniques).

Department of Electric Power Engineering (electric power stations, networks and systems; electrification of industrial enterprises; high tension techniques).

Department of Radio Electrical Engineering (radio techniques; automation and kinomatics; mathematics and calculation instruments).

Mechanics and Mathematics (department not yet determined).

11. *China University of Science and Technology,* Peking:

Departments: Nuclear Physics and Engineering; Technical Physics; Applied Geophysics; Chemical Physics; Radio Electronics; Radiation Chemistry; Thermodynamics; High Polymer Chemistry; Applied Mathematics and Computers; Dynamics; Biophysics; Automation; and Geochemistry and Rare Elements.

12. *Chungking Institute of Architectural Engineering* (5), Chungking:
Department of Architecture.
Department of Building Construction (4) (industrial and civil building construction).
Department of Health Engineering (4) (water supply and drainage; heating, gas supply and ventilation).

13. *Chungking University* (5), Chungking:
Department of Mining (mining of mineral deposits).
Department of Metallurgy (refining and processing of steel and iron).
Department of Machine Making (technology of machine making and lathes and tools for metal cutting; machinery and equipment for metal refineries; pressure processing of metals and machinery for the purpose).
Department of Dynamics (thermal energy dynamic equipment).
Department of Electrical Engineering (electric power stations, networks and systems; electrical machines and appliances).

14. *Dairen Engineering Institute* (5), Dairen:
Department of Mechanical Engineering (technology of machine making and lathes and tools for metal cutting; technology of and machinery for casting; cranes and transport machinery and equipment; electrification of industrial enterprises).
Department of Chemical Engineering (inorganic matter engineering; organic dyestuff and intermediary engineering; fuel chemical engineering; synthetic rubber engineering).
Department of Machinery for Chemical Engineering (machinery and equipment for production of chemicals).
Department of Water Conservancy Engineering (structure of rivers and water conservancy engineering construction for hydroelectric power stations; water conservancy engineering construction for waterways and ports).

15. *Dairen Institute of Marine Navigation* (5), Dairen:
Department of Navigation (navigation of ships).
Department of Turbines (dynamic equipment for ships; ship repairs).
Department of Navigation Management (management of marine navigation).

16. *East China Engineering Institute* (5), Shanghai:
Department of Chemical Engineering (machinery and equipment for production of chemicals).
Department of Inorganic Industrial Engineering (silicate engineering; inorganic matter engineering).
Department of Organic Industrial Engineering (basic organic compound engineering; fuel chemical engineering; organic dyestuff and intermediary engineering; pharmaceutic chemical engineering; antibiotics engineering; chemical engineering).

17. *East China Institute of Textile Industry* (4), Shanghai:
Department of Textile Engineering (fiber material mechanical engineering).

Department of Textile Mechanics (machinery and equipment for light industry; industrial thermal engineering).

Department of Chemical Engineering in Dyeing (fiber material chemical engineering; synthetic fiber engineering).

18. *East China Institute of Water Conservancy* (5), Nanking:
Department of Hydrography (land hydrography).
Department of River and Port Engineering (water conservancy engineering construction for hydroelectric power stations).

19. *Foochow University,* Foochow:
Departments of Mathematics; Physics; Chemistry; Mechanical Engineering; Civil Engineering; Electrical Engineering; Chemical Engineering; Mining and Metallurgy.

20. *Harbin University of Technology* (5), Harbin:
Department of Electrical Engineering (electric power stations, networks and systems; electrification of industrial enterprises; dynamos and electrical appliances; automation and kinomatics).
Department Mechanical Dynamics (boilermaking; turbine building; hydraulic machines).
Department of Machine Building (technology of machine building; lathes and tools for metal cutting).
Department of Mechanical Technology (metallography and heat treatment workshop equipment; welding technology and equipment; technology of and machinery for casting; pressure processing of metals and machinery; technology of and equipment for steel rolling).
Department of Instrument Making (precision machines and instruments; technology for making of instruments; electric automatic installations and measuring equipment; mathematics and calculating apparatus; spinning top instruments).
Department of Civil Engineering (industrial and civil building construction; heating, gas supply and ventilation; water supply and drainage).
Department of Engineering Economics (economy and organization of machine building industry; economy and organization of dynamic enterprises).
Department of Radio Engineering (radio techniques).

21. *Hofei Institute of Mining* (4), Hofei:
Department of Mining (mining of mineral deposits).
Department of Electro-Mechanical Mining (electromechanical mining; mining machinery).
Department of Mineral Geology and Shaft Construction (building construction for mining enterprises; mineral geology and survey).

22. *Kunming Engineering Institute* (4), Kunming:
Department of Mining (geological surveying and mineral prospecting; refining and processing of nonferrous metals).

23. *Nanking Engineering Institute* (5), Nanking:
Department of Dynamic Engineering (electric power stations, networks and systems; thermal energy dynamic equipment; electrification of industrial enterprises; industrial thermal engineering).

Department of Machine Building Engineering (technology of machine building and lathes and tools for metal cutting; technology of and machinery for casting; agricultural machines; machinery and equipment for building construction and roadbuilidng; machine designing).

Department of Radio Engineering (radio techniques; electronic appliances; industrial electronics).

Department of Chemical Engineering (silicate engineering; machinery and equipment for production of chemicals).

Department of Food Industry (fermentation engineering; food processing and storing industry; oil and fat engineering; food processing machines).

Department of Civil Engineering (industrial and civil building construction; highways and roads in cities; production of products and members for installation type structural concrete and reinforced concrete).

24. *Nanking Institute of Aeronautics* (5), Nanking:
Department of Aircraft.
Department of Engines.
Department of Aircraft Equipment.

25. *Nanyang Engineering Institute* (5), Shanghai:
Department of Machine Building (technology of machine building and lathes and lathes and tools for metal cutting; metallography and heat treatment workshop equipment).

Department of Electrical Engineering (electrical machines and appliances; electrical insulation and telegraph cable techniques).

26. *Northeast Engineering Institute* (5), Shenyang:
Department of Mining (mining of mineral deposits; building construction for mining enterprises).

Department of Steel and Iron Refining and Processing (refining and processing of steel and iron; furnaces).

Department of Steel and Iron Technology (pressure processing of steel and iron; casting; metallography and heat treatment of steel and iron).

Department of Non-Ferrous Metals (ore dressing; refining and processing of nonferrous metals; pressure processing of nonferrous metals and their alloys).

Department of Mechanical Engineering (technology of machine building and lathes and tools for metal cutting; machinery for mining; machinery and equipment for metal refineries).

Department of Electro-Mechanical Mining (electromechanical mining).

Department of Electric Power (electrification of industrial enterprises; engineering economics (now under the Department of Steel and Iron Refining and Processing: economy and organization of metallurgical industry).

27. *Northwest Engineering Institute* (5), Hsienyang:
Department of Mechanical Engineering (technology of machine building and lathes and tools for machine cutting; pressure proc-

essing of metals and machinery for the purpose; metallography and heat treatment workshop equipment).

Department of Textile Industry (fiber material mechanical engineering).

Department of Mining (mining of mineral deposits).

28. *Peking Institute of Aeronautics* (5), Peking:
Department of Aircraft.
Department of Engines.
Department of Aircraft Equipment.
Department of Air Navigation Technology and Economy.

29. *Peking Institute of Geological Survey* (5), Peking:
Department of Mineral Geology and Survey (mineral geology and survey; geological surveying and mineral prospecting).
Department of Geological Survey for Petroleum and Natural Gases (geology and survey of petroleum and natural gases).
Department of Geophysics and Survey (geophysical survey of metals and nonmetals; geophysical survey of petroleum and natural gases).
Department of Hydrographic Geology and Engineering Geology (hydrographic geology and engineering geology).
Department of Mineral Prospecting Engineering (mineral prospecting engineering).

30. *Peking Institute of Mining* (5), Peking:
Department of Mining (mining of mineral deposits; surveying of mineral deposits).
Department of Mining Machinery (mining machinery).
Department of Electro-Mechanical Mining (electromechanical mining; ore dressing).
Department of Shaft Building (building construction for mining enterprises).
Department of Colliary Geology (geology and survey of mineral products).
Department of Engineering Economy (economy and organization of mining industry).

31. *Peking Institute of Petroleum Engineering* (5), Peking:
Department of Petroleum Geology (geology and survey of petroleum and natural gases; geophysical drilling for petroleum and natural gases).
Department of Petroleum Drilling (petroleum and natural gas engineering; synthetic petroleum).
Department of Petroleum Machinery (machinery and equipment for oilfields; machinery and equipment for oil refineries; transportation and storage of petroleum and natural gases).
Department of Economics of Petroleum Industry (economy and organization of petroleum industry).

32. *Peking Institute of Posts and Telecommunications* (5), Peking:
Department of Cable Communication Engineering (telephonic and telegraphic communications).
Department of Radio Communication Engineering (radio communications and broadcasting).

Department of Economics (economy and organization of posts and telecommunications).

33. *Peking Institute of Steel and Iron Technology* (5), Peking:
Department of Physical Chemistry (physics of metals; physical chemistry of metals).
Department of Mining.
Department of Metallurgy (refining of processing of iron and steel; casting).
Department of Technology (metallography and heat treatment for steel and iron; pressure processing of steel and iron).
Department of Mechanical Engineering (machinery and equipment for metal refineries).

34. *Peking Institute of Technology* (5), Peking:
Department of Mechanical Engineering.
Department of Chemical Engineering.
Department of Instruments.
Department of Radio Engineering.

35. *Peking Railway Institute* (5), Peking:
Department of Rail Traffic (railway management).
Department of Telecommunications (automatic and remote control of rail transport and communications).
Department of Supplies (economy and organization of material and technical supplies in rail transport).
Department of Construction (construction of railways).
Department of Economics (economy and organization of rail transport).

36. *Shanghai Ship Building Institute* (5½), Shanghai:
Department of Ship Building (shipbuilding; ship dynamics; steam engines for ships and their installation; internal combustion engines for ships and their installation).
Department of Electrical Engineering for Ships.
Department of Machine Building (5) (technology of machine building and lathes and tools for metal cutting; welding technology and equipment).
Department of Engineering Economics (5) (economy and organization of shipbuilding industry).

37. *Shanghai University of Science and Technology*, Shanghai:
Probable Departments: Nuclear Physics and Engineering; Technical Physics; Applied Geophysics; Chemical Physics; Radio Electronics; Radiation Chemistry; Thermodynamics; High Polymer Chemistry; Applied Mathematics and Comuters; Dynamics; Biophysics; Automation; and Geochemistry and Rare Elements.

38. *Shantung Engineering Institute* (4), Tsinan:
Department of Machine Building (technology of machine building; lathes and tools for metal cutting; metallography and heat treatment workshop equipment; pressure processing of metals and machinery for the purpose; technology of and machinery for casting).
Department of Electrical Engineering (electric power stations, networks and systems; electrical machines and appliances).

39. *Sian Construction Engineering Institute* (6), Sian:
Department of Architecture.
Department of Construction Engineering (5) (industrial and civil building construction; heating, gas supply and ventilation; water supply and drainage).
Department of Construction Technology (production of products and members for installation type structural concrete and reinforced concrete).

40. *Sian Institute of Aeronautics* (5), Sian:
Department of Aircraft.
Department of Engines.
Department of Aeronautic Heat Processing Technology.

41. *Sian Institute of Dynamics* (5), Sian:
Department of Electric Power (electric power stations, networks and systems).
Department of Thermodynamics (thermal energy dynamic equipment).
Department of Hydraulics (structure of rivers and water conservancy engineering construction for hydroelectric power stations; hydraulic and dynamic equipment).
Department of Mechanical Engineering (technology of machine building and lathes and tools for metal cutting; hydraulic machinery).

42. *South China Engineering Institute* (5), Canton:
Department of Architecture.
Department of Paper-Making (4) (papermaking machinery; papermaking with vegetable fibers).
Department of Mechanical Engineering (4) (technology of machine building; lathes and tools for metal cutting).
Department of Chemical Engineering (4) (rubber engineering; silicate engineering; sugar produce engineering; food engineering; synthetic petroleum; machinery and equipment for production of chemicals).
Department of Civil Engineering (4) (industrial and civil building construction).
Department of Radio (4) (radio techniques).

43. *Taiyuan Engineering Institute* (5), Taiyuan:
Department of Electrical Engineering (electric power stations, networks and systems; electrification of industrial enterprises).
Department of Mechanical Engineering (technology of machine building and lathes and tools for metal cutting; technology of and machinery for casting).
Department of Chemical Engineering (inorganic matter engineering).
Department of Civil Engineering (industrial and civil building construction).

44. *Tangshan Railway Institute* (5), Tangshan:
Department of Mechanical Engineering (rail transport machines).
Department of Railway Construction.

Department of Bridges and Tunnels (railway bridges and tunnels).

Department of Electrified Transportation (electrification of railways).

Department of Rail Transport (railway management).

45. *Tientsin University* (5), Tientsin:

Department of Electric Power (electric power stations, networks and systems; electrification of industrial enterprises; electrical heating equipment; radio techniques).

Department of Mechanical Engineering (technology of machine building, and lathes and tools for metal cutting; internal combustion engines; machinery and equipment for production of chemicals; automation and conditioning of technological process for production of chemicals; precision machines and instruments; welding technology and equipment).

Department of Chemical Engineering (fuel chemical engineering; inorganic matter engineering; silicate engineering; organic dyestuff and intermediary engineering; basic organic composition; electrochemical production engineering; chemical engineering; papermaking vegetable fiber engineering).

Department of Water Conservancy (structure of rivers and water conservancy engineering construction for hydroelectric power stations; water conservancy engineering construction for waterways and ports).

Department of Architecture

Department of Civil Engineering (industrial and civil building construction; production of products and members for installation type structural concrete and reinforced concrete; water supply and drainage; heating, gas supply and ventilation).

Department of Textile Industry (mechanical engineering for fiber materials).

46. *Tsinghua University* (5), Peking:

Department of Architecture (6)

Department of Mechanical Dynamics (thermal energy dynamic equipment; automobiles and tractors; building of gas turbines; industrial thermo engineering).

Department of Electrical Engineering (electrification of industrial enterprises; electric power stations, networks and systems; dynamos and electrical applicances; automation and kinematics; science of operation; high tension technique).

Department of Machine Building (technology of machine building, and lathes and tools for metal cutting; technology of and machinery for casting; machinery for pressure processing of metals; metallography and equipment for heat treatment workshop; welding technology and equipment).

Department of Radio Engineering (radio techniques; electronic apparatus; mathematics and calculating instruments).

Department of Engineering Physics.

Department of Civil Engineering (industrial and civil building construction; water supply and drainage; heating, gas supply and ventilation).

Department of Water Conservancy Engineering (structure of rivers and water conservancy engineering construction for hydroelectric power stations; hydrodynamic equipment).

47. *Tungchi University* (5), Shanghai:
Department of Architecture (architecture; town planning) (6).
Department of Structure (industrial and civil building construction).
Department of Building Construction Technology (production of products and members for installation type structural concrete and reinforced concrete).
Department of Roads and Bridges (highways and roads in cities; roads, bridges and tunnels).
Department of Health Engineering (water supply and drainage; heating, gas supply and ventilation).
Department of City Construction (construction and management of cities).
Department of Railways.
Department of Economics (economy and organization of building construction enterprises).

48. *Wuhan Institute of Water-Borne Transport Engineering* (5), Wuchang:
Department of Ship Machinery (ship engines and machinery).
Department of Water-Borne Transport Management.
Department of Port Machinery (cranes and transportation machinery and equipment for ports).
Department of Water-Borne Transport Economics (economy and organization of waterborne transport).

49. *Wuhan Institute of Water Conservancy* (5), Wuchang:
Department of Water Conservancy Engineering Construction (structure of rivers and water conservancy engineering construction for hydroelectric power stations).
Department of Water Conservancy (conservancy of water and soil).

50. *Wuhan Surveying and Map-Making Institute* (5), Wuchang:
Department of Engineering Surveying.
Department of Aerial Photogrammetry and Mapmaking.
Department of Astronomical and Geodetic Surveying.

INSTITUTIONS OF MEDICINE

1. *Anhwei Medical College* (5), Hofei:
Major: Therapeutics.
2. *Canton College of Chinese Medicine* (5), Canton:
Major: Chinese medicine.
3. *Canton Medical College* (5), Canton:
Major: Therapeutics.
4. *Chekiang Medical College* (5), Hangchow:
Major: Therapeutics.
5. *Chengtu College of Chinese Medicine* (5), Chengtu:
Major: Chinese medicine.
6. *Chungking Medical College* (5), Chungking:
Majors: Therapeutics; pediatrics.

7. *Chungking Medical College* (5), Kweiyang(?):
   Major: Therapeutics.
8. *Dairen Medical College* (5), Dairen:
   Major: Therapeutics.
9. *Fukien Medical College* (5), Foochow:
   Major: Therapeutics.
10. *Harbin Medical College* (5), Harbin:
    Majors: Therapeutics; hygiene.
11. *Honan Medical College* (5), Kaifeng:
    Major: Therapeutics.
12. *Hopei Medical College* (5), Paoting:
    Major: Therapeutics.
13. *Hunan Medical College* (5), Changsha:
    Major: Therapeutics.
14. *Hupeh Medical College* (5), Wuchang:
    Major: Therapeutics.
15. *Inner Mongolia Medical College* (5), Huhehot:
    Major: Therapeutics.
16. *Kiangsi Medical College* (5), Nanchang:
    Major: Therapeutics.
17. *Kiangsu Medical College* (5), Nanking:
    Major: Therapeutics.
18. *Kunming Medical College* (5), Kunming:
    Major: Therapeutics.
19. *Kwangsi Medical College* (5), Nanning:
    Major: Therapeutics.
20. *Kweiyang Medical College* (5), Kweiyang:
    Major: Therapeutics.
21. *Lanchow Medical College* (5), Lanchow:
    Major: Therapeutics.
22. *Nanking College of Pharmacology* (4), Nanking:
    Major: Pharmacology.
23. *Nantung Medical College* (5), Nantung:
    Major: Therapeutics.
24. *Peking College of Chinese Medicine* (5), Peking:
    Major: Chinese medicine.
25. *Peking Medical College* (5), Peking:
    Majors: Therapeutics; hygiene; pediatrics; oralogy (4); pharmacology (4).
26. *Shanghai College of Chinese Medicine* (5), Shanghai:
    Major: Chinese medicine.
27. *Shanghai Medical College No. 1* (5), Shanghai:
    Majors: Therapeutics; hygiene; pharmacology (4).
28. *Shanghai Medical College No. 2* (5), Shanghai:
    Majors: Therapeutics; pediatrics; oralogy (4).
29. *Shansi Medical College* (5), Taiyuan:
    Majors: Therapeutics; hygiene.
30. *Shantung Medical College* (5), Tsinan:
    Major: Therapeutics.

31. *Shenyang College of Pharmacology* (4), Shenyang:
   Major: Pharmacology.
32. *Shenyang Medical College* (5), Shenyang:
   Major: Therapeutics.
33. *Sian Medical College* (5), Sian:
   Major: Therapeutics.
34. *Sinkiang Medical College* (5), Urumchi:
   Major: Therapeutics.
35. *Szechwan Medical College* (5), Chengtu:
   Majors: Therapeutics; hygiene; oralogy (4); pharmacology (4).
36. *Tientsin Medical College* (5), Tientsin:
   Major: Therapeutics.
37. *Tsingtao Medical College* (5), Tsingtao:
   Major: Therapeutics.
38. *Wuhan Medical College* (5), Hankow:
   Majors: Therapeutics; hygiene.
39. *Yenpien University (Medical College)* (5), Yenchi:
   Major: Therapeutics.

INSTITUTIONS OF AGRICULTURE AND FORESTRY

1. *Anhwei Institute of Agriculture* (4), Hofei:
   Majors: Agriculture; tea; sericulture and mulberry cultivation; forrest management.
2. *Central China Institute of Agriculture* (4), Wuhan:
   Majors: Agriculture; fruit trees and garden vegetables; protection of plants; soil and agricultural chemistry; sericulture and mulberry cultivation; agricultural economy and organization.
3. *Changchun Institute of Veterinary Science* (4), Changchun:
   Majors: Animal husbandry; veterinary science.
4. *Chekiang Institute of Agriculture* (4), Hangchow:
   Majors: Agriculture; protection of plants; fruit trees and garden vegetables; soil and agricultural chemistry; teas; sericulture and mulberry cultivation.
5. *Fukien Institute of Agriculture* (4), Foochow:
   Majors: Agriculture; fruit trees and garden vegetables; protection of plants; forest management.
6. *Honan Institute of Agriculture* (4), Chengchow:
   Majors: Agriculture; afforestation and improvement of soil for forestry.
7. *Hopei Institute of Agriculture* (4), Paoting:
   Majors: Agriculture; fruit trees and garden vegetables; protection of plants.
8. *Hunan Institute of Agriculture* (4), Changsha:
   Majors: Agriculture; forest management.
9. *Inner Mongolia Institute of Animal Husbandry and Veterinary Science* (4), Huhehot:
   Majors: Animal husbandry; veterinary science.
10. *Kiangsi Institute of Agriculture* (4), Nanchang:
   Majors: Agriculture; veterinary science.

11. *Kwangsi Institute of Agriculture* (4), Kweilin:
Majors: Agriculture; protection of plants; forest management.
12. *Kweichow Institute of Agriculture* (4), Kweiyang:
Majors: Agriculture; animal husbandry.
13. *Nanking Institute of Agriculture* (4), Nanking:
Majors: Agriculture; protection of plants; soil and agricultural chemistry; agricultural economy and organization; animal husbandry; veterinary science (5); mechanization of agricultural production (5).
14. *Nanking Institute of Forestry* (5), Nanking:
Majors: Forest management; afforestation and improvement of soil for forestry; forestry chemistry; mechanized processing of timber.
15. *North Kiangsu Institute of Agriculture* (4), Yangchow:
Majors: Agriculture; animal husbandry; veterinary science.
16. *Northeast Institute of Agriculture* (4 years and 7 months), Harbin:
Majors: Agriculture; animal husbandry; veterinary science (5); mechanization of agricultural production (5); consolidation of land (5).
17. *Northeast Institute of Forestry* (5), Harbin:
Majors: Forest management; afforestation and improvement of soil for forestry; mechanized processing of timber; mechanization of transportation in lumbering.
18. *Northwest Institute of Agriculture* (4), Wukung:
Majors: Agriculture; fruit trees and garden vegetables; protection of plants; agricultural economy and organization; mechanization of agricultural reduction; soil and agricultural chemistry; animal husbandry; forest management; afforestation and improvement of soil for forestry; improvement of water conservancy and soil (5).
19. *Northwest Institute of Animal Husbandry and Veterinary Science* (4 years and 7 months), Lanchow:
Majors: Animal husbandry; veterinary science (5).
20. *Peian Institute of Agriculture* (4), Peian:
Majors: Agriculture; soil and agricultural chemistry.
21. *Peking Institute of Agricultural Mechanization* (5), Peking:
Mechanization of agricultural reduction.
22. *Peking Institute of Forestry* (5), Peking:
Majors: Forest management; afforestation and improvement of soil for forestry; tree planting in cities and residential districts.
23. *Peking University of Agriculture* (4 years and 7 months), Peking:
Majors: Agriculture; fruit trees and garden vegetables; protection of plants; soil and agricultural chemistry; animal husbandry; agricultural economy and organization; veterinary science (5); agricultural meteorology (5).
24. *Shanghai Institute of Fishery* (5), Shanghai:
Majors: Industrial fishery; processing of marine produce; cultivation of marine produce.
25. *Shansi Institute of Agriculture* (4), Taiku:
Majors: Agriculture; animal husbandry.

26. *Shantung Institute of Agriculture* (4), Tsinan:
    Majors: Agriculture; fruit trees and garden vegetables; protection of plants; soil and agricultural chemistry; animal husbandry; forest management.
27. *Shantung University (Fishery Department)* (5), Tsingtao:
    Major: Cultivation of marine produce.
28. *Shenyang Institute of Agriculture* (4), Shenyang:
    Majors: Agriculture; fruit trees and garden vegetables; protection of plants; soil and agricultural chemistry; agricultural economy and organization; mechanization of agricultural reduction; afforestation and improvement of soil for forestry.
29. *Sinkiang Institute (Agricultural Section)* (3), Urumchi:
    Majors: Agriculture; animal husbandry.
30. *South China Institute of Agriculture* (4), Kuangchou:
    Majors: Agriculture; fruit trees and garden vegetables; protection of plants; soil and agricultural chemistry; sericulture and mulberry cultivation; animal husbandry; veterinary science; forest management; afforestation and improvement of soil for forestry.
31. *Southwest Institute of Agriculture* (4), Chungking:
    Majors: Agriculture; fruit trees and garden vegetables; protection of plants; soil and agricultural chemistry; agricultural economy and organization; sericulture and mulberry cultivation.
32. *Szechwan Institute of Agriculture* (4), Yaan:
    Majors: Agriculture; animal husbandry; veterinary science; forest management.
33. *Yenpien University (Department of Agriculture)* (3), Yenchi:
    Majors: Argiculture; animal husbandry.
34. *Yunnan University (Department of Agriculture and Forestry)* (4), Kunming.
    Majors: Agriculture; forest management.

TEACHER TRAINING INSTITUTES

1. *Anhwei Normal College,* Wuhu:
    4-year courses:
        Departments of Chinese Language and Literature; History; Mathematics; Physics; and Chemistry.
    2-year courses:
        Departments of Chinese Language and Literature; Russian Language; History; Mathematics; Physics; Chemistry; Biology; Geography; Music; and Drawing.
2. *Canton Special Course Normal School,* Kuangchou:
    2-year courses:
        Departments of Chinese Language and Literature; History; Mathematics; Physics; Chemistry; Biology; and Geography.

3. *Central China Normal College,* Wuhan:
   4-year courses:
   > Departments of Chinese Language and Literature; Russian Language; History; Education; Mathematics; Physics; Chemistry; and Biology.

4. *Changsha Special Course Normal School,* Changsha:
   2-year courses:
   > Departments of Chinese Language and Literature; Mathematics; and Physics.

5. *Chekiang Normal College,* Hangchow:
   4-year courses:
   > Departments of Chinese Language and Literature; Foreign Languages (Russian language and English language); History; Education; Mathematics; Physics; Chemistry; Biology; and Geography.

   2-year courses:
   > Departments of Biology; Geography; and Physical Culture.

6. *Chengchow Special-Course Normal School,* Chengchow:
   2-year courses:
   > Departments of Chinese Language and Literature; History; Physical culture; Music; and Drawing.

7. *Chufow Normal College,* Chufow:
   4-year courses:
   > Department of Mathematics.

   2-year courses:
   > Departments of Chinese Language and Literature; History, Mathematics; and Physics.

8. *Chungking Special-Course Normal School,* Chungking:
   2-year courses:
   > Departments of Chinese Language and Literature; Mathematics; Physics; and Geography.

9. *Dairen Special-Course Normal School,* Dairen:
   2-year courses:
   > Departments of Mathematics; Physics; Biology; and Geography.

10. *East China Normal College,* Shanghai:
    4-year courses:
    > Departments of Chinese Language and Literature; Foreign Language (majors for Russian language and English language); History: Education; Mathematics; Physics; Chemistry; Biology; and Geography.

11. *Fukien Normal College,* Foochow:
    4-year courses:
    > Departments of Chinese Language and Literature; Foreign Languages (majors for Russian language and English language); History; Mathematics; Physics; Chemistry; Biology; Geography; and Physical Culture.

    2-year courses:
    > Departments of Physics; Chemistry; Biology; Physical Culture; Music; and Drawing.

12. *Hangchow Special-Course Normal School,* Hangchow:
   2-year courses:
   > Departments of Chinese Language and Literature; History; Mathematics; Physics; and Chemistry.

13. *Harbin Normal College,* Harbin:
   4-year courses:
   > Departments of Chinese Language and Literature; Russian Language; Mathematics; and Chemistry.
   2-year courses:
   > Departments of Chinese Language and Literature; Mathematics; Chemistry; and Biology.

14. *Hofei Special-Course Normal School,* Hofei:
   2-year courses:
   > Departments of Chinese Language and Literature; History; Mathematics; Biology.

15. *Hopei Peking Normal College,* Peking:
   4-year courses:
   > Department of Mathematics.
   2-year courses:
   > Departments of Mathematics; Physics; and Chemistry.

16. *Hopei Tientsin Normal College,* Tientsin:
   4-year courses:
   > Departments of Chinese Language and Literature; Foreign Languages (majors for Russian language and English language); History; and Education.
   2-year courses:
   > Departments of Chinese Language and Literature; and History.

17. *Hunan Normal College,* Changsha:
   4-year courses:
   > Departments of Chinese Language and Literature; History; Education; Mathematics; Physics; Chemistry; and Biology.
   2-year courses:
   > Departments of Russian Language; History; Chemistry; and Biology.

18. *Hupeh Special-Course Normal School,* Wuhan:
   2-year courses:
   > Departments of Mathematics; Physics; Chemistry; Biology; and Geography.

19. *Inner Mongolia Normal College,* Huhehot:
   4-year courses:
   > Departments of Chinese Language and Literature; and Mathematics.
   2-year courses:
   > Departments of Chinese Language and Literature; History; Mathematics; Physics; Chemistry; Biology; Geography; and Physical Culture.

20. *Kaifeng Normal College,* Kaifeng:
    4-year courses:
    > Departments of Chinese Language and Literature; Foreign Languages (majors for Russian and English languages); History; and Geography.

    2-year courses:
    > Departments of Chinese Language and Literature; Foreign Languages (majors for Russian language and English language).

21. *Kaifeng Special-Course Normal School,* Kaifeng:
    2-year courses:
    > Departments of Mathematics; Physics; Chemistry; Biology; and Geography.

22. *Kiangsi Normal College,* Nanchang:
    4-year courses:
    > Departments of Chinese Language and Literature; History; Mathematics; Physics; Chemistry; and Biology.

    2-year courses:
    > Departments of History; Mathematics; Physics; and Biology.

23. *Kiangsu Normal College,* Soochow:
    4-year courses:
    > Departments of Foreign Languages (majors for Russian language and English language); History; Mathematics; Physics; and Chemistry.
    > Departments of Russian Language; Mathematics; Physics; and Physical Culture.

24. *Kirin Special-Course Normal School,* Changchun:
    2-year courses:
    > Departments of Chinese Language and Literature; History; Mathematics; and Geography.

25. *Kunming Normal College,* Kunming:
    4-year courses:
    > Departments of Chinese Language and Literature; History; Mathematics; Physics; and Chemistry.

    2-year courses:
    > Departments of Chinese Language and Literature; History; Mathematics; Physics; Chemistry; and Biology.

26. *Kwangsi Normal College,* Kweilin:
    4-year courses:
    > Departments of Chinese Language and Literature; History; Mathematics; Physics; and Chemistry.

    2-year courses:
    > Departments of Chinese Language and Literature; History; Mathematics; Physics; and Chemistry.

27. *Kweiyang Normal College,* Kweiyang:
    4-year courses:
    > Departments of Chinese Language and Literature; Russian Language; History; Mathematics; and Chemistry.

2-year courses:
>
> Departments of Chinese Language and Literature; Mathematics; Biology; Geography; and Physical Culture.

28. *Nanchang Special-Course Normal School,* Nanchang:

    2-year courses:

    > Departments of Chinese Language and Literature; Russian Language; Mathematics; and Geography.

29. *Nanchung Special-Course Normal School,* Nanchung:

    2-year courses:

    > Departments of Chinese Language and Literature; History; Mathematics; Chemistry; and Biology.

30. *Nanking Normal College,* Nanking:

    4-year courses:

    > Departments of Chinese Language and Literature; Education (majors on school education and preschool education); Chemistry; Biology; and Geography.

    2-year courses:

    > Departments of Chinese Language and Literature; Biology; and Geography.

31. *North Kiangsu Special-Course Normal School,* Yangchow:

    2-year courses:

    > Departments of Chinese Language and Literature; History; Mathematics; and Chemistry.

32. *Northeast Normal University,* Changchun:

    4-year courses:

    > Departments of Chinese Language and Literature; Russian Language; History; Education; Mathematics; Physics; Chemistry; Biology; Geography; and Physical Culture.

33. *Northwest Normal College,* Lanchow:

    4-year courses:

    > Departments of Chinese Language and Literature; History; Education; Mathematics; Physics; Chemistry; Biology; and Geography.

    2-year courses:

    > Departments of Chinese Language and Literature; History; Mathematics; Physics; Chemistry; Biology; Geography; Physical Culture; Music; and Drawing.

34. *Peking Normal College,* Peking:

    4-year courses:

    > Departments of Chinese Language and Literature; History; Mathematics; Physics; Russian Language.

    2-year courses:

    > Departments of Chinese Language and Literature; History, Mathematics; Physics; Chemistry; Biology; and Geography.

35. *Peking Normal University,* Peking:

    4-year courses:

    > Departments of Chinese Language and Literature; Russian Language; History; Education (majors on school education and preschool education); Mathematics; Physics; Chemistry; Biology; and Geography.

36. *Shanghai Normal College No. 1,* Shanghai:
    4-year courses:
    Departments of Chinese Language and Literature; English Language; and History.
    2-year courses:
    Departments of Chinese Language and Literature; and History.
37. *Shanghai Normal College No. 2,* Shanghai:
    4-year courses:
    Departments of Mathematics; Physics; Chemistry; Biology; and Geography.
    2-year courses:
    Departments of Mathematics; Physics; Chemistry; Biology; Geography; and Physical Culture.
38. *Shansi Normal College,* Taiyuan:
    4-year courses:
    Departments of Chinese Language and Literature; Foreign Languages (majors for Russian language and English language); History; Mathematics; and Chemistry.
    2-year courses:
    Departments of Chinese Language and Literature; History; Mathematics; Physics; Biology; Geography; and Physical Culture.
39. *Shantung Normal College,* Tsinan:
    4-year courses:
    Departments of Chinese Language and Literature; History; Mathematics; Physics; Chemistry; Biology; and Geography.
    2-year courses:
    Departments of Russian Language; Mathematics; Biology; Geography; Physical Culture; Music; and Drawing.
40. *Shensi Normal College,* Sian:
    4-year courses:
    Departments of Chemistry and Biology.
    2-year courses:
    Departments of Chinese Language and Literature; Mathematics; Chemistry; and Biology.
41. *Shenyang Normal College,* Shenyang:
    4-year courses:
    Departments of Chinese Language and Literature; Russian Language; History; and Mathematics.
    2-year courses:
    Departments of Chinese Language and Literature; English Language; History; Mathematics; Physics; and Drawing.
42. *Shihchiachuang Normal College,* Shihchiachuang:
    4-year courses:
    Departments of Mathematics; Physics; Chemistry; Biology; Geography; and Physical Culture.
    2-year courses:
    Departments of Biology; Geography; and Physical Culture.

43. *Sian Normal College,* Sian:
   4-year courses:
   > Departments of Chinese Language and Literature; History; Mathematics; Physics; and Geography.

   2-year courses:
   > Departments of History; Physics; and Geography.

44. *Sinkiang Normal College,* Urumchi:
   2-year courses:
   > Departments of Uighur Language; History; Mathematics; Physics; Chemistry; Biology; and Geography.

45. *Sinsiang Normal College,* Sinsiang:
   4-year courses:
   > Departments of Mathematics; Physics; Chemistry; and Biology.

   2-year courses:
   > Departments of Mathematics; Physics; and Biology.

46. *South China Normal College,* Kuangchou:
   4-year courses:
   > Departments of Chinese Language and Literature; Foreign Languages (majors for Russian language and English language); History; Education; Mathematics; Physics; Chemistry; Biology; Geography; and Physical Culture.

47. *Southwest Normal College,* Chungking:
   4-year courses:
   > Departments of Chinese Language and Literature; Foreign Languages (majors for Russian language and English language); History; Education; Mathematics; Physics; Chemistry; Biology; and Geography.

   4-year courses:
   > Department of Physical Culture.

48. *Szechwan Normal College,* Chengtu:
   > Departments of Chinese Language and Literature; History; Mathematics; Physics; and Chemistry.

49. *Tientsin Normal College,* Tientsin:
   4-year courses:
   > Departments of Chinese Language and Literature; Foreign Languages (majors for Russian language and English language); History; Mathematics; Physics; Chemistry; Biology; and Geography.

   2-year courses:
   > Departments of Chinese Language and Literature; History; Mathematics; Physics; and Geography.

50. *Wuhan Special-Course Normal School,* Hankow:
   2-year courses:
   > Departments of Chinese Language and Literature; and History.

51. *Wuhan Special-Course Normal School of Physical Culture,* Wuchang:

2-year course:
Department of Physical Culture.
52. *Yenpien University* (*Normal School Section*), Yenchi:
4-year courses:
Departments of Chinese Language and Literature; Korean Language; History; Mathematics; Physics; and Chemistry.

INSTITUTIONS OF FINANCE AND ECONOMICS

1. *Central South Institute of Finance and Economics* (4), Wuhan:
Departments of Economic Planning (planning of national economy and agricultural economics); Industrial Economics; Statistics; Accountancy; Finance and Credit (public finance and money and credit); Trade Economics (including supply and marketing co-operatives).
2. *Peking Institute of Foreign Trade* (5), Peking:
Department of Foreign Trade Economics: (including international finances.
3. *Northeast Institute of Finance and Economics* (4), Shenyang:
Departments of Industrial Economics; Agricultural Economics; Statistics; Finance and Credit (public finance, money and credit, accountancy); Trade Economics (including supply and marketing cooperatives).
4. *Shanghai Institute of Finance and Economics* (4), Shanghai:
Departments of Industrial Economics; Statistics; Accountancy; Finance and Credit (public finance and money and credit); Trade Economics (including supply and marketing cooperatives).
5. *Szechwan Institute of Finance and Economics* (4), Chengtu:
Departments of Industrial Economics; Agricultural Economics; Statistics; Accountancy; Public Finance.

INSTITUTIONS OF POLITICAL SCIENCE AND LAW

1. *Central South Institute of Political Science and Law* (4), Wuhan.
2. *East China Institute of Political Science and Law* (4), Shanghai.
3. *Peking Institute of Political Science and Law* (4), Peking.
4. *Southwest Institute of Political Science and Law* (4), Chungking.

INSTITUTIONS OF LANGUAGES

1. *Harbin Institute of Foreign Languages* (4), Harbin:
Russian language and literature.
English language and literature.
2. *Northwest Russian Language Special-Course School* (3), Sian:
Russian language and literature.
English language and literature.
3. *Peking Institute of Foreign Languages* (5), Peking:
English language and literature.
German language and literature.
French language and literature.

Spanish language and literature.
Rumanian language and literature.
4. *Peking Russian Language Institute* (4), Peking:
   Russian language and literature.
   Polish language and literature.
   Czechoslovak language and literature.
5. *Shenyang Russian Language Special-Course School* (3), Shenyang:
   Russian language and literature.
6. *Sinkiang Institute of Languages* (4), Urumchi:
   Russian language and literature.
   English language and literature.
   German language and literature.
   French language and literature.
7. *Southwest Russian Language Special-Course School* (3), Chungking:
   Russian language and literature.

INSTITUTIONS OF ARTS

1. *Central Conservatory* (5), Tientsin:
   Majors: Composition of music; directing of music; musical science; vocal music; musical instruments of nationalities; piano; strings and pipes.
2. *Central Institute of Fine Arts* (5), Peking:
   Majors: Water-color and plain-brush painting; oil painting; engraving; sculpture; history of fine arts.
3. *Central Institute of Technological Fine Arts* (5), Peking:
   Majors: Textile designing; ceramic designing; decoration and art designing; interior decoration and art designing.
4. *Central South Special-Course School of Fine Arts* (5), Wuhan:
   Majors: Water-color and plain-brush painting; oil painting; sculpture.
5. *Central South Special-Course School of Music* (5), Wuhan:
   Majors: Composition of music; vocal music; musical instruments of nationalities; piano; strings and pipes.
6. *Central Theatrical Institute,* Peking:
   Directing (5).
   Acting (4).
7. *Hangchow Institute of Fine Arts* (5), Hangchow:
   Majors: Water-color and plain-brush painting; oil painting; engraving; sculpture; decoration and art designing; textile designing.
8. *Peking Institute of Cinematography* (4), Peking:
   Majors: Film directing; acting, film shooting.
9. *Northeast Special-Course School of Music* (5), Shenyang:
   Majors: Composition of music; vocal music; piano; strings and pipes; folksongs; musical instruments of nationalities.
10. *Northwest Special-Course School of Arts* (3), Sian:
    Majors: Composition of music; vocal music; musical instruments of nationalities; piano; strings and pipes.

11. *Northwest Special-Course School of Arts* (3), Sian:
    Majors: Painting; textile designing.
12. *Shanghai Conservatory* (5), Shanghai:
    Majors: Composition of music; directing of music; musical science; piano; strings and pipes; musical instruments of nationalities.
13. *Shanghai Theatrical Institute,* Shanghai:
    Stage-setting art (5).
    Acting (4).
14. *Southwest Special-Course School of Fine Arts* (3), Chungking:
    Majors: Painting; ceramic designing; lacquerware designing.
15. *Southwest Special-Course School of Music* (5), Chengtu:
    Majors: Composition of music; vocal music; musical instruments of nationalities; piano; strings and pipes.

INSTITUTIONS OF PHYSICAL CULTURE

1. *Chengtu Institute of Physical Culture* (4), Chengtu.
2. *Peking Institute of Physical Culture* (4), Peking.
3. *Shanghai Institute of Physical Culture* (4), Shanghai.
4. *Shenyang Institute of Physical Culture* (4), Shenyang.
5. *Sian Institute of Physical Culture* (4), Sian.
6. *Wuhan Institute of Physical Culture* (4), Wuhan.

INSTITUTIONS FOR NATIONALITIES

1. *Central Institute for Minorities* (4) Peking:
   Departments of Languages and Literature (languages of national minorities) and History (histories of national minorities (5) and nationality science).
2. *Central South Institute for Nationalities* (2), Wuhan:
   Arts: Chinese language; history.
3. *Kweichow Institute for Nationalities* (2), Kweichow:
   Arts: Music; fine arts.
4. *Northwest Institute for Nationalities* (4), Lanchow:
   Arts: Department of Nationalities Languages (majors for Tibetan language, Mongolian language, and Uighur language).
5. *Sinkiang Institute* (3), Urumchi:
   Arts: Chinese language and literature; history; arts.
   Science: Mathematics; physics; chemistry; zoology.

INSTITUTIONS UNDER THE CHINESE PEOPLE'S LIBERATION ARMY

1. *Institute of Tele-Communications* (5), Kalgan:
   Departments of Telegraphic Engineering; Radio Engineering; and Radar Engineering.
2. *Fourth Military Medical University* (6), Sian:
   Major: Therapeutics.
3. *First Naval School* (4), Dairen.
4. *Second Naval School* (4), Dairen.

APPENDIX D

Announced List of Institutions Offering Postgraduate Courses, and Courses Offered

AUTHOR'S NOTE.—In practice, this impressive list may lose some of its luster because in some cases the actual work performed by the so-called postgraduates may be difficult to relate to the listed subjects. See chapter IV for a discussion of advanced studies in Communist China.

COMPREHENSIVE UNIVERSITIES

	Number of students
Amoy University:	
Differential geometry	2
Chemical dynamics	2
Optical analysis	1
Cytology	2
Chungshan University:	
Theory of Lie group	1
Geometrical theory of function of a complex variable	1
Theory of probability	1
Spectroscopy	1
X-ray crystal structure	1
Synthesis of medicine	1
Classification of higher vegetation	1
Vertebrate	1
Archaeology of Neolithic Age in China	1
History of Sui and T'ang dynasties	1
Fight of Kwangtung people against aggression in 1911 revolution	1
History of international relation and modern world history	1
Futan University:	
Functional theory of approximation	3
Geometrical theory of function	2
Differential geometry of general space	1
Geometry of differentiable manifold	1
Rare elements	1
Analysis of rare elements	1
Physical and chemical analysis of rare elements	1
Silicium compounds	1
Organic synthesis	2
Electrochemistry	1
Optics (luminescence)	1
Physical theory of semiconductors	2
Genetics (animals, plants or microbes)	2
Nerve physiology	1
Endocrinology	1
Mycology	1
Anthropology	1
Physiology of water in plants	1
Historical geography of China	1
Modern and contemporary history of the world	1
Modern English (pronunciation and grammar)	1
Lanchow University:	
Nuclear theory	2
Organic theory	2

Lanchow University—Continued

Biological alkali	2
Topography	2
History of Chinese Peasants' Wars	2

Nankai University:

Optics	1
Cosmic ray	1
Experimental nuclear physics	1
Nuclear theory	1
Elements, organic compounds and organic insecticides	3
Theoretical organic chemistry and organic synthesis	2
Organic phosphides and organic insecticides	2
Synthetic drugs	2
Ionic exchange process and organic insecticides	2
Organic analysis and organic phosphides	2
Thermodynamics	2
History of Ming and Ch'ing dynasties	2

Nanking University:

History of pre-Chin and Han literature	2
History of literature of Sung, Yüan, Ming and Ch'ing dynasties	2
Critical history of Chinese literature	2
English history	1
Modern history of China	1
English literature	4
Differential geometry (with topology as supplementary subject)	1
Functional analysis	1
Physical acoustics and supersonic physics	4
Composition of matter (nuclear physics)	2
X-ray metallic physics	1
Radio physics (microwave optics)	2

Northeast People's University:

Modern algebra	1
Functional analysis	1
Approximation	1
Theoretical nuclear physics	2
Metallic physics	1
Inscriptions on metalware, shells, and bones	1

Northwest University:

Study of optical rotation	1
Geology of Chinese Zone	1
History of Chinese system of nomination by examination	1
Mongolian history or Uighur history	1

Peking University:

Department of mathematics and mechanics	11
Department of physics	7
Department of chemistry	18
Department of biology	11
Department of geology and geography	1
Department of Chinese language and literature	6
Department of philosophy	4
Department of Western languages and literature	6

Shantung University:

History of the spring and autumn period and the warring states	1
History of East and West Han dynasties	1
Vegetable anatomy	2
Electrochemistry	2

Szechwan University:

Literature of T'ang and Sung dynasties	1
History of pre-Chin Era	1
History of Wei and Tsin dynasties and epoch of division between north and south	1
Theory of numbers	2
Classification of floriferous plants	1
Organic synthesis	1
Equilibrium of cobalt complex	1

Tientsin University:
 Internal combustion engines_____ 1
 Chemical engineering machinery_____ 1
 Precision mechanical instruments_____ 1
 Fiber chemistry_____ 2
 Organic dyestuffs and intermediates_____ 1
 Basic organic composition engineering_____ 1
 High molecular chemical engineering_____ 1
 Theory of chemical engineering_____ 1
Wuhan University:
 Function of a complex variable_____ 3
 History of mathematics_____ 1
 Research in metal inscriptions of Shang and Chou dynasties___ 1
 Modern history of China_____ 1
Yunnan University:
 Ecological geobotany_____ 2
 History of Thai nationality_____ 2

INSTITUTIONS OF TECHNOLOGY

Chekiang University:
 Building of electric machines_____ 1
 Fuel chemical engineering_____ 1
 Architectural structure_____ 1
 Theoretical physics_____ 2
Chengtu Engineering Institute:
 Chemical engineering_____ 1
 Leather chemistry_____ 1
 Plastics_____ 1
 Earth mechanics and foundation_____ 1
Chungking Institute of Architectural Engineering:
 Mechanics of elastic molding in engineering structure_____ 2
Dairen Engineering College:
 Fuel chemistry_____ 1
 Bed foundation_____ 1
East China Chemical Engineering Institute:
 Physical chemistry and electrochemistry_____ 1
 Catalyst chemistry_____ 1
 Synthetic drugs_____ 1
 Theory of chemical engineering_____ 2
East China Textile Institute:
 Textile raw material_____ 1
East China Water Conservancy Institute:
 Harbor and harbor building_____ 1
 River current dynamics_____ 1
Nanking Engineering Institute:
 Chinese architecture_____ 1
Northeast Engineering Institute:
 Mining method_____ 1
 Drilling and dynamiting of rock in mines_____ 1
Peking Institute of Aeronautics:
 Aircraft structural mechanics and elastic mechanics_____ 1
 Automatons for air navigation instruments_____ 1
Peking Institute of Iron and Steel Technology:
 Steel refining_____ 1
 Electrometallurgy_____ 1
 X-ray_____ 2
 Metallographic heat treatment_____ 2
Peking Institute of Petroleum Engineering:
 Theory of chemical engineering_____ 1
 Petroleum engineering_____ 1
 Synthetic petroleum_____ 1
 Organic synthesis_____ 2
Sian Institute of Aeronautics:
 Aircraft structural mechanics_____ 1
 Aerodynamics_____ 1

Tangshan Railway Institute:
 Railroad building_____ — 1
 Electrical haulage_____ — 1
Tsinghua University:
 Alloy casting_____ — 1
 Metal cutting lathe_____ — 1
 Comprehensive utilization of solid fuel_____ —
 Gas turbine_____ — 1
 Reinforced concrete structure_____ — 1
 Earth mechanics and bed foundation_____ — 1
 Automobile_____ — 1
 Bridge_____ — 1
 Elastic and plastic mechanics_____ — 1
 Hydraulics (question of soil and land)_____ — 1
Wuhan Water Conservancy Institute:
 Hydraulic structure_____ — 1
 Water and soil conservancy_____ — 1
 Hydraulics and riverbed dynamics_____ — 1
 Structural mechanics_____ — 2

INSTITUTIONS OF AGRICULTURE AND FORESTRY

Central China Institute of Agriculture:
 Crop cultivation_____ — 2
 Vegetable pathology_____ — 2
Chekiang Institute of Agriculture:
 Crop cultivation_____ — 1
 Seed selection for crops_____ — 1
 Vegetable cultivation_____ — 1
 Vegetable pathology_____ — 1
 Entomology_____ — 2
 Selection of breed in sericulture_____ — 1
 Anatomy and physiology of silkworm_____ — 1
 Soil chemistry_____ — 2
 Agricultural chemistry_____ — 1
Fukien Institute of Agriculture:
 Crop cultivation (sugarcane)_____ — 1
 Crop heredity and seed selection (superiority of crops of mixed strains) __ 1
 Subtropical fruit trees_____ — 1
 Entomology (systematic entomology)_____ — 1
Nanking Institute of Agriculture:
 Vegetable physiology_____ — 2
 Entomology_____ — 1
 Vegetable pathology_____ — 2
 Soil geography_____ — 1
 Breeding of domestic animals_____ — 1
 Veterinary science and microbiology_____ — 1
Nanking Institute of Forestry:
 Dendrology_____ — 2
 Tree cultivation_____ — 2
Northwest Animal Husbandry and Veterinary Institute:
 Sheep breeding_____ — 2
Peking Agricultural University:
 Hereditary seed selection_____ — 3
 Animal heredity_____ — 2
 Veterinary science and parasitology_____ — 1
 Sheep breeding_____ — 1
 Vivisection of domestic animals_____ — 1
 Infectious diseases of domestic animals_____ — 1
Peking Institute of Agricultural Mechanization and Chemistry:
 Repairing of agricultural machines and tractors_____ — 1
Peking Institute of Forestry:
 Forest management_____ — 2

Shenyang Agricultural College:
    Crop cultivation_____ 1
    Selection of paddy seed_____ 1
    Agricultural chemistry_____ 1
    Soil_____ 1
South China Agricultural College:
    Infectious diseases of domestic animals_____ 2
    Vegetable pathology_____ 2
    Fruit tree cultivation_____ 3
    Crop cultivation_____ 2
    Soil_____ 1
    Vegetable physiology_____ 1
Southwest Institute of Agriculture:
    Cotton cultivation_____ 1
    Fruit tree cultivation_____ 1
    Vegetable pathology_____ 1
    Vegetable physiology_____ 1

INSTITUTIONS OF LANGUAGES

Peking Foreign Languages School:
    English department_____ 5

Sources: *Kuang-ming Jih-pao* [Kuang-ming Daily], Aug. 9 and Sept. 3, 1957.

APPENDIX E

List of Specializations in Higher Technological Institutions

AUTHOR'S NOTE.—It must be pointed out that because of intensive specialization (see ch. IV) a student usually concentrates on only one of the subdivisions under the major headings.

Geological Survey

Geological survey and exploration of mines
Mining product geology and exploration
Petroleum and natural gas geology and exploration
Geophysical exploration of metals and nonmetals
Geophysical exploration of petroleum and natural gas
Geophysical well surveying of petroleum and natural gas
Exploration engineering
Hydrological geology and engineering geology

Mining

Mine exploration
Mine selection
Mine surveying
Mining electrical and mechanical technology
Mining industrial structure
Economic and organizational aspects of mining industry
Dual exploitation of petroleum and natural gas
Drilling of petroleum and natural gas
Economic and organizational aspects of petroleum industry

Dynamics

Hydroelectric installation
Heat power installation
Industrial heat energy
Powerplant network and distribution system
High tension electricity technology
Industrial electrification
Prime mover installation on ships
Economic and organizational aspects of electric power
Power for textile industry
Power transmission

Metallurgy

Metallurgy of iron and steel
Pressure processing of iron and steel
Heat treatment of iron and steel
Pressure processing of nonferrous metals
Metallurgy of nonferrous metals
Heat treatment of nonferrous metals and their alloys
Foundry work
Cupola practice
Economic and organizational aspects of metallurgy
Metallurgical physics
Foundry chemistry

Machinery Manufacture and Machine Tool Manufacture

Machinery manufacturing industry and its equipment
Foundry industry and machinery
Metal pressure processing and its machinery
Metallurgy and heat treatment shop equipment
Gas and electric welding industry and its equipment
Metal rolling industry and its equipment
Material handling machinery and equipment
Mining machinery
Metal melting shop machinery and equipment
Petroleum drilling machinery and its equipment
Petroleum refinery machinery and its equipment
Chemical processing machinery and equipment
Light industry machinery and equipment
Food machinery
Paper machinery
Agricultural machinery
Automatic tractor
Passenger car manufacture
Marine engines and their associated machinery
Shipbuilding
Marine engine installation
Boiler manufacture
Turbine
Marine steam engine technology
Internal combustion engines
Steam locomotive construction
Diesel locomotive construction
Hydraulic machinery
Refrigeration, compressors and their installation
Optical instruments
Precision instruments
Instrument manufacturing industry
Economic and organizational aspects of machinery building
Economic and organizational aspects of shipbuilding
Operation and repair of automobiles

Transportation and storage of petroleum and natural gas
Principles of machine design

Electrical Machinery and Electrical Equipment Manufacture

Electric machinery and electrical appliances
Electrical insulation and electric cable technology
Electric locomotive manufacture
Electric equipment in ships
Electric measuring equipment
Automation and dynamics
Transitional automatic control of chemical processing industry
Mathematical computer and instruments
Electronics technology
Design and manufacture of electronic equipment
Electronic devices
Industrial electronics
Electronic material and equipment
Semiconductors
Electronic automatic control: design and manufacture
Electric equipment: design and manufacture

Chemical Engineering

Chemical engineering
Petroleum and natural gas (industry) engineering
Synthetic petroleum
Fuel chemistry engineering
Inorganic chemical engineering
Silicate technology
Electrochemical processing technology
Organic dye technology
Elementary organic synthesis
Synthetic rubber technology
Natural rubber technology
Plastic technology
Chemical pharmacy technology
Antibody manufacture technology

Food Industry

Food processing and storage industry
Fermentation technology
Sugar product technology
Food technology
Fat technology

Paper Manufacture

Plant fiber paper manufacture

Light Industry

Cellulose material mechanical technology
Cellulose material chemical technology
Synthetic fiber technology
Leather, fur, and tanning agent technology

Survey, Mapping, and Hydrology

Astronomical terrestrial survey
Aerial photographic survey
Engineering survey
Mapping
    (Hydrology)
    (Continental hydrology)

Civil Engineering and Architecture

Architecture
Industrial and civil structures
Concrete engineering and structure products
Economic and organizational aspects of architecture
Water supply and water expulsion
Heating supply, gas supply, and ventilation
City planning
City construction and administration
Railroad construction
Highway and thoroughfare construction
Bridges and tunnels
Industrial transportation
River pitot and hydroelectric construction
Waterway and port construction
Improvement of irrigation and soil

Transportation

Railroad Transportation

Railroad management
Rail transportation machinery
Rail transportation automatic control, remote control, and communication
Railroad electrification
Railroad material technical supply
Economic and organizational aspects of railroad transportation

Transoceanic Transportation

Pilotship of ocean liner
Repair of ocean liner (drydocking)
Transoceanic transportation administration

Internal Waterway Transportation

River transportation administration
Dock crane and equipment
Economic and organizational aspect of waterway transportation

Communication

Telegraph and telephone communication
Radio communication and broadcasting
Economic and organizational aspect of postal and electric communication

Miscellaneous

Practical mathematics
Mechanics
Mathematics
Physics

Source: *Kao-teng Hsueh-hsiao Chao-sheng Sheng-hsueh Chih-tao* [Students' Guide to Higher Education] (Peking: Ministry of Higher Education, 1958). Translated by Jennings L. Wong in *Information on Education Around the World*, No. 13 (Washington, D.C.: U.S. Department of Health, Education, and Welfare, May 1959).

Regulations Governing the Enrollment of New Students by Institutions of Higher Education in 1959

Following are the regulations governing the enrollment of new students by institutions of higher education in 1959 as promulgated by the Ministry of Education of the People's Republic of China.

The work of enrolling students for institutions of higher education in 1959 must be based on the work of 1958 in giving continued implementation to the principle of recognizing the leadership of party committees and the class line, in soberly implementing the principle of insuring the quality of the students enrolled according to the conditions of the schools, and in fulfilling the student-enrollment plans of the different kinds of institutions of higher education.

According to the above requirement, the following regulations are hereby laid down to govern the enrollment of students by institutions of higher education this year:

(1) The institutions of higher education shall adopt the method of combining unified leadership with decentralized handling in the enrollment of students. The different provinces, municipalities, and autonomous regions shall deal with the student-enrollment work according to the expediency of their places in accordance with the provisions of these regulations and the unified arrangements made pertaining to the enrollment of students. The education departments (bureaus) and higher education departments (bureaus) of the different provinces, municipalities, and autonomous regions shall, under the leadership of the people's councils in their respective provinces, municipalities, and autonomous regions, and in conjunction with the establishments concerned, organize the institutions of higher education under their jurisdiction to set up student-enrollment organizations for the purposes of handling student-enrollment work in their respective provinces, municipalities, and autonomous regions.

Schools whose entrance examinations have special requirements may enroll students independently.

All institutions of higher education wanting to enroll students should carry out student-enrollment work under the unified leadership of the party committees and student-enrollment committees in their places.

(2) The Ministry of Education shall consult with the provinces, municipalities, autonomous regions, and institutions concerned in formulating plans to determine the number of students to be enrolled by institutions under the leadership of the different

agencies of the Central Government from the different provinces, municipalities, and autonomous regions, and the number of students to be transferred from provinces and municipalities with an abundant supply of candidates to provinces, municipalities, and autonomous regions which are in short supply of candidates. The different provinces, municipalities, and autonomous regions shall consult with each other over the transfer of small numbers of students among themselves.

The student-enrollment organizations of the different provinces, municipalities, and autonomous regions shall, before the registration of candidates, announce the names of the institutions of higher education and their departments and courses (special courses) deciding to enroll students from the different provinces, municipalities, and autonomous regions.

(3) All citizens of the People's Republic of China who have a senior secondary school education or its equivalent and are under 30 years of age (the age limit for workers, peasants, demobilized and rehabilitated soldiers, and cadres on active duty may be extended properly in different places) may apply for enrollment in institutions of higher education provided they are able to meet any one of the following requirements:

(a) Graduates from senior secondary schools of this year who are in possession of letters of introduction issued by their schools.

(b) Graduates from secondary vocational schools of this year who have been authorized by the competent business establishments or local educational administrations to further their studies in a higher school and are in possession of letters of introduction issued by the work units employing them.

(c) Personnel on active duty in party and Government organs, business and enterprise units, and mass organizations who have obtained the approval of the work units employing them, and are in possession of letters of introduction from such units.

(d) Rehabilitated, demobilized, and discharged soldiers who are in possession of letters of identification issued by Government civil affairs establishment of the *hsien* level or above (or of the *ch'u* level in large and medium size cities), or armed force units of the regiment level or above.

(e) Returned overseas Chinese students, or students from Hong Kong and Macau who are in possession of letters of identification issued by overseas Chinese affairs organs in China, or "the Committee to Guide Senior Secondary School Graduates From Hong Kong and Macau to Seek Higher Study in Canton."

(f) Other intellectual youth who are in possession of letters of identification issued by people's communes, or people's councils of the *ch'u* level and above.

(4) The institutions of higher education shall this year divide their examinations into three classes according to the nature of the

special courses, and candidates shall be examined in the following subjects:

(a) For special courses of all kinds in science and engineering colleges (including the courses in the geography department in normal colleges and schools, and the special course in natural geography in universities), special courses in mechanization of agricultural production, agricultural meteorology, land planning, farm irrigation, crop management, agricultural chemistry, agricultural electrification, designing and building of agricultural machines, lumbering and transport, water transport, lumbering machines, manufacture of forestry machines, chemical technology for forestry products, mechanical processing of timber, industrial fishery, and processing of marine product in colleges and schools of agriculture and forestry, and special courses in pharmacology in colleges and schools of medicine, candidates shall be tested in the Chinese language, political science, mathematics, physics, chemistry, and foreign languages.

(b) For special courses of all kinds (special courses listed under "(a)" excepted) in the colleges of medicine, agriculture, and forestry, and courses in the departments of biology and physical culture, and the special course in psychology, candidates shall be tested in the Chinese language, political science, physics, chemistry, biology, and foreign languages.

(c) For special courses of all kinds in colleges of literature, history, political science and law, finance and economics, and arts, and the special course in economic geography in universities, candidates shall be tested in the Chinese language, political science, history, geography, and foreign languages.

Candidates who sit for the different special courses in colleges of finance and economics, the special course in economic geography, and the special course in philosophy, shall be tested in mathematics in addition (cadres specialized in financial and economic work who sit for the different special courses in finance and economics may apply for exemption). For candidates who sit for special courses in arts, physical culture, etc. (departments in courses included) which have special requirements, the additional subjects of examination shall be stipulated by the schools concerned.

The foreign language in which candidates are to be tested may be either Russian or English according to the option of the candidates. Those who have not studied any foreign language may apply for exemption. Candidates sitting for special courses in foreign languages, however, may not apply for exemption.

(5) The joint entrance examinations for institutions of higher education are scheduled to be held on July 20. The dates of examination for institutions of higher education enrolling students independently shall be fixed by these institutions themselves.

(6) The different provinces, municipalities, and autonomous regions shall determine the examination districts and examination centers to be set up themselves, and shall announce the same for the information of the candidates.

(7) In enrolling new students, the institutions of higher education shall observe the principle of enrolling candidates with the best scholastic and health conditions, provided their political quality is assured.

The method of recommending candidates for examination shall be applicable to the workers, peasants, cadres of worker and peasant status, and veteran cadres. These recommended candidates shall not participate in the nationwide joint examination, but shall be examined independently by institutions to which they are sent. The educational administrations of the different provinces, municipalities, and autonomous regions shall be held responsible for recommending candidates.

Workers, peasants, cadres of worker and peasant status, and veteran cadres who participate in the joint examination because they have not been recommended, and candidates who are demobilized or rehabilitated soldiers, cadres on active duty with long service in revolutionary work, national minorities, children of martyrs, oversea Chinese students, or students from Honk Kong and Macau are entitled to enrollment with priority.

(8) All expenses incurred by candidates of all kinds during the time of the entrance examination shall be borne by the candidates themselves. After their enrollment, in case they are personnel on active duty, rehabilitated soldiers, or graduates of this year from secondary vocational schools, the units (schools) to which they belong shall pay for their traveling expenses to their schools. In the case of other new students, they are in principle required to bear the traveling expenses themselves. In some individual cases, because the candidates have a relatively long way to travel, and they are really unable to raise the money for traveling expenses due to the straitened circumstances their families are in, they may apply to the student-enrollment organizations or the local educational administrations of their own provinces, municipalities, of autonomous regions for a subsidy grant.

(9) Institutions of higher education should subject the new students to another political and health checkup after their enrollment. If they fail to pass this checkup, they shall be disqualified for enrollment.

(10) The student-enrollment organizations and the schools which enroll students independently in the different provinces, municipalities, and autonomous regions shall, in accordance with these regulations, and the concrete demands of their provinces, municipalities, autonomous regions, and schools, formulate separate abridged regulations governing the enrollment of students for announcement to the candidates.

Source: *New China News Agency,* June 10, 1959.

APPENDIX G

Outlines of Selected Examinations for Matriculation to Institutions of Higher Education for 1959

AUTHOR'S NOTE.—In May 1959 the Higher Education Publishing House in Peking published outlines of the examinations for matriculation to institutions of higher education, as compiled by the Ministry of Education of the Chinese People's Republic, in the following subjects: Chinese language, politics, mathematics, physics, chemistry, biology (replacing a course in fundamentals of Darwinism), history, geography, Russian, and English. Reproduced in this appendix are the outlines only for the examinations in mathematics, physics, chemistry, and biology, as interesting examples of the Chinese approach to their required standards. It seems most unlikely that large numbers of secondary school graduates would successfully pass the tests based on these outlines. The introductory explanation pointed out that because "conditions of secondary education were not uniform," the candidates must make special efforts to "make up what they did not study last year." It must also be pointed out that since these outlines "only serve as a guide to the scope of the examinations," the actual examination may have a much narrower scope and may vary regionally with the standards established by the secondary schools. The translation had not been checked for technical accuracy.

Source: *Current Background,* American consulate general, Hong Kong, No. 587, Aug. 17, 1959.

SELECTED EXAMINATIONS

OUTLINE OF EXAMINATION IN MATHEMATICS

Candidates in mathematics will be required—

1. To have clear knowledge of the definitions and formulae set out under various items in this outline, to prove the theorems, and to deduce the formulae.

2. To state correctly and briefly the mathematical knowledges contained in this outline (especially the theorems and definitions).

3. To demonstrate ability of applying theories in the solution of problems and of obtaining correct results by calculation or inference. The solution of problems must be as concise as possible, but attention should be paid to the completeness of steps.

4. To show ability of quick numerical calculation, of obtaining approximations of the required accuracy, and of using mathematical tables (e.g., tables of trigonometrical functions and the logarithmic table).

5. To know the contributions of the motherland's laboring people and mathematicians to mathematics and the significance of mathematics for natural science and industrial and agricultural production (provided such knowledge shall be confined to the textbooks now in use).

ARITHMETIC AND ALGEBRA

I. Real Quantities and Mixed Numbers

1. Natural numbers; expression of a natural number as the continued product of prime factors. H. C. F. and L. C. M.
2. Rational quantities; four fundamental operations of arithmetic and their properties; decimals and fractions; recurring decimals.
3. Squares and square roots; the idea of irrational quantities; approximations of square roots with an error of not more than $\frac{1}{10^n}$; the idea of indices; operations of roots and exponents involving rational indices.
4. The idea of weights and measurements; the standard system and the municipal system; operations of compound numbers; percentages and ratios.
5. Real quantities and mathematical axes.
6. The absolute value of real quantities; fundamental properties of equality and inequality of numbers.
7. Mixed numbers and their four fundamental operation; expression of mixed numbers as trigonometrical functions.

II. Algebraical Expressions

1. Four fundamental operations of simple and compound expressions and the following formulae:
$$(a \pm b)^2 = a^2 \pm 2ab + b^2$$
$$(a+b)(a-b) = a^2 - b^2$$
$$(a \pm b)^3 = a^3 \pm 3a^2b + 3ab^2 \pm b^3$$
$$(a \pm b)(a^2 + ab + b^2) = a^3 \pm b^3$$
2. Factorization of compound expressions; the Remainder Theorem and its application in the factorization of compound expressions.
3. Fractions and their operations.
4. Operations of roots; rationalization of denominators expressed as roots of the second order; operations of roots and exponents involving rational indices.

III. Equations

1. Identities, equations, and their fundamental properties.
2. Linear equations containing one unknown quantity.
3. Systems of linear equations containing two or three unknown quantities; discussion of two systems of linear equations containing two unknown quantities.
4. Quadratic equations containing one unknown quantity; relations between radicals and coefficients of quadratic equations; discussion of solution of quadratic equations with literal coefficients; double quadratic equations $(ax^4 + bx^2 + c = 0)$; binomial equations of the third, fourth, or sixth degree.

5. Systems of quadratic equations containing two unknown quantities (confined to systems of two equations of which one is linear and the other quadratic and to extraordinary cases of systems of two equations of which both are quadratic).

6. Application of equations in solving practical problems (including all the above-mentioned equations and their systems).

7. Fundamental properties of inequalities; solution of inequalities of the first degree containing one unknown quantity and inequalities of the second degree containing one unknown quantity.

8. The idea of functions; independent variables and functions; graphs of the following functions:

$$y = kx;\ y = \frac{k}{x};\ y = kx + b;\ y = ax^2;\ y = ax^2 + bx + c$$

IV. Series

1. The idea of series; enumeration of different kinds of series; general terms of series.

2. Arithmetic series; calculation of the general term and the sum of all terms of arithmetic series.

3. Geometric series; calculation of the general term and the sum of all terms of geometric series.

4. The idea of limits of series; finding, by the definition of limits, the sum to infinity of diminishing geometric series.

V. Logarithms

1. The idea of logarithms; fundamental properties of logarithms; graphs of exponent functions and logarithmic functions.

2. Logarithms of products, quotients, exponents, and roots; derivations of logarithmic expressions (that is, addition, subtraction, multiplication, and division of logarithms).

3. Properties of logarithms with 10 as base; application of logarithmic tables in working out sums.

4. Solution of simple exponent equations and logarithmic equations.

VI. Permutations, Combinations, and the Binomial Theorem

1. The idea of unrepeated permutations and combinations and their formulae; proof of the identity $C\frac{n}{m} = C\frac{m-n}{m}$ (that is, the number of combinations when each selection out of m elements consists of n elements is equal to the number of combinations when each selection consists of $m - n$ elements).

2. The binomial theorem.

GEOMETRY

I. Plane Geometry

1. Straight lines; curves; segments of lines; sum and difference of segments.

2. Angles; sum and difference of angles; vertically opposite angles.

3. Triangles; types of triangles; perpendicular bisectors of sides of triangles; bisectors of internal angles of triangles; and medians, altitudes, ex-centers, in-centers, centers of gravity, and orthocenters of triangles.
4. Properties of isosceles triangles.
5. Identity of triangles.
6. Properties of external angles of triangles; relationship between sides and angles of triangles; sum and difference of two sides of triangles.
7. Properties of perpendiculars and obliques.
8. Properties of perpendicular bisectors of lines; properties of angular bisectors; the idea of loci.
9. Fundamental constructions:
   a. Construction of an angle equal to a given angle.
   b. Bisection of a given angle.
   c. Construction of a perpendicular to a given straight line and through a given point.
   d. Bisection of a given line.
   e. Construction of a triangle when three sides, two sides, and the included angle, or two angles and the included side are given.
10. Parallel lines; theorems involving parallel lines; conditions of two lines being parallel; construction of a line parallel to a given line from a point beyond that line.
11. Two angles whose corresponding sides are parallel or perpendicular.
12. Sum of internal angles and external angles of triangles and convex polygons.
13. Parallelograms and trapeziums; properties of sides and angles of parallelograms; properties of diagonals of parallelograms, rectangles, rhombuses, and squares.
14. Properties of lines joining the middle points of two sides of a triangle and the middle points of the two nonparallel sides of a trapezium; division of a given line into a number of equal segments.
15. Circles, centers, radii, and diameters; angles at the center of a circle, arcs, chords, and distance of a chord from the center; tangents; properties of the radius meeting the point of tangent; circumscribed and inscribed circles of triangles.
16. Magnitude of an angle (angle at the center, angle at the circumference, angle inside the circle, and angle outside the circle) the two sides of which intersect with the circumference of a circle; construction of a tangent to a circle from a point outside it.
17. Lines with or without coinciding portions; lines bearing a definite ratio to one another; properties of segments formed when parallel lines pass through two sides of an angle; division of a given line into a number of segments which bear a definite ratio to one another; construction of the fourth line bearing a definite ratio to the three segments.
18. Similar triangles and similar polygons; construction of triangles (or polygons) similar to a given triangle (or polygon) when one side is given; conditions of similarity of two triangles.
19. Properties of bisectors of internal angles and external angles of triangles.

20. The theorem involving the altitude of a right-angled triangle from the hypotenuse and the projections on the hypotenuse of the two sides containing the right angle; the Theorem of Pythagorus and its extension.
21. The ratio of segments formed when two intersecting straight lines are cut by the circumference of a circle.
22. Construction of a line x when lines a, b, and c are given, where—

$$x = \sqrt{a^2 \pm b^2} \qquad x = \frac{bc}{a}$$

$$x = \frac{a^2}{c} \qquad x = \sqrt{ab}$$

23. Construction of circumscribed circles and inscribed circles of regular polygons. Similarity of two regular polygons with the same number of sides and relationship of their perimeters.
24. Construction of inscribed and circumscribed squares, regular hexagons, and regular triangles of a circle of given radius.
25. Calculation of area; areas of rectangles; parallelograms, trapeziums, triangles, and regular polygons; application of the formula which expresses the area of a triangle in terms of its three sides; ratio of areas of similar triangles and of similar polygons.
26. Circumference of a circle as the limit of the perimeter of the inscribed regular polygon whose number of sides is doubled indefinitely; the formula for circumference; the idea of the Ludolphian number and its approximation; area of a circle as the limit of the area of the inscribed regular polygon; the formula for the area of a circle.

II. Solid Geometry

1. Straight lines perpendicular to a plane and conditions of straight lines being perpendicular to a plane; the theorem of three perpendiculars and its converse.
2. Conditions of straight lines being parallel to a plane; conditions of two planes being parallel.
3. Dihedral angles; dihedral angles and plane angles; perpendicular planes; conditions of two planes being perpendicular to each other.
4. Angles formed by straight lines and planes; straight lines in different planes and the angles formed by them.
5. Prisms; area of surfaces of prisms; parallelepipeds; properties of diagonals of rectangular blocks.
6. Pyramids; properties of sections of a pyramid parallel to its base.
7. Area of surfaces of regular pyramids and frustums of regular pyramids; volume of prisms, pyramids, and frustums of pyramids.
8. Area of surfaces and volume of right circular cylinders, right circular cones, and frustums of right circular cones.
9. Spheres; plane sections of spheres; tangent planes of spheres; the theorem of great circles of spheres; area of spheres; area of zones and crowns of spheres; volume of spheres and sectors of spheres.

TRIGONOMETRY

I. Definition of Trigonometrical Functions and Their Properties

1. Angular measure and circular measure of angles; positive angles and negative angles.
2. Definition of trigonometrical functions of any angle; variations in value of trigonometrical functions as the magnitude of angles vary from 0 to 2π; the value of trigonometrical functions of the following angles:

$$0, \frac{\pi}{6}, \frac{\pi}{4}, \frac{\pi}{3}, \frac{\pi}{2}, \pi, \frac{3\pi}{2}, 2\pi.$$

The periodicity of trigonometrical functions.
3. Relationship of trigonometrical functions of the same angle.
4. Finding the general value of an angle when the value of one of its trigonometrical functions is given.
5. Formula for converting the trigonometrical functions of any angle into those of a regular acute angle.
6. Graphs of trigonometrical functions (sine, cosine, and tangent).

II. Derivations of Trigonometrical Functions and Trigonometrical Equations

1. Formulae for compound angles:

$$\sin(\alpha \pm \beta) = \sin\alpha\cos\beta \pm \cos\alpha\sin\beta;$$
$$\cos(\alpha \pm \beta) = \cos\alpha\sin\beta \mp \sin\alpha\cos\beta;$$
$$\tan(\alpha \pm \beta) = \frac{\tan\alpha \pm \tan\beta}{1 \mp \tan\alpha\tan\beta}.$$

2. Trigonometrical functions of double angles and half angles.
3. Converting the following sums and differences into products:

$$\sin\alpha \pm \sin\beta; \quad \cos\alpha \pm \cos\beta; \quad \tan\alpha \pm \tan\beta.$$

4. Converting expressions of trigonometrical functions into expressions which will facilitate calculation.
5. Simple trigonometrical equations.
6. Reciprocals of trigonometrical functions and their important values.

III. Solution of Different Types of Triangles

1. Use of logarithmic tables of trigonometrical functions.
2. Solution of right-angled triangles.
3. The theory of sine and the theory of cosine; area of triangles.
4. Solution of oblique angled triangles with the theory of sine and the theory of cosine.
5. Solution of simple geometrical problems with trigonometrical functions.

OUTLINE OF EXAMINATION IN PHYSICS

Candidates will be required to have clear knowledge of physical phenomena; of the basic ideas, principles, and laws of physics; of the formulae involved in the study of physics; of the physical significance of the quantities expressed by these formulae; and of their internal relationship to one another. Candidates will also be required to adapt them to and apply them in the explanation of phenomena and the solution of concrete problems. Candidates should at the same time pay attention to the relations among the different branches of physics and to their joint application.

Candidates will also be required to be thoroughly acquainted with the knowledge of physics contained in the textbooks, with the application of such knowledge in production, and with the important experiments.

I. Mechanics

1. Mechanical motion; the velocity of motion and its units; formula for motions with uniform velocity; lines representing the course and velocity of motions with uniform velocity.
2. Composition of two rectilinear motions with uniform velocity; composition and resolution of velocity (graphical solution).
3. Rectilinear motions with variable velocity; average velocity; instant velocity; acceleration and its units; motions with uniform acceleration; velocity of motions with uniform acceleration and its line; course of motions with uniform acceleration; formula for motions with uniform acceleration; motion of bodies falling freely; acceleration of freely falling bodies; motion of bodies thrown vertically downward and vertically upward.
4. Newton's first law; force; gravitational force and elasticity; balance of forces; magnitude of a force; statis friction; kinetic friction; and the law of friction.
5. Composition of forces; resolution of a force into two component forces acting at an angle.
6. Conditions of equilibrium of a lever; composition of parallel forces with the same sense; center of gravity; states of equilibrium; stability.
7. Mass; Newton's second law; formula for Newton's second law; time of application of a force and the change in velocity; mass and weight; density and specific gravity; system of units for mechanics.
8. Newton's third law; momentum; the law of conservation of momentum; reaction and its application; impact and its application.
9. Work; magnitude of work; units of work; power; units of power; the principle of work of machines; efficiency of machines; inclined plane; wedge; screw; energy; potential energy; kinetic energy; transformation of mechanical energy and the law of conservation of energy.
10. Motion in a curve; motion of horizontal projectiles; circular motion with uniform velocity; angular velocity and linear velocity; centripetal acceleration; centripetal force and centrifugal force; several kinds of machines which make use of the phenomena of circular motion; displacement of solids; three devices for transmission of motion.
11. The law of universal attraction; variation in weight of matters on earth.

12. Simple harmonic vibration; amplitude, period, and frequency of vibration; the law of oscillation of a simple pendulum; damped oscillation; forced vibration; resonance and its technological significance.
13. Transmission of vibration in matters; transverse waves and longitudinal waves; wave length; relationship of wave length, frequency, and the velocity of waves.
14. Occurrence and transmission of sounds; velocity of transmission of sound; pitch, loudness, and intensity of sound; reflection of sound waves; resonance of sound.
15. Liquid pressure; upthrust experienced by substances immersed in liquid; atmospheric pressure; the action of siphons; pressure inside moving fluids; suction and its application.

II. Molecular Physics and Heat

1. Brownian movement; phenomenon of diffusion; force of interaction of molecules; thermal movement of molecules.
2. Temperature; internal energy of matters and its variation; heat and its units; specific heat of matters and its determination; work equivalent of heat; change of energy and the law of conservation of energy.
3. Linear expansion and cubical expansion of solids; heat expansion of liquids; technological significance of heat expansion.
4. Boyle-Mariette's Law; Charles' Law; Gay-Lussac's Law; absolute temperature scale; equations for the gaseous state.
5. Surface tension; phenomenon of wetting; capillarity.
6. Deformity of solids; fundamental types of elastic deformity; Hooke's Law; elastic limit and index of safety.
7. Melting and solidification; heat of fusion; volumetric changes in matters when melting or solidifying.
8. Evaporation; saturated steam and unsaturated steam; saturated vapor pressure; boiling; heat of vaporization; liquefaction of gases.
9. Humidity of air; dew point; measurement of humidity.
10. Fundamental parts of thermal machines and characteristics of the work of thermal machines; steam engine; steam turbine; internal combustion engine.

III. Electricity

1. Electric charge on matters; Coulomb's law; units of electricity; Coulomb's law in electric media; explanation of the electronic theory and the phenomenon of electric charge; distribution of electric charge on conductors.
2. Electric field; intensity of electric field; lines of electric force; electric field of uniform intensity; electric potential and potential difference; relationship between potential difference and intensity of electric field; electric potential of conductors; electrical capacity; capacitors.
3. Conditions of occurrence and existence of an electric current; intensity and direction of an electric current; voltage of a conductor carrying an electric current; Ohm's law for part of a circuit; electrical resistance and its units; rate of electrical resistance; combination of conductors in series and in parallel; resistors and resistance boxes.

4. Internal resistance of a source of electricity; Ohm's law for the complete circuit; electromotive force of a source of electricity and voltage of terminals; battery resistance.
5. Work and power of an electric current; Joule-Lenz's law; choice of cross sections of conductors.
6. Electrolysis; Faraday's law of electrolysis; electricity needed to liberate one gram-atomic weight of matters by electrolysis.
7. Magnetic phenomena of permanent magnets; magnetic field; intensity of magnetic field; lines of magnetic force.
8. Magnetic field of an electric current; electromagnetic iron; effect of magnetic field on an electric current; measurement of electric currents; measurement of amperes and volts.
9. Electromagnetic induction; direction of the induced current; Lenz's law; right hand rule; electromotive force of induced current; self-induction.
10. Alternate current; alternate current dynamos; electronically controlled commutators; direct current dynamos; direct current electric motors; long-distance transmission of electricity; transformers.
11. Electromagnetic vibration; electromagnetic waves; transmission of electromagnetic waves; electrical harmonic vibration; detection of waves.

IV. Light

1. Propagation of light in a uniform medium; velocity of light.
2. Luminous intensity and its units; general measurement of light; intensity of illumination and its units; the law of illumination; determination of luminous intensity of a source of light.
3. The law of reflection of light; image in a plane mirror; formulae for concave mirrors (deduction not required); construction of images in a concave mirror; convex mirrors.
4. The law of refraction of light; refractive index; total reflection; rays passing through a transparent body having two parallel sides; rays passing through a prism.
5. Lenses; formulae for lenses (deduction not required); construction of images formed by lenses.
6. The eye; short sight and long sight; glasses; microscopes; telescopes.
7. Interference of light.
8. Dispersion of light; emission spectra; absorption spectra; spectrum analysis; ultrared ray and ultraviolet ray; Rëntgen's rays; the electromagnetic theory of light.
9. Lighting effect of electricity; fluorescent tubes and their application; photons; current position of the light theory.

V. Atomic Structure

Nuclear structure of atoms; distribution of electrons outside the nucleus of an atom; composition of an atomic nucleus; the idea of atomic energy; fission of uranium nucleus and application of atomic energy; thermal nuclear reaction; radioactive isotopes and their uses.

NOTE.—Candidates may base their preparations for the examination on the textbook of physics for senior secondary school students, book one (2nd edition of 1956), book two (2nd edition of 1957), and book three (2nd edition of 1958), published by the People's Education Publishing House.

OUTLINE OF EXAMINATION IN CHEMISTRY

Candidates in chemistry will be required—

1. To have clear knowledge of the basic ideas and basic laws of chemistry.

2. To be able to understand correctly and use the basic nomenclature of chemistry.

3. To be thoroughly acquainted with the properties, manufacture, and uses of some important substances.

4. To be able to write down correctly the molecular formulae of substances and equations of chemical reactions and to use them in basic calculations.

5. To know (a) Mendelyev's periodic law and the periodic table of elements; (b) the structure of atoms; (c) the basic content of the ionic theory; and (d) to be able to explain, by these theories, the relevant properties of certain elements and the law of their changes.

6. To systemically understand, by the theory of chemical structure, the molecular structure and properties of the most basic organic substances.

7. To understand the principles and process of production of some materials of importance in the national economy as well as their role in socialist construction.

8. To master the basic processes and methods of chemical experiments and to be able to recognize some substances.

The concrete requirements of the examination in chemistry are as follows:

I. Basic Knowledge of Substances

1. Physical and chemical properties of substances; physical phenomena and chemical phenomena.
2. Mixtures; compounds; elements; simple substances.
3. Decomposition; composition; replacement; double decomposition.
4. Law of indestructibility of matter, law of constant composition (law of definite proportions); Avogadro's law.

II. Basic Knowledge of Atoms and Molecules

1. The idea of atom and molecule and the main points of the atomic-molecular theory.
2. Atomic weight and molecular weight; gram atom and gram mole; gram-molecular volume of gases.
3. Composition of atoms and their valence; positive valence and negative valence; radicals and their valence.
4. Determination of valence of different atoms from the molecular formulae of compounds; correctly writing down the molecular formulae of compounds when the valence of atoms is known.
5. Different meanings expressed by molecular formulae.
6. Different meanings contained by chemical equations and the writing of chemical equations.

227

7. Nucleus of an atom and its electric charges; distribution of electrons outside the nucleus (confined to elements of atomic numbers from 1 to 20); isotopes.
8. Explanation of the following ideas from the theory of structure of atoms:
   a. Formation of simple substances and compounds (atomic bonds and ionic bonds); valence.
   b. Oxidation; reduction; oxidizing agents; reducing agents.
   c. Elements; isotopes.

III. Basic Calculations

1. Calculating the molecular weight of a gas from its density; determination of the molecular weight of a gas from its relative density.
2. Determination of the empirical formula of a substance from its percentage composition and atomic weights; determination of its molecular formula from its empirical formula and its molecular weight.
3. Determination of the molecular weight and percentage composition of a compound from its molecular formula and atomic weights; determination of the gram-atomic number and gram-molecular number of substances from atomic weights and molecular weights.
4. Determination of the density of a gas from its molecular formula and atomic weights.
5. Determination of the weight of different substances and the volume of gaseous substances from chemical equations (including calculation by means of gram atom, gram molecule, and gram-molecular volume).

IV. The Periodic Law and the Periodic Table of Elements

1. Mendelyev's periodic law.
2. Knowledge of the periodic law of elements; short period and long period; main groups and auxiliary groups; elements in the same period and the regularity of variation of properties of their compounds; similarity of the properties of elements within the same main groups and the regularity of variation of properties.
3. Explanation of the periodic law and the nature of the periodic table of elements from the point of atomic structure.

V. Hydrogen

1. Manufacture; reaction between metals and acids (mastery of laboratory experiments is required); reaction between metals and water; reaction between carbon and water.
2. Properties; combustibility and reducing property.
3. Uses; as a reducing agent, for hydrogenation of oils and fats, and in synthesis of hydrochloric acid and ammonia.

VI. Water and Solutions

1. Composition of water; volumetric and quantitative.
2. Chemical properties of water.
3. The idea of solution; heat absorption and heat release in dissolving
4. The idea of solution, saturated solution, and solubility.
5. Effect of temperature on solubility of gases and solids in water.

6. Strength of solutions and determination of such strength; percentage strength; gram-molecular strength; preparation of a solution of required strength.

VII. The Ionic Theory

1. Electric conductivity of solutions; electrolytes and nonelectrolytes.
2. Main points of Arrhenius' theory; distinction between ions and atoms.
3. Ionization of acids, alkalis, and salts; explanation, by the ionic theory, of the common properties of acids and those of alkalis.
4. Ionization; neutralization; hydrolysis of salts.
5. Replacement of hydrogen ions and the ions of other metals by a metal; electrochemical series.
6. Explanation, by the ionic theory, of the process of electrolysis.

VIII. Oxides and Acids, Alkalis, and Salts

1. Acidic oxides and basic oxides; their properties.
2. Oxyacids and nonoxyacids; properties of acids.
3. Soluble alkalis and insoluble alkalis; properties of alkalis.
4. Formation of salts: normal salts; acid salts; solubility or insolubility of important salts.
5. Relationship of simple substances, oxides, acids, alkalis, and salts.

IX. Halogens

1. Manufacture and occurrence of chlorine; electrolysis of common salt solution (knowledge of principles of reaction is required); reaction of concentrated hydrochloric acid with oxidizing agents (knowledge of principles of reaction and mastery of laboratory experiments are required).
2. Properties of chlorine; reaction with metals, nonmetals, water, and alkalis; bleaching action.
3. Uses of chlorine.
4. Hydrogen chloride and hydrochloric acid; manufacture; synthesis (knowledge of principles of reaction, process of production, and conditions of reaction is required); reaction of common salt with concentrated hydrochloric acid (mastery of laboratory experiments is required).
5. Properties and uses of hydrochloric acid; distinction between hydrochloric acid and soluble chlorides.
6. Common properties of halogens.

X. The Oxygen Group

1. Laboratory preparation of oxygen; decomposition of potassium chlorate; decomposition of potassium permanganate (mastery of laboratory experiments is required in both instances).
2. Properties and uses of oxygen.
3. Manufacture of ozone and its properties; allotrophic forms.
4. Oxidation and oxidizing agents; slow oxidation and combustion; catalysis and catalysts.
5. Chemical properties and uses of sulphur.
6. Manufacture of sulphurated hydrogen and its properties.
7. Manufacture of sulphur dioxide and its properties; formation of sulphur trioxide.

8. Manufacture of sulphuric acid by the "contact" method (knowledge of principles of reaction, process of production, and conditions of reaction is required).
9. Properties and uses of sulphuric acid; dilution of sulphuric acid.
10. Distinction between sulphuric acid and soluble sulphates.

XI. The Nitrogen Group

1. Properties of nitrogen.
2. Chemical equilibrium.
3. Manufacture of ammonia; synthesis (knowledge of principles of reaction and conditions of reaction is required); reaction between ammonium salts and alkalis (mastery of laboratory experiments is required).
4. Properties of ammonia and ammonium hydroxide; recognition of ammonium salts.
5. Manufacture of nitric acid; oxidation of ammonia (knowledge of principles and conditions of reaction is necessary); reaction between saltpeter and concentrated sulphuric acid.
6. Properties of nitric acid; as an acid, as an oxidizing agent; action on organic substances.
7. Uses of nitric acid and nitrates.
8. Comparison of properties of yellow phosphorus and red phosphorus; properties of phosphoric anhydride and orthophosphoric acid.
9. Chemical fertilizers; nitrogenous fertilizer, phosphorous fertilizer, and potassium fertilizer.

XII. The Carbon Group

1. Properties of carbon and its allogropic forms.
2. Occurrence and properties of carbon monoxide; water gas and producer gas (knowledge of principles of production is required).
3. Manufacture and properties of carbon dioxide; recognition of carbonates.
4. Silicon dioxide and the silicate industry.
5. Principal constituents of soil and soil fertility.

XIII. General Discussion of Metals

1. Positions of metals in the periodic table of elements and characteristics of the atomic structure of metals.
2. Physical properties and chemical properties of metals.
3. Basic principles and ordinary methods in the smelting of metals.

XIV. Alkaline Metals

1. General properties of alkaline metals; properties of sodium and potassium.
2. Manufacture of caustic soda (knowledge of principles of electrolysis of common salt solution is required); properties and uses of caustic soda.
3. Manufacture of sodium carbonate; the ammonia and alkali method (Solvay process; explanation of the industrial process is not required).

XV. Alkaline Earth Metals

1. General properties of alkaline earth metals.

2. Properties and uses of calcium carbonate, calcium oxide, and calcium sulphate.
3. Hard water and its softening.

XVI. Aluminum

1. Smelting of aluminum (explanation of the industrial process is not required); properties and uses of aluminum.
2. Compounds of aluminum; properties and uses of aluminum hydride, aluminum hydroxide, and alum.

XVII. Iron

1. Principal iron ores and smelting of pig iron (knowledge of raw materials used in blast furnaces or native-type blast furnaces and principal chemical reactions is required).
2. Properties and uses of wrought iron and steel; ordinary steel and special steel.
3. Steel refining (it is required to pay attention to the principles of steel refining in converters or native-type converters and open-hearth furnaces).
4. Ferric salts and ferrous salts.

XVIII. Organic Compounds

1. Chain hydrocarbons:
   a. Saturated chain hydrocarbons; manufacture of methane and its properties; substitution with halogens.
   b. Structural formulae of alkanes; isomers.
   c. Unsaturated chain hydrocarbons; structural formulae; manufacture, properties, and uses of ethylene and ethine; addition reaction of unsaturated chain hydrocarbons.
   d. Fractional distillation and thermal dissociation of petroleum; principal products in the fractional distillation of petroleum.
   e. Derived products of chain hydrocarbons; the meaning of functional group; the functional classification of different derived products.
      (1) Alcohols; properties and manufacture of ethyl alcohol.
      (2) Aldehydes; properties, manufacture, and uses of formaldehyde.
      (3) Carboxylic acids; uses and manufacture of acetic acid.
      (4) Esters; manufacture and properties of ethyl acetate.
      (5) Oils and fats; manufacture of soap; esterification and saponification.
   f. Carbohydrates; simple sugar and complex sugar; properties of grape sugar and cane sugar; properties and water solubility of starch; properties and water solubility of cellulose; cellulose nitrate.
2. Naphthene:
   a. Structural formulae of benzene; properties of benzene.
   b. Derived products of benzene; properties and uses of toluene, benzyl phenol, introbenzene, and aniline; DDT (structural formula not required).
   c. Dry distillation of coal; principal products of fractional distillation of gas tar.

OUTLINE OF EXAMINATION IN BIOLOGY

When preparing for the examination in various branches of biology, candidates should aim at consolidating the basic knowledge of biology which they have already acquired so as to insure good examination results and lay the foundations for the further studies they may wish to undertake: studies of agriculture, medicine, and biology.

This outline comprises three parts: Botany, zoology, and anatomy and physiology of the human body. The outline requires the candidates, in reviewing their lessons, to master selectively and systematically basic knowledge of the structure, mode of life, and development of living organisms, basic knowledge of the structure and functions of the human body, knowledge of biology concerned with agricultural production, and theoretical knowledge for maintaining and promoting the health of a human body.

In reviewing their lessons, candidates should try to understand and master the above knowledges in the spirit of the Michurin theory and the Pavlov theory (namely, that a living body is unified with its living conditions and that both the human body and any other living body are unified and integral bodies).

Where methods are concerned, candidates should review their lessons selectively and systematically. They should try to really understand what they learn and should avoid memorization without comprehension.

Whatever the candidates have learned about botany, zoology, and anatomy and physiology of the human body constitutes the basic knowledge of biology. However, in view of the fact that the time for revision is rather short and that revision covers a variety of subjects, the outline selects only a portion of such knowledge for systematic revision. The revision of this portion, it is estimated, will take 25 hours' classroom revision (8 hours for botany, 7 hours for zoology, and 10 hours for anatomy and physiology of the human body).

The outline is drawn up mainly in accordance with the (draft) teaching program of secondary school biology course, textbooks of botany published in 1953, textbooks of zoology published in 1954, and textbooks of anatomy and physiology of the human body published in 1956. If there are difficulties in securing these books, candidates may base their preparations on the textbooks they are now using.

Botany

I. Organs of Plants

Clear notion of the roots, stem, and leaves of a plant as its nutritive organs and flowers and fruits as its reproductive organs. The organs combine to form the integral plant body.

II. Cells of Plants

Clear knowledge of the cellular structure of plants. Cells are the smallest units in the composition of a plant body.

III. Seeds and Seed Germination

1. Clear knowledge of the structure and composition of seeds; the notion of organic matters and inorganic matters.

2. Clear knowledge of the conditions of seed germination; clear knowledge of the fact that for different kinds of plants the conditions of seed germination are different.
3. Necessity of nutrition and respiration during germination; clear knowledge of the fact that the gases exchanged in the respiration of plants are the same as those in the case of animals.
4. Preparations for sowing; the notion of rate of seed germination and methods for determining such a rate; time for sowing, methods for sowing, and the depth of sowing.

IV. Roots

1. Morphology of roots; internal structure of roots; absorption of water and inorganic salts by roots. When refreshing their knowledge of the above, candidates should pay attention to the relations of morphology and structure to functions.
2. Roots are organs for absorbing nutrition from the soil. Substances absorbed by roots from the soil; measures and methods for insuring that the soil will regularly provide these substances.

V. Leaves

1. Leaves are the organs where plants manufacture organic substances. When refreshing their knowledge of the parts of leaves, the arrangements of leaves, and the internal structure of leaves, candidates should pay attention to their adaptation for the purpose of obtaining sunlight.
2. Clear knowledge of the conditions under which leaves manufacture organic substances; the notion of photosynthesis.
3. Importance of green plants in nature and their value in the national economy.

VI. Stems

1. Stems are organs through which plants transport water, inorganic salts, and organic substances. Structure of seedlings; growth of seedlings into adult plants. When refreshing their knowledge of internal structure of stems, candidates should try to clearly understand the characteristics of the compatibility between structure and transportation functions of cortex and pith.
2. Transportation of water and inorganic salts within the plant body; transportation and storage of organic substances within the plant body.

VII. Reproduction of Plants

1. The notion of asexual reproduction of plants and the methods for effecting same; the notion of grafting and separate planting of tubers and the methods for effecting same.
2. The notion of sexual reproduction of plants; structure of flowers; self-pollination and cross-pollination; characteristics of flowers of anemophilous plants and flowers of entomophilous plants; fertilization; formation of fruits and seeds.

VIII. Transformation of Plants—Michurin's Theory

The basic direction of Michurin's work—to transform the plant kingdom according to a set plan; Michurin's methods for creating new fruit trees: cross-fertilization, grafting, selection, and fostering of young plants.

Zoology

I. Candidates should, by referring to the rabbit as their example, clearly understand the morphology of animal bodies, internal structure, and living functions, for the purpose of realizing the general characteristics of animals, their metabolism, and their close relations to living conditions.

When refreshing their knowledge of the organs and systems of rabbits, candidates should lay emphasis on the following points:

1. Locomotion of rabbits completed through the cooperation of muscles and the skeleton.
2. Functions of the different parts of the digestive tract and the digestive glands, the notion of digestion, and the process of absorption.
3. Where respiratory organs are concerned, candidates should above all understand the structure and function of the lungs (absorption of oxygen and excretion of carbon dioxide).
4. Where the circulation system is concerned, candidates should above all understand the structure of the heart, the types of blood vessels, and routes and functions of circulation.
5. Where excretory organs are concerned, candidates should clearly understand the function (excretion of wastes) of the kidneys.
6. Where the nervous system is concerned, candidates should above all understand the structure of the brain and the functions of sense organs.
7. Knowledge of rabbits as viviparous animals and the fact that young rabbits are nursed by the milk of their mothers.

II. The animal kingdom is divided into eight phyla: Protozoa, Porifera, Coelenterata, Annelida, Mollusca, Arthropoda, Echinodermata, and Chordata. Key points in the revision are animal parasites, arthropods, and vertebrates in the phylum Chordata.

1. Adaptation of ascarids and tapeworms to parasitic life; the harmful effect of ascarids, tapeworms, schistosomes, and hookworms and the methods for their control.
2. When refreshing their knowledge of arthropods, candidates should understand, by referring to the locust as their example, the morphology of arthropods, their structure, and their living functions.

Candidates should understand the external features of locusts, their internal structure, and their living functions. They should above all understand the following points: The fact that arthropods are characterized by the possession, as in the case of locusts, of external skeletons consisting of chitinous integuments; ingestion of food through the mouth parts; respiration through trachea; possession of simple hearts with open circulation; composition of the excretory system of many tubules concentrated just outside the intestines; possession of the cranial ganglion and special sense organs; distinct sexual forms where reproduction is concerned; metamorphosis— incomplete metamorphosis—in growth. The harmful effect of locusts and the methods for their control.

When refreshing their knowledge of harmful insects, stress should be laid on the harmful effect of caterpillars, cotton aphides, mosquitoes, and flies and the methods for their eradication (eradication at the weak links in their life history).

3. Classification of vertebrates into five classes: Pisces, Amphibia, Reptilia, Aves, and Mammalia.
   a. Knowledge of the characteristics of fish, amphibious animals, reptiles, birds, and mammals and their adaptation to living conditions.
   b. When studying the structure of the animals of these five classes, candidates should, by means of comparison, understand the structural difference of their respiratory systems, their circulation systems, and their brains. When studying the reproduction of the animals of these five classes, candidates should contrast their different forms of reproduction. In this way, they will be able to have a clear picture of the evolution of mammals from lower forms to higher forms.
   c. Knowledge of the origin of amphibious animals and birds and the fact that mammals have evolved from reptiles of the past.

Anatomy and Physiology of the Human Body

I. The Human Body as a Unified and Integral Body

1. Distinction between the cellular structure of an animal body and that of a human body, between that of an animal body and that of a plant body; metabolism of cells; multiplication of cells by fission.
2. The notion of tissues of animals and human beings; structure and function of the epithilial tissue, the connective tissue, the muscular tissue. When revising their lessons, candidates should stress the structure and functions of nerve tissues. The notion of organ and systems of organs and the principal systems composing the human body.
3. Clear knowledge that "the human body is a unified and integral body" is the basic principle in the understanding of the human body; the unification of the human body depends primarily on the function of the nervous system; reflex action is the foundation of nerve activities. The student should have a knowledge of the notion of reflex arc and the five constituents of the reflex arc.

II. Circulation System

1. Blood circulation; systematic circulation and pulmonary circulation; the significance of blood circulation; relationship of blood, tissue fluid, and lymphatic system to metabolism.
2. Structure of the heart with attention to the relationship between structure and functions of the various parts; physiology of the heart; distinction between a healthy heart and a weak heart; importance of training the heart; significance of physical culture and physical labor for strengthening of the work ability of the heart.
3. Blood vessels; structural characteristics of arteries, capillaries, and veins with attention to the relations between structure and functions. Blood pressure is the condition of the motion of blood; pulse.

4. Effect of the nervous system on the work of the heart and the blood vessels.
5. Composition and functions of blood; free matrix and the three kinds of blood corpuscles (red blood corpuscles, white blood corpuscles, and small blood plates); haemoglobin and its functions; protective function of blood; significance of immunization, prophylactical innoculation, and antiserum.

III. Respiratory Organs

1. The notion of respiration; functions of respiratory organs; structure of respiratory organs.
2. Exchange of gases in the lungs and in the tissues.
3. Respiratory movements; shallow breathing and deep breathing; principles and methods of artificial respiration.
4. Effect of the nervous system on respiratory movements; effect of carbon dioxide on the central respiratory system.

IV. Digestive Organs

1. Significance of digestion.
2. Digestive functions of digestive organs with stress on digestive functions of the buccal cavity, the stomach, and the intestines.
3. Structure and absorption function of small intestines.
4. Functions of the liver.
5. Regulation of the work of digestive glands. The work of digestive glands is regulated by the nerves and blood circulation. Under the effect of the nervous system, the various digestive organs work in coordination.

V. Metabolism

1. Significance of metabolism: metabolism is the essential to life of living organisms. Material metabolism and energy metabolism constitute a unified process. Metabolism and catabolism are two sides of a unified process.
2. Metabolism of proteins, fats, and sugars inside the human body.
3. Energy spent by a man in 1 day and the supply of food.

VI. Excretion

Significance of excretion in metabolism; structure and functions of kidneys; formation of urine.

VII. Nervous System

1. Significance of nervous system; constituents of nervous system (central nervous system and peripheral nervous system); structure and properties of nerves.
2. Medulla; structure and functions of grey matters and white matters of the medulla; the notion of the central nervous system; the spinal nerves.
   Reflex action of the medulla; external stimulation; the notion of restraint of reflex; relationship between restraint of reflex and coordination of reflex.
3. Brains; the structure of brains; functions of brains; functions of the covering of cerebrum, cerebellum, and medulla oblongata; the guiding function of the covering of cerebrum.

4. Vegetable nervous system, including associate and coassociate nervous systems with stress on the structural and functional characteristics of the vegetable nervous system.
5. Sense organs; the notion of receptor organs and sensory organs; their functions inside the human body.
6. Pavlov's theory of conditional reflex; the notion of unconditional reflex and conditional reflex; signal effect of conditional stimulus; formation of conditional reflex; importance of conditional association of the covering of cerebrum in the formation of conditional reflex; restraint of conditional reflex; significance of conditional reflex.
7. Characteristics of higher nerve activities and of human beings; the notion of the first and second signal systems; significance of the second signal system in human life. The establishment of the theory of conditional reflex overthrows the unscientific grounds of the idealist contention for the existince of soul and mental activities inside a man.

APPENDIX H

Constitution of All-China Federation of Students

The 17th Congress of the All-China Federation of Students on February 10, 1960, adopted a constitution for the organization. The text of the constitution is as follows:

CHAPTER I. *General Principles*

ARTICLE 1. This association is named the All-China Federation of Students.

ART. 2. The tasks of this federation are: Under the leadership of the Chinese Communist Party, to unite the students throughout the country, in enthusiastic response to Chairman Mao's call "to have good health, to study well, and to work properly"; to thoroughly implement the party's policy of "letting education serve the political interests of the proletariat, and combining education with productive labor"; to make efforts to cultivate ourselves to be both red and expert intellectuals of the working class, so as to struggle to build China into a great and strong Socialist country with highly developed modern industry, modern agriculture, and modern science and culture; to strengthen the unity with the students of Socialist countries; to develop friendship and cooperation with students of various countries; to support the struggle against imperialism and colonialism, so as to exert efforts for the cause of bringing about a lasting peace and the progress of mankind.

ART. 3. This federation joins the All-China Federation of Youths as a group member.

CHAPTER II. *Membership*

ART. 4. Those students' associations of higher educational institutions which agree to the constitution of this federation may join this federation as members.

ART. 5. The rights and the duties of members are:

(1) The right to discuss, to make suggestions, and to criticize the work of this federation.

(2) The right to vote and stand for election.

(3) The duties to abide by the constitution of the federation, to carry out the decisions of the federation, and to pay membership dues.

Source: *New China News Agency,* Feb. 10, 1960.

Chapter III. *Organizations and Functions and Powers*

Art. 6. The principle of the organization of the federation is democratic centralization.

Art. 7. The National Committee is the highest organ of authority of this federation. The National Committee is formed through election and by consultation among the member associations. The members of the National Committee are elected for a term of 4 years. Member associations may withdraw and change their own representatives to the National Committee whenever they deem this necessary.

Art. 8. The National Committee shall elect one member as the chairman and a certain number of members as vice chairmen to form a presidium. When the National Committee is not in session, the presidium is responsible for conducting the affairs of the federation.

Art. 9. The National Committee exercises the following functions and powers:

(1) To hear and examine the work report of the presidium.

(2) To discuss and decide the work and tasks of the federation.

(3) To revise the constitution of the federation.

(4) To elect the chairman and vice chairmen of the National Committee.

Chapter IV. *Students' Associations of Higher Educational Institutions and Municipal Federations of Students*

Art. 10. The tasks of the students' associations of higher educational institutions are, under the leadership of the party and with the assistance of the Young Communist League: To urge fellow students to continuously raise their Communist consciousness and to study hard, and to organize fellow students to take part in social and political activities, productive labor, scientific research, and cultural and athletic activities. Any student now studying in school may be a member of a students' association, irrespective of nationality, sex, and religious belief. The representative meeting of all students in a school (or the general meeting of all students in a school) examines and decides on the work of the students' association, and elects a students' committee. The students' committee is composed of a chairman and a certain number of vice chairmen to be responsible for the daily work.

Art. 11. In the municipalities where there are comparatively many higher educational institutions, member associations of this federation may form a municipal federation of students; that is, a joint council of the chairmen of students' associations of higher educational institutions of the whole municipality. Its functions and duties are to assist the students' associations of various schools in carrying out their work and to conduct activities concerning the students of the municipality as a whole. A chairman and a certain number of vice chairmen are elected by the Municipal Federation of Students to be responsible for the council and its work.

APPENDIX I

Scientific Research Institutes in China

AUTHOR'S NOTE.—The following list of institutes and other institutions affiliated with the Chinese Academy of Sciences and the institutes of the Academy of Medical Sciences and the Academy of Agricultural Sciences was compiled by Mr. Wang Chi of the Science and Technology Division of the Library of Congress. Since no such list has ever been published by the Communists, it had to be compiled from many different sources over a long period of time. It will comprise a section of a projected publication tentatively entitled "Institutions of Higher Education and Research in Communist China." The location and/or date of founding have not been determined unless indicated in the list.

I. CHINESE ACADEMY OF SCIENCES: INSTITUTES AND AFFILIATED INSTITUTIONS

Department of Physics, Mathematics, and Chemistry

Institute of Atomic Energy (Yuan-tzu-li yen-chiu so), Peking.

Institute of Chemistry (Hua-hsueh yen-chiu so), Peking. Founded in 1956.

Institute of Dynamics (Tung-li yen-chiu so), Peking.

Institute of Mathematics (Shu-hsueh yen-chiu so), Peking. Founded in 1941. Reorganized in 1952.

Institute of Mechanics (Li-hsueh yen-chiu so), Peking.

Institute of Organic Chemistry (Yu-chi hua-hsueh yen-chiu so), Shanghai. Founded in 1950.

Institute of Physical Chemistry (Wu-li hua-hsueh yen-chiu so), Shanghai. Founded in 1950.

Institute of Semiconductors (Pan-tao-t'i yen-chiu so), Peking. Founded in 1956.

Institute of Upper Atmospheric Physics (Kao-k'ung ta-ch'i wu-li yen-chiu so).

Sian Institute of Chemistry (Hsi-an hua-hsueh yen-chiu so), Sian, Shensi.

Lanchow Research Laboratory of Chemistry (Lan-chou hua-hsueh yen-chiu shih), Lanchow, Kansu.

Wuhan Institute of Chemistry (Wu-han hua-hsueh yen-chiu so), Wuhan, Hupeh.

Department of Biological Sciences

Institute of Agrobiology (Nung-yeh sheng-wu hsueh yen-chiu so), [Wukung, Kansu?].

Institute of Applied Mycology (Ying-yung chen-chun hsueh yen-chiu so), Peking. Founded in 1958.

Institute of Biochemistry (Sheng-wu hua-hsueh yen-chiu so), Shanghai. Founded in 1958.

Institute of Biophysics (Sheng-wu wu-li yen-chiu so).

Institute of Botany (Chih-wu yen-chiu so), Peking. Founded in 1950.

Institute of Botany, South China Branch (Hua-nan chih-wu yen-chiu so), Canton. Founded in 1954.

Institute of Entomology (K'un-ch'ung yen-chiu so), Peking. Founded in 1950.

Institute of Experimental Biology (Shih-yen sheng-wu yen-chiu so), Shanghai. Founded in 1950.

Institute of Limnology (Tan-shui sheng-wu yen-chiu so), Wuhsi, Kiangsu.

Institute of Marine-biology (Shui-sheng sheng-wu yen-chiu so), Shanghai. Founded in 1950.

Institute of Materia Medica (Yao-wu yen-chiu so), Shanghai. Founded in 1953.

Institute of Microbiology (Wei-sheng-wu hsueh yen-chiu so), Peking.

Institute of Paleontology (Ku-sheng-wu yen-chiu so), Nanking. Founded in 1950.

Institute of Physiology (Sheng-li yen-chiu so), Shanghai. Founded in 1950.

Institute of Plant Physiology (Chih-wu sheng-li yen-chiu so), Shanghai. Founded in 1944. Reorganized in 1953.

Institute of Plant Taxonomy (Chih-wu fen-lei yen-chiu so), Peking.

Institute of Vertebrate Paleontology (Ku chi-chui tung-wu yen-chiu so), Peking. Founded in 1928. Reorganized in 1953.

Institute of Zoology (Tung-wu yen-chiu so), Peking. Founded in 1950.

Amoy Institute of Marine Biology (Hsia-men hai-yang sheng-wu yen-chiu so), Amoy, Fukien. Founded in 1950.

Laboratory of Developmental Physiology of the Institute of Experimental Biology (Shih-yen sheng-wu yen-chiu so fa-sheng sheng-li yen-chiu shih), Shanghai.

Laboratory of Plant Physiology (Chih-wu sheng-li shih-yen shih), Peking. Founded in 1957.

Laboratory of Nutrition Research (Ying-yang yen-chiu shih), Shanghai.

Research Institute of Yellow Sea Fisheries (Huang-hai shui-ch'an yen-chiu so), Tsingtao, Shantung.

Genetic Laboratory of Institute of Botany (Chih-wu yen-chiu so i-ch'uan yen-chiu shih), Peking.

Northwestern Institute of Biology and Pedology (Hsi-pei sheng-wu t'u-jang yen-chiu so) [Sian, Shensi?].

Tsingtao Marine Life Museum (Ch'ing-tao shui-chu kuan), Tsingtao, Shantung.

Wuhan Microbiological Laboratory (Wu-han wei-sheng-wu yen-chiu shih), Wuhan, Hupeh. Founded in 1957.

Department of Geography and Geology

Institute of Forestry and Pedology (Lin-yeh t'u-jang yen-chiu so), Shenyang, Liaoning.

Institute of Forestry Science (Lin-yeh k'o-hsueh yen-chiu so), Peking.

Institute of Geography (Ti-li yen-chiu so), Peking. Founded in 1950. Reorganized in 1953.

Institute of Geography, Nanking Branch (Nan-ching ti-li yen-chiu so), Nanking.

Institute of Geology (Ti-chih yen-chiu so), Peking. Founded in 1950.

Institute of Geophysics (Ti-ch'iu wu-li yen-chiu so), Peking. Founded in 1952.

Institute of Meteorology and Geophysics (Ch'i-hsiang ti-chiu wu-li yen-chiu so), Shanghai.

Institute of Mineralogy (K'uang-yeh yen-chiu so), Peking. Founded in 1958.

Institute of Oceanography (Hai-yang yen-chiu so), Tsingtao, Shantung. Founded in 1950.

Institute of Pedology (T'u-jang yen-chiu so), Nanking. Founded in 1952.

Laboratory of Pedology (T'u-jang shih-yen shih), Chungking, Szechwan.

Research Laboratory of Geology (Ti-chih shih-yen shih), Changchun, Kirin.

Changsha Institute of Mineralogy (K'uang-yeh yen-chiu so Ch'ang-sha fen-so), Changsha, Hunan.

Hunan Institute of Geology (Hu-nan ti-chih yen-chiu so) [Changsha?], Hunan.

Lanchow Geological Research Laboratory (Chung-kuo k'o-hsueh yuan Lan-chou ti-chih yen-chiu shih), Lanchow, Kansu.

Department of Technical Sciences

Institute of Applied Chemistry (Ying-yung hua-hsueh yen-chiu so), Changchun, Kirin. Founded in 1948. Reorganized in 1954.

Institute of Applied Physics (Ying-yung wu-li yen-chiu so), Peking. Founded in 1950.

Institute of Automation and Remote Control (Tzu-tung-hua yen-chiu so), Peking. Founded in 1956.

Institute of Chemical Engineering and Metallurgy (Hua-kung yeh-chin yen-chiu so), Peking.

Institute of Civil and Architectural Engineerings (T'u-mu chien-chu yen-chiu so), Harbin, Heilungkiang.

Institute of Computing Technology (Chi-shuan chi-shu yen-chiu so), Peking. Founded in 1956.

Institute of Electrical Engineering (Tien-kung yen-chiu so) [Peking?].

Institute of Electronics (Tien-tzu hsueh yen-chiu so), Peking. Founded in 1956.

Institute of Iron and Steel (Kang-t'ieh yen-chiu so) [Shenyang], Liaoning.

Institute of Mechanical and Electrical Engineerings (Chi-hsieh tien-chi yen-chiu so), Changchun, Kirin. Founded in 1950.

Institute of Metallurgy and Ceramics (Yeh-chin t'ao-t'zu yen-chiu so), Shanghai. Founded in 1929. Reorganized in 1952.

Institute of Metals (Chin-shu yen-chiu so), Peking. Founded in 1953.

Institute of Optics and Precision Instruments (Kuang-hsueh ching-mi chi-hsieh i-ch'i yen-chiu so), Changchun, Kirin. Founded in 1957.

Institute of Petroleum (Shih-yu yen-chiu so), Dairen, Liaoning. Founded in 1952.

Research Academy of Hydrology (Shui-li k'o-hsueh yen-chiu yuan), Peking. Founded in 1958.

Changsha Institute of Metallurgy and Ceramics (Chung-kuo k'o-hsueh yuan yeh-chin t'ao-t'zu yen-chiu so Ch'ang-sha fen-so), Changsha, Hunan.

Canton Institute of Applied Chemistry (Kuang-chou ying-yung hua-hsueh yen-chiu so), Kuangchou, Kuangtung.

Lanchow Institute of Petroleum (Shih-yu yen-chiu so Lan-chou fen-so), Lanchow, Kansu.

Department of Philosophy and Social Sciences

Institute of Archeology (K'ao-ku yen-chiu so), Peking. Founded in 1950.

Institute of Economics (Ching-chi yen-chiu so), Peking. Founded in 1949. Acquired present name in 1950.

Institute of Ethnology (Min-tsu yen-chiu so), Peking. Founded in 1958.

First Institute of History (Li-shih yen-chiu so ti-i so), Peking. Founded in 1954.

Second Institute of History (Li-shih yen-chiu so ti-erh so), Peking. Founded in 1954.

Third Institute of History (Li-shih yen-chiu so ti-san so), Peking. Founded in 1950.

Institute of International Relations (Kuo-chi kuan-hsi yen-chiu so), Peking.

Institute of Law (Fa-hsueh yen-chiu so), Peking.

Institute of Languages and Linguistics (Yu-yen yen-chiu so), Peking. Founded in 1950.

Institute of Literature (Wen-hsueh yen-chiu so), Peking. Founded in 1956.

Institute of National Minority Languages (Shao-shu min-tsu yu-yen yen-chiu so), Peking.

Institute of Natural Science History (Tzu-jan k'o-hsueh shih yen-chiu so), Peking. Founded in 1954.

Institute of Philosophy (Che-hsueh yen-chiu so), Peking.

Institute of Psychology (Hsin-li yen-chiu so), Peking. Founded in 1952.

Observatories

Feng-huang-shan Astronomical Observatory (Feng-huang-shan t'ien-wen t'ai), Kunming, Yunnan.

Hangchow Astronomical Observatory (Hang-chou t'ien-wen t'ai), Hangchow, Chekiang.

Hsu-chia-hui Astronomical Observatory (Hsu-chia hui t'ien-wen t'ai), Shanghai. Founded in 1873. Reorganized in 1950.

Peking Astronomical Observatory (Pei-ching t'ien-wen t'ai), Peking.

She-shan Astronomical Observatory (She-shan t'ien-wen t'ai), Kiangsu.

Tzu-chin-shan Astronomical Observatory (Tzu-chin-shan t'ien-wer t'ai), Nanking.   Founded in 1928.

Library, Documentation, and Publication Offices

Institute of Scientific and Technical Information (K'o-hsueh chi-shu ch'ing-pao yen-chiu so), Peking.   Founded in 1956.
Library of the Chinese Academy of Sciences (Chung-kuo k'o-hsueh yuan t'u-shu kuan), Peking.   Founded in 1954.
Science Press (K'o-hsueh ch'u-pan she), Peking.   Founded in 1954.

Botanical Gardens

Botanical Garden of Lushan (Chih-wu yen-chiu so Lu-shan chih-wu yuan), Lushan, Kiangsi.   Founded in 1934.   Reorganized in 1950.
Botanical Garden of Nanking (Chih-wu yen-chiu so Nan-ching chih-wu yuan), Nanking.   Founded in 1929.   Reorganized in 1954.
Botanical Garden of Peking (Chih-wu yen-chiu so Pei-ching chih-wu yuan), Peking.   Founded in 1954.
Botanical Garden of Wuhan (Wu-han chih-wu yuan), Wuhan, Hupeh.

Branch Academies

Chinese Academy of Sciences, Anhwei Branch (Chung-kuo k'o-hsueh yuan An-hui fen-yuan), Hofei, Anhwei.   Founded in 1959.
Chinese Academy of Sciences, Chekiang Branch (Chung-kuo k'o-hsueh yuan Che-chiang fen-yuan), Hangchow, Chekiang. Founded in 1958.
Chinese Academy of Sciences, Kirin Branch (Chung-kuo k'o-hsueh yuan Chi-lin fen-yuan), Changchun, Kirin.   Founded in 1958.
Chinese Academy of Sciences, Kiangsi Branch (Chung-kuo k'o-hsueh yuan Chiang-hsi fen-yuan), Nanchang, Kiangsi.   Founded in 1958.
Chinese Academy of Sciences, Kiangsu Branch (Chung-kuo k'o-hsueh yuan Chiang-su fen-yuan), Nanking.   Founded in 1958.
Chinese Academy of Sciences, Hopei Branch (Chung-kuo k'o-hsueh yuan Ho-pei fen-yuan), Paoting, Hopei.   Founded in 1958.
Chinese Academy of Sciences, Sinkiang Branch (Chung-kuo k'o-hsueh yuan Hsin-chiang fen-yuan).
Chinese Academy of Sciences, Canton Branch (Chung-kuo k'o-hsueh yuan Kuang-chou fen-yuan), Kuangchow, Kuangtung.   Founded in 1958.
Chinese Academy of Sciences, Kweichow Branch (Chung-kuo k'o-hsueh yuan Kuei-chou fen-yuan), Kweiyang, Kweichow.   Founded in 1958.
Chinese Academy of Sciences, Lanchow Branch (Chung-kuo k'o-hsueh yuan Lan-chou fen-yuan), Lanchow, Kansu.   Founded in 1959.
Chinese Academy of Sciences, Shantung Branch (Chung-kuo k'o-hsueh yuan Shan-tung fen-yuan), Tsinan, Shantung.   Founded in 1958.
Chinese Academy of Sciences, Shanghai Branch (Chung-kuo k'o-hsueh yuan Shang-hai (fen-yuan), Shanghai.   Founded in 1958.
Chinese Academy of Sciences, Shensi Branch (Chung-kuo k'o-hsueh yuan Shen-hsi fen-yuan), Sian, Shensi.   Founded in 1958.

Chinese Academy of Sciences, Szechwan Branch (Chung-kuo k'o-hsueh yuan Ssu-ch'uan fen-yuan), Szechwan. Founded in 1958.

Chinese Academy of Sciences, Wuhan Branch (Chung-kuo k'o-hsueh yuan Wu-han fen-yuan), Wuhan, Hupeh. Founded in 1959.

Chinese Academy of Sciences, Yunnan Branch (Chung-kuo k'o-hsueh yuan Yun-nan fen-yuan), Kumning, Yunnan. Founded in 1958.

II. CHINESE ACADEMY OF MEDICAL SCIENCES: INSTITUTES

Chinese Academy of Medical Sciences (Chung-kuo i-hsueh k'o-hsueh yuan), Peking.

Institute of Anti-biotics (K'ang-sheng shu yen-chiu so), Peking.

Institute of Parasitology (Chi-sheng-ch'ung ping yen-chiu so), Peking.

Institute of Pharmacology (Yau-wu yen-chiu so), Peking.

Institute of Micro-biology (Wei-sheng-wu hsueh yen-chiu so), Peking.

Institute of Tuberculosis (Chieh-ho ping yen-chiu so), Peking.

Institute of Oncology (Chung-liu yen-chiu so), Peking.

Institute of Internal Medicine (Nei-k'o yen-chiu so), Peking.

Institute of Surgery (Wai-k'o yen-chiu so), Peking.

Institute of Acupuncture and Moxabustion (Chen-chiu yen-chiu so), Peking.

Institute of Traditional Chinese Drugs (Chung-yao yen-chiu so), Peking.

Institute of Pediatrics (Erh-k'o yen-chiu so), Peking.

Institute of Medical Radiology (Fang-she i-hsueh yen-chiu so), Peking.

Institute of Hypertension (Kao-hsueh-ya yen-chiu so), Peking.

Institute of Labor Hygiene, Labor Protection, and Occupational Diseases (Lao-tung wei-sheng lao-tung pao-hu yu chih-yeh ping yen-chiu so), Peking.

Institute of Epidemiology and Microbiology (Liu-hsing-ping hsueh yu wei-sheng-wu hsueh yen-chiu so), Peking.

Institute of Biological Products (Sheng-wu chih-p'in yen-chiu so), Peking.

Institute of Blood Transfusion and Hemopathology (Shu-hsueh hsueh-yeh-ping hsueh yen-chiu so), Peking.

Institute of Dermatology (P'i-fu-hsing ping yen-chiu so), Peking.

Laboratory of Isotopes (T'ung-wei-su shih), Peking.

Fukien Institute of Epidemiology (Fu-chien liu-hsing-ping hsueh yen-chiu so) [Amoy?]

Fukien Institute of Epidemiology (Fu-chien liu-hsing-ping yen-chiu so), Foochow.

Shensi Institute of Traditional Chinese Medicine (Shen-hsi chung-i yen-chiu so) [Sian?].

Shensi Institute of Acupuncture and Moxabustion (shen-hsi fen-yuan chen-chiu yen-chiu so) [Sian?]

III. CHINESE ACADEMY OF AGRICULTURAL SCIENCES: INSTITUTES

Central Research Institutes

Chinese Academy of Agricultural Sciences (Chung-kuo nung-yeh k'o-hsueh yuan), Peking. Founded in 1957.

Institute of Agricultural Economics (Nung-yeh ching-chi yen-chiu so), Peking. Founded in 1958.
Institute of Agricultural Mechanization (Nung-yeh chi-hsieh-hua yen-chiu so), Peking.
Institute of Animal Husbandry (Hsu-mu yen-chiu so), Peking. Founded in 1958.
Institute of Breeding and Cultivation (Tso-wu yu-chung tsai-p'ei yen-chiu so), Peking. Founded in 1957.
Institute of Chinese Veterinary Science (Chung shou-i yen-chiu so), Peking. Founded in 1958.
Institute of Cotton (Mien-hua yen-chiu so), Peking. Founded in 1957.
Institute of Olericulture (Shu-ts'ai yen-chiu so), Peking. Founded in 1958.
Institute of Plant Protection (Chih-wu pao-hu yen-chiu so), Peking. Founded in 1957.
Institute of Pomology (Kuo-shu yen-chiu so), Peking. Founded in 1958.
Institute of Soil and Fertilizer (T'u-jang fei-liao yen-chiu so), Peking. Founded in 1957.
Research Laboratory of Agricultural Heredities (Nung-yeh i-ch'an yen-chiu shih), Peking. Founded in 1958.
Research Laboratory of Agricultural Meteorology (Nung-yeh ch'i-hsiang yen-chu shih), Peking. Founded in 1958.
Research Laboratory of Atomic Energy Applications (Yuan-tzu-li ying-yung yen-chiu shih), Peking. Founded in 1958.
Chenchiang Sericultural Research Institute, Chinese Academy of Agricultural Sciences (Chung-kuo nung-yeh k'o-hsueh yuan Chen-chiang ts'an-yeh yen-chiu so), Chenchiang, Kiangsu.

Branch Research Institutes of the Academy of Agricultural Sciences

Central China Institute of Agricultural Sciences (Hua-chung nung-yeh k'o-hsueh yen-chiu so). Wuhan, Hopei.
East China Institute of Agricultural Sciences (Hua-tung nung-yeh k'o-hsueh yen-chiu so), Nanking.
Northern China Institute of Agricultural Sciences (Hua-pei nung-yeh k'o-hsueh yen-chiu so) [Paoting, Hopei ?].
Northeastern China Institute of Agricultural Sciences (Tung-pei nung-yeh k'o-hsueh yen-chiu so), Kungchuling, Kirin.
Northwestern China Institute of Agricultural Sciences (Hsi-pei nung-yeh k'o-hsueh yen-chiu so), Sian, Shensi.
Southern China Institute of Agricultural Sciences (Hua-nan nung-yeh k'o-hsueh yen-chiu so), Kuangchou, Kuantung.
Hunan Institute of Agricultural Sciences (Hu-nan sheng nung-yeh k'o-hsueh yen-chiu so) [Changsha?].
Hupeh Institute of Agricultural Sciences (Hu-pei sheng nung-yeh k'o-hsueh yen-chiu so).
Kiangsu Institute of Agricultural Sciences (Chiang-su sheng nung-yeh k'o-hsueh yen-chiu so), Nanking.
Kirin Institute of Agricultural Sciences (Chi-lin sheng nung-yeh k'o-hsueh yen-chiu so), Changchun.

Liaoning Institute of Agricultural Sciences (Liao-ning sheng nung-yeh k'o-hsueh yen-chiu so), Shenyang.

Szechwan Institute of Agricultural Sciences (Ssu-ch'uan sheng nung-yeh k'o-hsueh yen-chiu so), Chengtu.

INDEX

A

Academia Sinica, Peking, 101; merged into the Academy of Sciences, 109.

Academy of Agricultural Sciences, physical labor required of research workers, 121; list of institutes and branches of, 245–247.

Academy of Medical Sciences, list of institutes of, 245.

Academy of Sciences, 25, 164; enforced labor by members of, 4; scientific research at, 7; budget, 15, 16–17, 114; responsibility for University of Science and Technology, 60; assignment of graduates to, 76; graduate work at, 78–79, 80; Kuo Mo-jo, president of, 101; extension of branches of, 103–104; level of scientific work at, 104; friction between agencies and, for control of research and development, 106–107; establishment, functions, controls, quality of work, and organization, 109–113 (chart, 110; personnel and institutes, 111 table 1); mission to Soviet Union, 116; Soviet specialists in China under auspices of, 117; plan for scientific co-operation with Soviet Academy of Sciences, 117; complaints of members of, during the period of "blooming and contending," 118–120; "rectification" following complaints, 120–122; awarding body for prizes and awards for scientific research, 122–123; list of institutes and affiliated institutions, 240–244; branch academies, 244–245.

Adult education, 48–55.

Advanced studies, 77–80. *See also* Postgraduate work and research.

Agricultural sciences, list of institutes of the Academy of Agricultural Sciences, 245–247.

Agricultural secondary schools, 37. *See also* Agriculture; Agriculture and forestry; Secondary schools.

Agriculture, work-study policy in training in, 59; as research category in 12-year plan, 104–105; development of, as task set forth by scientific and technological work conference, 105.

Agriculture and forestry, vocational-school enrollment in, 46; enrollment in, related to other fields, 68–71; graduates in, 72–74; assignment of graduates to, 76; research personnel in, 115; graduates in, related to those in other specializations, 128–130; women students in, 144, 172; number of graduates in, from higher educational establishments related to graduates in other fields, 171; higher educational institutions listed, 192–194; higher educational institutions for, offering postgraduate courses, listed with courses and number of students, 207–208. *See also* Academy of Agricultural Sciences.

All-China Federation of Students, Constitution of, 238–239.

American universities, Chinese comment on curriculums in, 133.

Animal husbandry, research personnel in, 115.

Architecture, as specialization in higher technological institutions, 212.

Army. *See* Chinese People's Liberation Army.

Arts, work-study policy in training in, 59; graduates in literature and, related to those in other specializations, 128–130; women students in literature and, 144, 172; list of higher educational institutions for, 202–203. *See also* Fine arts; Literature and arts.

Atomic energy, peaceful uses of, as research category in 12-year plan, 104–105.

Atomic reactor, Sino-Soviet cooperation in construction of, 115.

Automation, as research category in 12-year plan 104–105; mission to Soviet Union to study conditions of research in, 116.

B

Biological Sciences, institutes affiliated with the department of, Academy of sciences, 240–241; in the Academy of Sciences, 109–113, *passim;* chart, 110.

Biology, outline of examination in, for matriculation to institutions of higher education, 232–237.

Biophysics, Soviet Union aid in, 116.

Birth control, 8. *See also* Population.

"Blooming and contending," 3; results of, on scientists, 107; scientists' opinions expressed during the period of, 118–120; "rectification" campaign against scientists and intellectuals, 120–122. *See also* "Hundred Flowers Movement"; "Rectification" campaign.

Botanical gardens, affiliated with the Academy of Sciences, 244.

Botany, excess of graduates over needs in, 94–95.

Budget for education, 14–17; for the Academy of Sciences, 15, 16–17, 114; for research by higher educational schools and institutions, 114.

Building industry, research in, 114.

C

California Institute of Technology, engineering curriculum compared with that of a Chinese and a Soviet university, 132–133.

Central Science Library, 112–113.

Chemical engineering, as specialization in higher technological institutions, 211. *See also* Chemistry; Engineering.

Chemical industry, research in, 114.

Chemistry, in the Academy of Sciences, 109–113, *passim;* chart, 110; outline of examination in, for matriculation to institutions of higher education, 227–231; institutes affiliated with the department of, Academy of Sciences, 240. *See also* Natural sciences; Physical chemistry; Sciences.

China Association for Dissemination of Scientific and Technical Knowledge, 104.

Chinese People's Liberation Army, assignment of graduates to, 76; list of higher educational institutions under, 203.

Chinese Youth League, 50.

Chou En-lai, 39, 122, 130, 131.

Civil engineering, as specialization in higher technological institutions, 212. *See also* Engineering; Engineers.

College entrance examinations, 218–237. *See also* Higher educational schools and institutions.

College graduates, quality of, 6–7; excess of Russian-language graduates, 94; assignment of, by the state, 94–96; over-specialization, surpluses, and deficiencies in fields of specialization, 94–96. *See also* Higher education; Higher educational schools and institutions.

Colleges, in educational-system chart, 11. *See also* Higher educational schools and institutions.

Colleges, normal: number, 57; specialized training in, 58; length of curriculum, 58. *See* Secondary schools—*Normal;* Secondary schools—*Specialized;* Teacher-training institutes.

Commission for Scientific and Technical Cooperation, cooperation with Soviet Union, 117.

Communications, research personnel in, 115. *See also* Transportation and Communications.

Confucius, early Chinese education based on, 9.

Conservation, water and soil: Soviet Union aid in, 116.

Construction, workers and employees in, in distribution within production categories, 162–163. *See also* Production categories of labor.

Correspondence schools, in educational-system chart, 11. *See also* Higher educational schools and institutions.

Curriculums, sample: elementary schools, 173; secondary schools, 174; normal schools, 175.

D

Death rate, 152.

Diseases, as research category in 12-year plan, 104–105; continuance of, in China, 152.

Dynamics, mission to Soviet Union to study conditions of research work in, 116; as specialization in higher technological institutions, 209.

E

Earth sciences, in the Academy of Sciences, 109–113, *passim;* chart, 110.
Economics. *See* Finance and economics.
Education, general comment on nature of statistics on, v-vi; quantity versus quality, 5, 18, 22, 81–100; broad conjectures on future of, 7–8; rural compared to urban, 8; quality affected by integration of education and production, 24, 25, 26 (*see also* "Walking on two legs"; Production, integration of education and); shortage of teachers and lowering of teacher qualifications, 82–84; shortage and incompetence of administrative personnel, 83–84; inadequacy of physical facilities, 84–88; withdrawals from primary and secondary schools, 88–89; problems in quality in vocational schools, 89–91; problems of quality in higher education, 91–94; effects of inadequate planning on quality, 96–99. *See also* Adult education; Colleges; Higher education; Higher educational schools and institutions; Institutes; Kindergartens; Literacy; On-the-job training; Postgraduate work and research; Preschool facilities; Primary education; Primary schools; Production, integration of education and: Secondary education; Secondary schools; Spare-time education; Universities.
Education (pedagogy), increase in graduates in, 6; enrollment in, related to other fields, 67, 68–71; graduates, 72, 73, 75; assignment of graduates to, 76; graduates in, related to those in other specializations, 128–130, 171; decrease in proportion of women in enrollment in, 144, 172.
Educational system, before 1950, 9–10; policies and problems, 9–28; structure of, 11–14; Communist reforms, 11–28; Soviet influence on, 12 (*see also* Soviet Union); budget, 14–17; significant features of, during Communist regime, 26; indications of future trends, 26–28.

See Education, above, and cross-references thereunder.
Electrical engineering, mission to Soviet Union to study conditions of research work in, 116. *See also* Engineering.
Electrical machinery and electrical equipment manufacture, as specialization in higher technological institutions, 211.
Electronic techniques, as research category in 12-year plan, 104–105.
Electronics, mission to Soviet Union to study conditions of research work in, 116.
Electrophysics, Soviet Union aid in, 116.
Employees. *See* Workers and employees.
Engineering, work-study policy in training in, 59; assignment of students to, 62; length of curriculums, 67; enrollment in, related to that in other fields, 67, 68–71; graduates, 72, 73, 74; assignment of graduates, 76; quality of teaching staff in courses at institutions of higher education, 91; overspecialization in (civil), 92–93; shortage of graduates related to need in some fields and excess of graduates in others, 94–95, 127; students and graduates in institutions of higher education, 127–133; graduates in, related to those in other specializations, 128–130, 171; distinction between graduates in, and persons performing engineering functions, 132; comparison of curriculums in China, Soviet Union, and U.S., 132–133; women students in, 144, 172; graduates in, as percent of workers and employees in production categories, 164; engineering and technical personnel as percent of total workers in production categories, 164–165 (see note to table 7). *See also* Chemical engineering; Electrical engineering; Engineers; Secondary schools —*Vocational education.*
Engineers, graduates, vii; percentage of, in population with higher degrees, 6; emphasis to continue on, 8; quality of, 8. *See also* Engineering.
Experimental farms. *See* Production, integration of education and.

F

Factories, part-time schools established by, 20; scientific industrial research at, 114.

Sciences), 106; statement of intent on role of scientists in scientific research, 107; failure of this role to develop, 107; statement on needs as to theoretical research and practical application of science, 108; report on research institutes and personnel, 115; statement on Soviet scientific cooperation, 115; content of Scientific Cooperation Agreement between China and Soviet Union explained by, 116; promises to scientists, 119; statement regarding Chinese scientists and students abroad, 125–127.

L

Labor force, limit to mass labor utilization under present policies, 154; analysis of, urban areas, 158–166; intellectuals in, 165–166. *See also* Construction; Industry; Production categories of labor; Transportation and communications.

Laboratories, responsibility of Science Planning Commission for, 106; at Academy of Sciences, 112. *See also* the Appendices.

Land survey, shortage of graduates related to need, 94–95.

Languages, required at the Academy of Sciences, 112; list of higher educational institutions for, 201–202; higher educational institutions for, offering postgraduate courses, listed with courses and number of students, 208. *See also* Oriental languages; Russian language.

Law, graduates in, related to other fields, 6; enrollment in political science and, related to other fields, 67, 68–71; graduates, see "Other" column, 75 table 5; graduates in social sciences and, related to other specializations, 128–130; women students in political science and, 144, 172. *See also* Political science.

"Leap forward," 2, 4, 5; in education, 18–24, 48, 66, 81–82; in science and technology, 102, 108, 111, 112, 120, 122; in the labor force, 161.

Libraries, responsibility of Science Planning Commission for, 106; of the Academy of Sciences, 112; cooperation with Soviet Union, 117; lack of, for scientists, 120; affiliated with Academy of Sciences, 244. *See also* Central Science Library.

Literacy, classes in the educational-system chart, 11; drive for, 48–55.

Literature and arts, enrollment in, related to other fields, 67, 68–71; graduates, 72, 75; graduates in, related to those in other specializations, 128–130, 171; women students in, 144, 172.

M

Machine-building industry, research in, 114.

Machinery, mission to Soviet Union to study conditions of research work in, 116.

Machinery manufacture and machine-tool manufacture, as specialization in higher technological institutions, 210–211.

Machines, heavy: as research category in 12-year plan, 104–105.

Mapping, as specialization in higher technological institutions, 212.

Mathematics, overspecialization within the field of, 93; in the Academy of Sciences, 108–113, *passim;* chart, 110; as specialization in higher technological institutions, 213; outline of examination in, for matriculation to institutions of higher education, 218–223; institutes affiliated with the department of, Academy of Sciences, 240.

Mechanics, as specialization in higher technological institutions, 213.

Medical colleges, number, 57. *See also* the Appendices.

Medical sciences, development of, as task set forth by scientific and technological work conference, 105; graduates in, related to those in other specializations, 128–130; shortage of trained personnel, 134–136; probable assignment of low priority to, 136; students and graduates in, 136; emphasis on native medicine, 137; formal medical-science education—institutes, graduates, conditions in, 138–142; medical personnel and hospital beds, 141 table 8; women students in, 144, 172; list of institutes of the Academy of Medical Sciences, 245; *see also* Health; Medicine; Pharmacy.

Medicine, increase in graduates in, 6; length of curriculum, 57, 67; work-study policy in training in, 59; enrollment in (health), related to other fields, 68–71; graduates, 72, 74; prestige of traditional Chinese medicine as opposed to Western medicine, 102; research personnel in, 115; higher educational institutions listed, 190–192. *See also* Health; Medical sciences; Pharmacy.

Metallurgical industry, research in, 114.

Metallurgy, shortage of graduates related to need, 94–95; as research category in 12-year plan, 104–105; Soviet Union aid in, 116; mission to Soviet Union to study conditions of research work in (titanium), 116; as specialization in higher technological institutions, 210.

Mineral resources, exploration of, as research category in 12-year plan, 104–105.

Mining, shortage of graduates related to need in some fields, excess of graduates in others, 94–95; as specialization in higher technological institutions, 209.

Ministries. *See* State ministries.

Ministry of Education, 13, 19, 49, 53, 54, 62, 88, 89, 97, 98, 125. *See also* Ministry of Higher Education.

Ministry of Higher Education, 13, 45, 79, 92, 93, 96. *See also* Ministry of Education.

Minpan. See "People's schools."

N

National Committee of College Enrollment, 62.

Nationalities (national minorities), higher educational institutions for, listed, 203.

Natural sciences, basic theoretical problems in, as research category in 12-year plan, 104–105; emphasis on, at Academy of Sciences, 120; graduates in, related to those in other specializations, 128–130; students and graduates in, institutions of higher education, 133–134, 135; quality of graduates in, 134; more qualified graduates in, probably trained in Soviet Union, 134; women students in, 144, 172.

Nieh Jung-chen, role of, in science and technology, and references to, 101–102, 104, 105; statement on scientific goals, 105; chairman, Scientific and Technological Commission and Science Planning Commission, 106; statement on Party leadership in scientific work, 107; statement on practical application of science, 108; statement on expansion of research into the provinces, 114.

Normal (teachers') schools. *See* Colleges, normal; Secondary schools; Teacher-training institutes.

Nurseries, development of kindergartens and, 29–30.

O

Observatories, affiliated with Academy of Sciences, 243–244.

On-the-job training, 52, 54, 142, 164; emphasis on, as opposed to vocational schools, 48; reliance upon Soviet experts for, 54; in engineering, 132.

Oriental languages, excess of graduates in, over needs, 94–95. *See also* Languages.

P

Paper manufacture, as specialization in higher technological institutions, 211.

Part-time schools, established by factories, 20. *See also* "Leap forward" in education; "Red and expert" universities; Spare-time education; "Walking on two legs."

Peking, educational center, 57.

Peking National Academy of Sciences, merged into the Academy of Sciences, 109.

Peking University, establishment of, 10; conditions at, reflected in professors' statements, 93–94; physical labor required of professors, 121.

"People's schools," 14, 18, 20, 21, 22.

"People's universities." See "Red and expert" universities.

Petroleum, surplus of graduates in (mining), 94; surveying and prospecting for, and other scarce materials, as research category in 12-year plan, 104–105.

Pharmacy, excess of graduates over needs in, 94–95; graduates in medicine and, related to those in other specializations, 128–130.

Philosophy, work-study policy in training in, 59; in the Academy of Sciences, 109–113, *passim;* chart, 110; institutes affiliated with the department of, Academy of Sciences, 243.

Physical chemistry, Soviet Union aid in, 116.

Physical culture, list of higher educational institutions for, 203.

Physical sciences. *See* Natural sciences.

Physics, in the Academy of Sciences, 109–113, *passim;* chart, 110; as specialization in higher technological institutions, 213; outline of examination in, for matriculation to institutions of higher education, 223–226; institutes affiliated with the department of, Academy of Sciences, 240. *See also* Biophysics; Electrophysics; Natural sciences; Sciences.

Political science, enrollment in law and, related to other fields, 67, 68–71; graduates in, see *"Other"* column, 75 table 5; women students in law and, 144, 172; graduates in law and, from higher educational establishments, related to graduates in other fields, 171; list of higher educational institutions for, 201.

Population, increase in, as factor limiting China's achievements, 8; factors in, pertinent to analysis of education and professional manpower related to goals of economic and social development, 147–148; total, 148; 1953 count, 148–149; post-1953 reports, 149–151; validity of reported vital-statistics rates, 151–152; rate of growth, 153–154; specific implications of factors, related to educational and manpower problems, 153–154; urban-rural distribution, 154–156; age and sex structure of, on mainland, 156–158.

Postgraduate work and research, in educational-system chart, 11; list of institutions offering courses, and number of students, 204–208. *See also* Advanced studies; Higher education.

Power stations, Soviet cooperation in building, 117.

Preschool facilities, 29–30.

Primary education, enrollment for China, U.S. and Soviet Union, 4; increase in enrollment under Communist regime, 5; broad conjectures on future of, 7–8; before 1950, 9–10; inadequacy of planning, 96–99, *passim;* population factors related to future of, 153–154. *See also* Budget; Primary schools.

Primary schools, in educational-system chart, 11; increased enrollment, 18; development of (enrollment, graduates, curriculum), 31–34; enrollment expected by 1962, 84; school-building construction related to enrollment, 85–86; inadequacy of physcal facilities, 84–88; withdrawals from, prior to completion of education, 88–89; female students as percent of enrollment, 145; curriculum, 173. *See also* Primary education.

Production, integration of education and: as part of the educational system, 5, 18–27, *passim;* in preschool facilities, 30; in primary schools, 20, 34, 99; in secondary schools, 20, 38–39, 99; in vocational schools, 48, 90; in higher education, 20, 58–59; at University of Science and Technology, 60; in institutions for higher education, 60, 61, 92; need for job holders to serve concurrently as teachers, 84; in the scientific field, 108, 121–122, 132. *See also* Secondary schools—*Vocational schools.*

Production categories of labor, comparison of workers in, with the engineering and technical personnel in, 164–165 (see note to table 7); workers and employees in, 162–163; ratio of workers and employees in, to engineering graduates, 164. *See also* Construction; Industry; Transportation and communications.

Production and precision equipment, automation in, as research category in 12-year plan, 104–105.

Professional manpower, statement on use of statistics concerning, vi; broad conjectures on future of, 7–8; inefficiency in estimated need for, and placement of college graduates, 94–96; Chapter VII, 125–146. *See also* Higher education; Population.

Public health, vocation-school enrollment in, 46; development of, as task set forth by scientific and technological work conference, 105. *See also* Health; Medical sciences; Medicine; Pharmacy.

Publication offices, affiliated with the Academy of Sciences, 244.

Q

Quality in education. *See* Chapter V, 81–100.

R

S

120; engineering curriculum in China compared with that in Soviet Union, 132–133; the more qualified science graduates probably trained in, 134; workers and employees in China compared with those in, as portion of urban labor force, 160, 161. *See also* Russian language.

Spare-time education, in educational-system chart, 11; emphasis on, as opposed to vocational-school training, 48; numbers of students in, and literacy classes, 49 table 9; enrollment (higher, secondar⁻, vocational, and primary schools), 49 table 9; provided by industrial plants, 52–53; peasants in, 53; low quality, 53–54; deterrents to, for workers, 54–55; comparison of, with full-time, in institutions of higher education, 66–67; as accepted part of the educational system, 82. *See also* Adult education; Factories; Part-time schools; Production, integration of education and; "Red and expert" universities.

Spare-Time Education Commission, creation of, 52.

State Council, 13, 50, 52, 76, 77, 101–102, 106, 109, 112, 119, 122–123.

State ministries, scientific research by, 113–115; industrial scientific research by, 114–115.

State Technological Commission, 106.

Surveying, as specialization in higher technological institutions, 212.

T

Teacher-training institutes, listed, 194–201. *See also* Colleges, normal; Secondary schools—*Normal (teachers') schools.*

Teachers, low qualifications, 82–84; inadequacy of living accommodations, 87. *See* Colleges, normal; Secondary schools—*Normal (teachers') schools;* Teacher-training institutes.

Technical institutes, in educational-system chart, 11.

Technical and industrial courses in vocational schools, graduates from, 47 table 8.

Technical personnel, shortage, at professional and semiprofessional levels, 7; emphasis to continue on, 8; quality

of, 8. *See also* Secondary schools—*Vocational schools;* Science and technology; Scientific personnel; Technical sciences; Technology.

Technical sciences, in the Academy of Sciences, 109–113, *passim;* chart, 110; institutes affiliated with the department of, Academy of Sciences, 242–243.

Technology, broad conjectures on future of, 7–8; higher educational institutions listed, 180–190; list of higher educational institutions offering postgraduate courses, with courses and number of students, 206–207; list of specializations in higher technological institutions, 209–213. *See also* Engineering; Science and technology.

Transportation, development of, as task set forth by scientific and technological work conference, 105; research on, 114. *See also* Transportation and communications.

Transportation and communications, assignment of graduates to, 76; shortage of graduates related to need, 94–95; workers and employees in, in distribution within production categories, 162–163; as specialization in higher technological institutions (railroad, transoceanic, internal waterways), 212. *See also* Production categories of labor.

Tsing-hua Polytechnical University, 84, 113, 114; curriculum, 132–133. *See also* the Appendices.

U

United States, explanation of noncomparative data on China and, vii; enrollment in higher, secondary, and primary education compared with that in Soviet Union and China, 4; Chinese advanced students in, 77–78.

University graduates, number and distribution, 125–127. *See also* Higher education; Higher educational schools and institutions.

University of Science and Technology, 112; departments, direction, and enrollment, 60; probability of advanced-degree level of study at, 80.

Universities, establishment of, 10, number (polytechnical and general), 57; general education provided by, 58; conditions in, reflected in professors' statements, 93–94; low quality of scientific research in, and absence of adequate facilities and funds, 101; scientific research at, 113–114; comprehensive, listed, 176–180; comprehensive, offering postgraduate courses, listed with courses offered and number of students, 204–206. *See also* Colleges; Higher education; Higher educational schools and institutions; "Red and expert" universities.

V

Vital statistics. *See* Population.
Vocational education. *See* On-the-job training; Production, integration of education and; Secondary education; Secondary schools—*Vocational schools;* Spare-time education.

W

"Walking on two legs," 24–26, 42, 82, 104.
Water conservancy, assignment of graduates to, 76.
Western-trained personnel (pre-1950), professional manpower core formed of post-1950 Soviet-trained personnel and, 6–7. *See also* Intellectuals.
Women, distribution of population with completed secondary and completed

higher education, by age and sex, 143–146; proportion of, in enrollment in secondary schools and institutions of higher education, 144–145; in the labor force, 158–159, 161, 162; proportion among students in institutions of higher education, 1932–46 (distributed by field of specialization, 1934–46), 172.
"Work and study" schools, 14, 18, 21. *See also* Production, integration of education and; Spare-time education.
Workers and employees, as nucleus of urban labor force and data on, 159–166; compared with those in Soviet Union as portion of urban labor force, 160, 161; distribution within production categories, 162–163; engineering graduates as percent of, 164; comparison of number of professionals and semiprofessionals with total number of, 164–166.

Y

Yangtze River, technical problems in exploration of, as category in 12-year plan, 104–105.
Yellow River, technical problems in exploration of, as category in 12-year plan, 104–105.

Z

Zoology, excess of graduates over needs in, 94–95.

U.S. GOVERNMENT PRINTING OFFICE: 1961